D1165802

INTERNATIONAL STUDIES

The Slovak Dilemma

INTERNATIONAL STUDIES

Published for the Centre for International Studies,
London School of Economics and Political Science

The Centre for International Studies at the London School of Economics was established in 1967 with the aid of a grant from the Ford Foundation. Its aim is to promote research and advanced training on a multi-disciplinary basis in the general field of International Studies, particular emphasis being given initially to contemporary China, the Soviet Union and Eastern Europe and the relationship between these areas and the outside world. To this end the Centre offers research fellowships and studentships and, in collaboration with other bodies (such as the Social Science Research Council), sponsors research projects and seminars.

The Centre is undertaking a series of publications in International Studies, of which this volume is the second.

Whilst the Editorial Board accepts responsibility for recommending the inclusion of a volume in the series, the author is alone responsible for the views and opinions expressed.

THE SLOVAK DILEMMA

EUGEN STEINER

CAMBRIDGE
AT THE UNIVERSITY PRESS · 1973

Published by the Syndics of the Cambridge University Press
Bentley House, 200 Euston Road, London NW1 2DB
American Branch: 32 East 57th Street, New York, N.Y. 10022

© Cambridge University Press 1973

ISBN 0 521 20050 4

Printed in Great Britain by
Western Printing Services Ltd, Bristol

CONTENTS

PREFACE

Twice in my life I have had to leave my native country: in the spring of 1939 when Hitler's soldiers marched into Czechoslovakia, and in the summer of 1968 when Brezhnev's soldiers did the same. In both cases I have chosen exile as a Jew, as a Communist and as a Slovak. But the reasons for going into exile were not quite the same each time. Perhaps on the second occasion I should have left out Communism because, when the Warsaw Pact armies decided to impose their political ideas on my country by force, I knew that once again my belief in Communism had been shaken.

The first eight months of 1968 in Czechoslovakia had raised in many of us the hope that after all it might be possible to combine justice and equality with freedom – without which Communism cannot be Communism. 1968 was more than an experiment. Although in the life of a nation eight months is not a long time, it is perhaps long enough to reshape the political ideas of an individual. Even if it was only an experiment, I believe that it did not fail. It was because it worked that it had to be prevented from succeeding. The Czechoslovak socialist laboratory had to be smashed by a hostile rival who thought, perhaps, that his laboratory was a better one. In 1968 my friends and I felt that we were on the way to being reconverted to the faith which we had lost. The Prague Spring was not a dream. It had already become reality. But, whether dream or reality, it was shattered by brute force.

Three decades ago I came to Britain with the Czechoslovak forces fighting on the side of the Allies against Hitler. When I was discharged from the Army my government gave me a grant to go to the London School of Economics and Political Science, where I read sociology as an undergraduate and later as a research student. When I returned to my native Slovakia in 1948 I soon discovered that Stalin's concept of socialism did not embrace sociology. I knew that I could not pursue my work in the social sciences. I took up instead the 'safer' career of journalism. Soon the Czech and Slovak executors of Stalin's will stopped me from my activities as a propagandist of Marxism–Leninism. I was not trusted. Only after the Twentieth Congress of the Soviet Communist Party was I again able to work as a journalist. Times have changed but not to the extent that we expected after those hopeful days following Khrushchev's 'revelations'. They were not revelations to me and my friends, most of whom had experienced Stalinism at first hand, either in prison or through other forms of persecution. For twenty years I lived in Gottwald's, Zápotocký's, Novotný's and for a very short time, Dubček's Czechoslovakia. In my native Slovakia I witnessed at first hand what the system meant to the Slovak people – to the working class and peasants and to the working intelligentsia, as the party phraseology goes. As a Slovak journalist, I could watch from very close quarters, the main participants in the Slovak act of the Czechoslovak drama which often was, and has again been turned into a tragedy. I was in personal contact with many leading Slovaks.

When I found myself by the end of August 1968 in Britain once more, this time not as a soldier in an army fighting against those who had invaded my country but as a bewildered and confused Slovak journalist, I was fortunate enough to enjoy again the hospitality of the London School of Economics, where I was a Visiting Fellow of the Centre for International Studies. I have done my best to repay the LSE by working on a subject which is of the deepest interest to me and which I felt had been neglected by Western research. In most works on Czechoslovakia, including the recent very able accounts of the Dubček era very little interest, if any, has been shown in Slovakia's particular problems.

As far as I know, this book is the only one dealing with this subject to be published in Britain in recent years. It is in part history; and in part it is a more direct description of events, based on my personal experience. The second half of the book has all the defects, and perhaps one or two of the virtues, of this more direct kind of approach. In the second part the reader will find fewer references to sources than in the first, more historical, chapters of the book. Throughout however I have drawn extensively on the works of modern Slovak and Czech historians, political writers and economists, many of whom contributed to the downfall of Novotný. I am not in full agreement with all their conclusions but I am indebted to their work. I have made use of documentary materials, for example those in the Archives of the Institute of History of the Slovak Communist Party, to which, unfortunately, I no longer have access.

It is a sad reflection on the nature of the present régime in still occupied Czechoslovakia that the progressive writers and journalists, so often mentioned in my book, have been prevented from continuing their work. All have lost their jobs – and some are languishing in Husák's jails.

I am grateful to the London School of Economics and Political Science for the hospitality and financial help which have enabled me to produce this book. In particular, I should like to thank Professor Geoffrey Goodwin, Professor Leonard Schapiro, Mr Philip Windsor and Mr Adam Roberts, all of the LSE, who read the manuscript and helped me with substantial suggestions. And last, but not least, I am most grateful to Miss Margaret Vallance and to Mr Richard Taylor, who were very helpful in putting my Slovak English into English English.

December 1972   EUGEN STEINER

INTRODUCTION

On 28 October 1968 the highest representatives of the Communist Party and the government of Czechoslovakia came to Bratislava Castle to declare that the Czechoslovak Socialist Republic was to become a federal state consisting of two national republics – a Czech one and a Slovak one. Fifty years after the foundation of Czechoslovakia in the aftermath of the First World War, the existence of the Slovaks as a nation entitled to a degree of autonomy was formally recognized. It was recognized in somewhat bizarre circumstances, being one of the few elements of the reform programme of Dubček and his colleagues which was allowed to survive the Soviet-led invasion of Czechoslovakia which had occurred two months earlier. The solemn ceremony on 28 October 1968 was marred only by the awareness that foreign troops were present in Czechoslovakia. It was reminiscent of a similar situation almost thirty years earlier when the independent Slovak State was proclaimed on 14 March 1939, after Czechoslovakia had been attacked not by fraternal socialist allies, but by Hitler.

This book describes the modern history of the Slovaks – the four-and-a-half million people who inhabit the eastern part of Czechoslovakia. Like the nine-and-a-half million Czechs in the western part of the country, they are Slavs. Their history is in many respects unusual or even unique. For many centuries they lived under foreign rule, yet they survived this experience with their culture and sense of national identity intact. Before 1918, as part of the sprawling Hapsburg Empire, they were dominated by the Hungarians. After the foundation of Czechoslovakia, they were in the uneasy position of junior partner to the Czechs. Apart from a brief, involuntary and limited 'independence' as the Slovak State during the Second World War, the Slovaks remained largely under the control of Prague. The situation was not radically changed by the Communist take-over in 1948. And one may doubt how much the status of Slovakia has changed even now, after the federalization of Czechoslovakia.

Because of this chequered history, one of the themes of this study is necessarily that of cultural survival under foreign domination. The extraordinary persistence of a sense of nationhood was a phenomenon under-estimated by liberal democrats and Communists alike, and is of special interest whether viewed from the perspective of political theory or international relations. It has been the fate of Slovaks to be the satellite of other more powerful nations and at present, as before 1918 under the Hungarians, they can in some respects even be called the satellite of a satellite – a position which may be unusual but is hardly enviable. Yet the modern history of the Slovaks is more than one of mere survival. Slovaks have played an important role in many key episodes in Czechoslovak political life. True, Slovak dissatisfaction was probably not very important as a cause of the dismemberment of Czechoslovakia in 1938 and 1939 in the face of Hitler's threats and attacks. But in the 1960s Slovak intellectual and political developments had a considerable impact on the advent and character of the 1968 democratization process.

Any attempt to explain Novotný's downfall by one single factor, whether it be the Slovak national one or the economic difficulties of Czechoslovakia, would lead only to vulgar simplifications and shallow generalizations. It may have been only a historical accident that it was a Slovak, Alexander Dubček, who in 1968 succeeded Antonin Novotný as leader of the Czechoslovak Communist Party; it was probably less of a coincidence, and more of a carefully manipulated affair, that Dubček's successor in April 1969 was another Slovak Communist, Dr Gustav Husák. But the overall role of Slovaks, and of the Slovak issue, in Czechoslovakia's recent politics has been considerable; it has been studied far too little, and understood hardly at all.

It is perhaps a paradox that nationalism should have played so significant a part in the development of a socialist society. The events and developments described in this book go some way towards explaining why so many Slovaks, including Slovak Communists, resented the centralization of 'socialist Czechoslovakia' as much as that of the pre-war republic. Partly, they resented the extreme Stalinism and orthodoxy of Prague, but the roots of Slovak nationalism go deeper than any particular issue of policy, however momentous and far-reaching its effects. It is one of my conclusions in this study that national sentiment is a normal part of the make-up of human beings, and that this national sentiment prevails irrespective of whether the national group to which an individual belongs lives in its own independent state or not.

One of the main fallacies in classical Marxism has been precisely an under-estimation of the impact of nationalism in all spheres. Marxists insist that they do not preach cosmopolitan universalism and they claim that they fully understand the needs and aspirations of various ethnic groups and nations. Yet Marxist theoretical writ-

ings have sometimes suggested that nationalism is a somewhat artificial creation, the product of modern capitalist development, rather
than a basic fact of life rooted deeply in human nature. The practice
of Marxists, and especially of the rulers in the Soviet Union, has
often been to ignore the force of nationalism, or else to suppress it
in a manner not so very different from that of the Tsars. This study,
in attempting to trace the Communist attitude to nationalism, and to
define the effects of this attitude as far as the Slovaks are concerned
deals in microcosm with a major problem which lies at the heart of
the Soviet Union's policies, internal and external.

Frustration of national hopes is one of the basic features of Slovak
history, and has done much to determine the Slovak 'national character', if one can speak of such a thing. The sense of frustration felt by
many Slovaks springs in large measure from the fact that other bigger nations, including the Czechs, have often let them down. Promises made in solemn terms on solemn occasions have repeatedly
been followed by disappointments.

This takes us to the very heart of the Slovak dilemma. As a small
nation, the Slovaks have always had to choose which larger grouping
they shall belong to or support. Their history is not one of independence but of interdependence. Such was their position in 1848, the
year of revolutions in Europe, when they had to decide whether to
support the Hungarians or the Hapsburgs. In the event they chose
to revolt against the Hungarians, who were their immediate neighbours and more visible oppressors, even though the leader of the
Hungarian rebellion was a liberal-minded radical, Lajos Kossuth; the
Hapsburgs in Vienna, against whom Kossuth was revolting, represented the forces of reaction and had joined forces with an even more
reactionary ally – the Russian Tsar. The Slovaks' revolt in 1848
brought them no gratitude from the Hapsburgs and inevitably resulted in the Hungarians becoming even more suspicious of the
Slovaks. Seventy years later, in 1918, the choice for most Slovaks was
easier, and therefore less of a dilemma. They expected more from the
Czechoslovak Republic than from their Hungarian rulers and their
hopes were not altogether misplaced, even if their ambition as a
nation remained unfulfilled. In 1938 there was again a dilemma,
though one might dispute whether the Slovaks really had a choice.
After Munich, and the German invasion of the Czech lands, which
of two evils was the lesser one? The so-called independent Slovak
State under Hitler, or total occupation by him and his allies or rivals
in Hungary and Poland? Again, after the end of the Second World
War and the collapse of the 'independent' Slovak State, there were

difficult dilemmas. The Slovaks were reunited with the Czechs once more in 1945, but in 1948 was there really a choice for either of these national groups between the existing democratic system and the political arrangement dictated by Stalin which replaced it? And in 1968 again there was not even much illusion of choice. In early 1968 the Slovaks at last had leaders whom they trusted to bring about the best solution to Slovak national problems. Expectations ran high; but this only made their frustrations the more desperate when Russia intervened and the Slovaks realized that once again there was no real choice. Although federalization was announced in 1968, and came into effect on 1 January 1969, Slovaks remained apprehensive both about the reality of this measure as far as effective decision-making was concerned, and about the general political situation as Czechoslovakia bowed to Soviet demands.

Although Slovakia's history has hardly been a happy one, this book is in no sense to be interpreted as a plea for some new 'Slovak state' or some simple cure-all for a complicated national and international problem. Moreover, it must be stated explicitly and categorically that the Slovaks have gained a great deal from their incorporation into Czechoslovakia. This has rightly been recognized by many modern Slovak historians. Whatever were the deficiencies of the pre-Munich Czechoslovak Republic in solving the Slovak problem, however unsound has been the theory of one 'Czechoslovak people', most Slovak politicians and historians today admit that the creation of a 'bourgeois' Czechoslovakia in 1918 meant for the Slovaks a positive step in their political, cultural and economic development. For example, L'ubomír Lipták, a progressive Slovak Marxist and a rather patriotically-inclined historian, saw in the founding of the Czechoslovak Republic in 1918 a real national democratic revolution, even if it had its limits as far as Slovakia was concerned. He wrote in 1968: 'The most conspicuous, self-evident result of the 1918 revolution has been the removal of the most brutal and primitive national oppression. Before the eyes of often surprised contemporaries a process took place which could perhaps be called an external re-Slovakization of Slovakia.'[1]

Since the invasion of Czechoslovakia in August 1968, the role of Slovakia has been interesting and sometimes controversial. In Slovakia, as in the Czech lands, there was initially very strong opposition to the invasion, and in general this study suggests that any claim that Slovakia was more pro-Russian than the Czech lands,

[1] L'ubomir Lipták, *Slovensko v 20. storočí* (Slovakia in the Twentieth Century), Bratislava, 1968, p. 97.

or more 'normalized', must be treated with extreme caution. In their feelings about the invasion, as in many other matters, Czechs and Slovaks felt themselves inextricably inter-twined. The federalization arrangement is unlikely to affect this basic political attitude, although unquestionably it does have its specific effects and even some potential for future instability. After all, a federalization system containing two component parts is unique and may conceivably be more liable to produce rivalry between the parts than a larger federal structure containing many different national or regional divisions.

However if Slovaks as a whole, even under the federal system, have not reacted to the invasion in a manner markedly different from the people in the Czech lands, it is nevertheless true that the Slovak Communist Party, and many leading Slovak Communist politicians, have played an important and in some respects characteristic role. Since there is no specifically Czech Communist Party (a remarkable and deliberate omission in the structure of federalization), the Slovak Party can at times be one of the most powerful pressure groups within the Czechoslovak Communist Party as a whole, and it has been used as such at several points since the invasion, including the appointment of Husák as First Secretary of the CPCz in 1969.

The roles of the successive First Secretaries of the Czechoslovak Communist Party, Dubček and Husák, in fact provide one of the many paradoxes of recent Czechoslovak political life. Both of them are Slovaks, but Dubček was always regarded more as a Communist than a Slovak. Husák, on the other hand, was always more of a Slovak than a Communist, as his many years in prison under Gottwald and Novotný for the crime of 'bourgeois nationalism' indicated. Yet it was Dubček who came to appeal more to the national and political needs of Slovakia than the nationalist Husák. Some of the material presented here on Husák – and especially on Husák's attitude to the Slovak State in the Second World War – may shed some light on his present attitudes; it suggests that Husák may have had a tendency to confuse the illusion of independence with the reality.

Recent developments in Czechoslovakia suggest that once again, despite the principles of federation laid down in the constitution, the Slovaks may be frustrated in their national aspirations – and again by a Slovak in Prague. The Slovaks have often had prime ministers in Prague, in the First Republic and after the Second World War. Most of them tended to be less Slovak than Czechoslovak. Whatever happens in the coming years, it looks as if the Slovaks, as so often in the past, will not be short of dilemmas – and will be less than completely free in responding to them.

I THE SLOVAKS AS A NATION

The long disputed question of whether the Slovaks are a separate nation has by now been answered by all Slovaks in the affirmative. They consider themselves to be a separate national group among the Slav peoples and not merely a branch of the Czechoslovak nation. This is a subjective criterion but, as national sentiment is fundamentally of a subjective nature, this is the most important factor to consider. On the level of objective criteria the Slovaks are a nation too. They speak, and for more than a century have written, in their own language, they inhabit a compact territory, and have their own history, which, for many hundreds of years, was different from that of their closest Slav neighbours, the Czechs. Without attempting to provide a precise definition of a nation, nobody would today seriously question the fact of Slovak nationhood. All theories attempting to deny this have been proved false, artifices put up to serve political purposes, in most cases sinister from the Slovak point of view, and in most cases directed against the interests of the Slovak people.

If we consider the rather broader and looser concept of 'national character', most Czechs would not only admit, but would argue with vehemence, that the Slovaks are different from them. But differences in national character may occur within the same old-established and recognized unified nations, in England, Germany, France or Italy, for example, where patterns of behaviour and attitudes differ between inhabitants of various regions. The most striking example of this is provided by the Germans. They were united into one nation-state only a century ago; before Bismarck the only bond that made them feel German, if such a bond was really felt, was the written language. Even after unification millions of Germans, such as the Austrians and the German-speaking Swiss, remained outside the Hohenzollern Empire. It was only Hitler who attempted to force all Germans, whether or not they lived in the Third Reich, to belong to one homogenous nation.

Unifying tendencies usually originate with the strongest and largest member of the family of similar ethnic groups, which then becomes the nucleus of centralization. In Germany the process of unification started in Prussia. The fact that the men who originally inspire the idea of unity often come from a peripheral area – Garibaldi was born in Nice, Napoleon in Corsica, Hitler in Austria, Stalin in Georgia, de Gaulle in Lorraine, Pilsudski in Lithuania – does not alter this historical tendency, and may be explained more in terms of psychology than political science.

One attempt at such a movement was the panslav idea. It originated in Tsarist Russia in the first half of the nineteenth century. It never became an official state ideology nor a policy of the Tsars and their governments. It reflected rather an intellectual ferment which had a certain impact on most of the Slav peoples, with the exception of the Poles who lived too close to Russia to be attracted by this basically pro-Russian idea. The smaller immediate neighbour is seldom, if ever, enthusiastic about joining the bigger one. Nevertheless, in the first half of the nineteenth century the Slav nations under the Austro-Hungarian monarchy, or at least some of their more articulate intellectual leaders, cherished the idea of belonging to a larger group of nations of the Slav race. They took a certain pride in the fact that the biggest brother of them all, the Russian, was the ruler of a great Empire stretching from the centre of Europe to the Pacific Ocean. In the northern part of Austria there was the former kingdom of Bohemia inhabited by the Czechs; and in the northern part of Hungary, in the region between the Carpathian range of mountains and the river Danube, another Slav people, the Slovaks.

The Czechs had lost their national independence, or more exactly their historical statehood, to the Hapsburgs after the battle of the White Mountain in 1620. The Slovaks had lost theirs seven centuries earlier. After the death of King Svätopluk, they lost their state when, partly due to the rivalry which broke out between his three sons, the territory was invaded by the Magyars (Hungarians) coming from the Central Asian steppes round AD 900. From that time on they were ruled by that Mongol race which settled and acclimatized itself in the Danubian basin, becoming eventually fully European.

This is a very long time for a nation to be under foreign rule. It is unique in Europe. Even the Turkish rule over some Balkan nations, which lasted to the very end of the nineteenth and the beginning of the twentieth century, was a relatively short one. It was remarkable that the Czechs survived three hundred years of Austrian supremacy; it was a miracle that the Slovaks did not lose their national identity during the thousand years of Hungarian rule. To some this historic fact serves as convincing evidence that closely-knit national groups can and usually do survive long years of foreign oppression without having their own nation-states.

In the nineteenth century, when the pressure from Vienna and Budapest grew stronger, panslavism, the feeling of spiritual and cultural unity with Russia, may offer one of the explanations why the Slav peoples, though ruled by alien races, survived. Among the Czechs and Slovaks the panslav movement was propagated by outstanding men, the poet Ján Kollár and the linguist and historian Pavel Šafárik. Both were Slovaks. They wrote in Czech because until the first half of the nineteenth century Czech was the usual written language of both Czechs and Slovaks. Kollár and Šafárik regarded themselves as Slovaks, but in a situation in which it was not yet clear why there should be a separate written language, or which of the many Slovak dialects should be adopted as such, they saw no reason to give up Czech.

Kollár and Šafárik were enthusiastic advocates of Slav unity but they thought of it more in cultural than political terms, and anyway they would never have dared to propagate any political adherence to Tsarist Russia. They remained loyal subjects and citizens of the Austrian monarchy. Stressing Slav cultural unity and mutuality, Kollár and Šafárik saw no point in tendencies which they thought worked against this aim, tendencies which might provoke disunity. They therefore opposed all the efforts of Slovak leaders like Bernolák, Štúr, Hodža and Hurban to establish a Slovak written language.[1] Kollár and Šafárik argued that it would serve no purpose to create a less accessible written language, which would make for provincialism. They were influenced by the German thinkers Herder and Hegel with their teleological view of history, of human progress. Herder believed that it was the historic mission of the Slav race to fulfil the idea of goodness, the role of the Germans was the realization of truth, while that of the classical world had been the materialization of beauty.

This concept of history left little room for the desire of small nations split into even smaller ones. Why should the Czechs and Slovaks divide into two different nations? Why not instead encourage a movement towards panslav unity under the moral and cultural leadership of the Russians, especially if mankind expected the Slavs to be the bearers of goodness, perhaps the most precious of all human values?

---

[1] The most prominent of them was L'udovít Štúr (1815–56), a poet, publicist and politician. He was the main advocate of the Central Slovak dialect being adopted as the literary language. This was agreed upon in 1843 after an attempt by a Roman Catholic priest, Anton Bernolák, to introduce the Western dialect had finally been abandoned.

Štúr and his group shared this philosophy rather than opposing it, but they believed that the Slovak people should enter the community of Slav nations as a separate ethnic unit, as a legitimate younger child in the family of which Russia, if not the mother, was the oldest and most powerful brother.

In the spring of 1848, the year which historians call 'the Spring of Nations', Štúr turned against the Hungarians who had revolted against imperial Vienna and the Hapsburg monarchy. The Hungarian democrats and liberal radicals led by Lajos Kossuth – allegedly of Slovak origin – and themselves imbued with their own nationalism, had little understanding for the national aspirations of the Slovaks and other minorities in their part of the Empire. Hungarian nationalism was turned against the Austrian feudal absolutist monarchy. The Slovak leaders thought, mistakenly as it turned out, that by damaging the cause of their immediate masters they might find gratitude and understanding in Vienna. But on the whole their rebellion was not a big affair, it was not even coordinated with the larger movements in Bohemia which were, of course, openly anti-Austrian. The Slovak rebellion was merely a counter-action against the Hungarian revolution which started a few weeks earlier. The Slovak rebels consisted of a few hundred volunteers who were quickly and brutally suppressed by the Hungarians. The subsequent Russian intervention helped to suppress the Hungarian revolt without paying the slightest consideration to the Slovak cause and their Slovak supporters. The Tsar came to help the Austrian Emperor, not the Slav peoples of the Austrian Empire. For him liberal ideas were more dangerous and their suppression of greater importance than his sympathy for the panslav ideals of the period.

Tsarist Russia was a natural and official ally of Imperial Austria. Therefore Štúr thought that, after Vienna, St Petersburg was the place to look for moral and even political support. Slovak national interests seemed to Štúr more important than the liberal democracy proclaimed by the Hungarian insurgents, although Štúr himself was not unsympathetic to democratic and liberal ideas. He expressed his progressive political views frequently in his writings and in his speeches in the Hungarian parliament.

Later it was an embarrassment to Slovak Communists that Marx criticized the Slovak leaders of 1848 because he saw in their anti-Hungarian attitude and their rebellion a betrayal of the democratic and liberal revolution. Marx, the internationalist, could not understand or sympathize with the nationalism of Slovak leaders. For him the fact that the Slovak rebels saw in the Russian Tsar and the

Austrian Emperor the protectors of their cause, was sufficient reason to condemn their attempt at revolution in 1948 although the Slovak leaders were just as democratically motivated as the Hungarians.

Incidentally, it was the Slovak Communist poet and publicist Ladislav Novomeský who in the 1930s in the pre-war Czechoslovak Republic criticized Marz for his views. Novomeský tried to explain why Marx was wrong, and Štúr right. In the 1950s, when Novomeský was accused and tried for bourgeois nationalism together with Husák and others, his heretical stand against Marx certainly could not have helped him. If it was not directly used as one of the actual charges by the secret police, it was only because they were not sophisticated enough to grasp the full implication of this early political deviation on the part of the old nationalist. However, in the days of Novomeský's trial even official Communist history held Štúr in higher regard than Marx had done. Marx's lack of sympathy for Slovak nationalism was played down and was treated in the way most Marxist historians deal with controversial matters which do not fit their immediate cause and purpose.

From the very beginning the Czechs opposed Štúr's Slovak cultural separatism. They saw in it a weakening of their own struggle for national recognition although it was only much later, in fact only a few years before the First World War, that some Czech politicians started to voice the idea of an independent Czech state. The idea of Czechoslovakia as a common state of Czechs and Slovaks (or Czechoslovaks) only became a political reality when the question of successor states arose after the defeat of the Hapsburg Empire in 1918.

Vienna had never attempted to prevent the Hungarians from Magyarizing their own minorities. The Hungarians were of course hardly a free nation themselves. The growing middle classes in particular were involved in a bitter struggle for the recognition of their Hungarian nationhood – a struggle which ended only in 1867 when the Hapsburg monarchy changed into a dual state, a kind of personal union between Austria and Hungary under a common emperor who was crowned as Hungarian king. For the minorities living in Hungary it meant national and political, if not economic, disaster. The Hungarians were in a minority against the combined number of other nationalities in their part of the common Empire, hence their deliberate policy of Magyarization of other national groups by suppressing their culture and closing their schools.

It was in this period of intensified national oppression that some Slovak intellectuals became politically conscious and active. They began to regard the Czechs in the Austrian half of the monarchy as their natural allies and thought that the Slovaks had the potential to form a real cultural unit with the Czechs. They also argued that cooperation with the Czechs would imply the acceptance of the principle of national unity with them, otherwise the Slovaks could not be saved from national extinction. The protagonists of this view, who were still emphasizing economic cooperation and cultural rather than political unity with the Czechs, were very careful to point out that it would not help the Slovak cause to antagonize Vienna – a concern which was rather important from the point of view of Czechs, as they were under direct Austrian rule. The Slovaks were ruled from Budapest which regarded with suspicion any contacts with the Czechs. The Hungarians considered any form of Czech–Slovak cooperation as a practical application of panslavism and this served as a good pretext for increased national oppression.

The Hungarian ruling classes thought that the non-Hungarian masses were inclined to accept nationalistic ideas, not as a result of political oppression but in reaction to economic pressure, and they therefore wanted to eliminate panslavism by economic methods. To this end they encouraged the industrialization of northern Hungary to placate the Slovaks. However, they overestimated the capacity of the industrialization process to prevent the growth of nationalistic movements. L'udovít Štúr had already realized this when he wrote in his article 'Where are the roots of our poverty' in 1867: 'Industrialization cannot prosper in an unfree country...It can flourish only as an organic part of national life under conditions of liberty... For industrial development independence, wealth and security are needed.'[2]

The slightest attempts to fight for Slovak national rights either together with or independently of the Czechs were suppressed by the authorities in Budapest. A few dissident voices were heard among the more enlightened and provident Hungarian intellectuals, but these went unheeded. One of them, the liberal thinker Oszkár Jászi wrote in 1910: 'The aim of Hungarian radical democrats is to abolish the old brutal national policy and introduce a system of education based on national liberty. Otherwise Hungary will never become a state based on law and culture.'[3] He realized that industry could not develop in a situation in which the illiterate masses could not and did not revolt against oppression. These were prudent views,

---

[2] L'udovít Štúr, *Prejavy a články* (Speeches and Articles), Bratislava, 1953, p. 167.
[3] 'A Nemzeti Kérdés' (The Problem of Nationality), *Világ* (weekly), Budapest, 29 January 1910.

but in the whole political context of the time they came only from the radical fringe and had no great influence on the powers that be.

The policy of the Budapest government seems to have been based on the belief that economic progress would automatically eliminate all 'panslav' tendencies. The notorious anti-panslav organization Felvidéki Magyar Egyesület (Cultural Association of Upper Hungary) whose aim was to protect Hungary from foreign influence, also put great emphasis on industrialization. As a result some Slovaks adopted an anti-industrialist attitude, although this might also have had its origins in the vested interests of the agricultural sections of the country and of its small native production. The daily *Slovenský denník* warned against the Hungarian industrialization policy and wrote: 'There is no doubt that the Hungarians conclude correctly that economic problem is closely related to the problem of nationality.'[4] It pointed out that economic aid to the Slovak region would in itself bring about Magyarization and harm native production although even this would pose a lesser threat than the outright industrialization of Slovakia.

To prevent this, the Slovak politician, Milan Hodža, who had represented agrarian interests even before the First World War, encouraged the Czechs to come and 'cultivate our lands in the interests of both our nations'.[5] He was worried that the national wealth of Slovakia might become prey to German speculation as he considered that the Hungarians themselves were too weak to compete successfully against German business enterprises. In fact substantial amounts of Czech capital continued to flow in. Those who supplied it were motivated not only by brotherly love for the 'Hungarian branch of the Czech nation', but by more practical considerations such as cheap labour and land and abundance of natural resources.

Tomáš G. Masaryk, the future first president of Czechoslovakia, wrote in 1910 that Slovakia was the most natural area for Czech economic expansion. Anticipating his later views, in which he vehemently defended the idea of a single Czechoslovak nation, he wrote: 'We need practical unity in the fields of economy and finance, and not just unity of culture. The Czechoslovak problem must be considered from an economic point of view. It is not as simple and easy as buying a textbook on Slovak grammar.'[6] Ironically enough,

---

[4] *Slovenský denník* (daily), Budapest, 1912, no. 14.
[5] M. Hodža, 'Hospodárska politika' (Economic Policy), *Slovenské Listy* (weekly) 1898, no. 6.
[6] T. Masaryk, *Prúdy*, 1910/11, p. 287.

this belief in an economic solution to almost all the difficulties arising out of national aspirations echoed the views held by some Hungarian politicians and writers who had preached the omnipotence of economics in dealing with the problem of nationalism. Some of them went so far as to believe that economic satisfaction could bring about political and cultural liquidation of the Slovaks as a nation. Some Slovak individuals did indeed lose their national identity. When they turned into 'genuine' Hungarians, some of them became prominent in industry, in the professions and in the church. Some even reached the highest ranks in the Roman Catholic hierarchy, as for example, Csernoch, the notorious archbishop of Esztergom, one of the most outspoken advocates of the Magyarization of Slovakia.

There is also little doubt that the territory inhabited by the Slovaks benefited from the general economic growth of the country and the industrial revolution which took place in Europe during the second half of the nineteenth century. Yet experience has shown that no amount of industrialization and economic advantage can eliminate deep-rooted national attitudes. National political movements may be the product of the capitalist age but nations as such are not. On the other hand these national attitudes need not necessarily be inimical to economic development and integration in a modern world in which cooperation is an absolute necessity. By the time the Hungarians became aware of this in relation to the Slovaks it was already too late. All the efforts made by Hungarian politicians immediately before the fall of the Hapsburg monarchy and especially after the proclamation of Karolyi's liberal democratic Hungarian Republic, which promised recognition of the national rights of Slovakia as an autonomous region within the old Hungarian fatherland, failed. The attempt by the Hungarian Communists in 1919 to set up a Slovak Soviet Republic did not succeed. The establishment of this 'independent' Slovak state in a small region based on the east-Slovakian town of Prešov was an artificial creation and gained no support from the Slovak people. Despite the official celebrations in 1969 at which this first Slovak Communist state was hailed as a victory, some Slovak Communist historians have admitted that the venture was a rather clumsy attempt to save the Slovak region for the greater fatherland which the Hungarian Communists did not intend to relinquish.[7] They were only following the example of the Russian Bolsheviks who neither willingly gave up any territories gained by the Tsars nor respected the national aspirations of the various peoples of the Russian Empire.

[7] J. Šolc 'Slovenská republika rád', *Nové Slovo*, Bratislava, 1969, nos, 21–3.

Before the founding of the first Czechoslovak Republic in 1918, which will be described later, Slovakia did in fact witness a relatively high level of industrial development. For example, big textile works in Žilina, cotton mills in Ružomberok and a considerable concentration of factories of all kinds in and around Bratislava, an important river port on the Danube. The Hungarian bourgeoisie, including that part which remained ethnically Slovak, pursued a policy of industrialization to the very end of the nineteenth century when economic stagnation set in. Despite this, Hungary had remained basically an agrarian country. Its agricultural system only gradually changed from a quasi-feudal system of land tenure to a more modern system, although even then very little of the land belonged to those who actually worked on it. But on the whole Hungarian agriculture learned modern methods of production and big landowners successfully imitated their western colleagues. Only the small landowners remained backward, and this was especially typical of Slovakia.

Apart from agriculture, in the northern, Slovak, part of Hungary emphasis was laid on heavy industry; more than a quarter of the country's iron was produced there but the machine industry represented only 4.1 per cent of the total. While this region produced 33.7 per cent of Hungarian textiles, only 5.8 per cent of the dress-making industry was situated there. Slovakia produced 53.7 per cent of the paper, but contained only 1.9 per cent of the printing works. Most of the processing industries, producing finished consumer goods were situated near Budapest.[8]

From a purely economic point of view, it is only natural in a liberal capitalist economy that iron should be produced where there is iron ore and where there are other favourable conditions for this kind of industry. It is logical that paper should be produced in a region with an abundance of forests and wood. But modern Slovak historians and economists (Lipták, Falťan, Pavlenda, Kočtúch) also argue that the products of heavy industry should be used locally in light industry. They object, not to the insufficient industrial development of Slovakia, but to its structure. This criticism does not apply only to the Hungarian context. It is mainly directed against similar practices in the Socialist Republic and its industrial policy which, in their view, amounts to the virtual exploitation of Slovakia. They maintain that when Slovakia became a part of the new state in 1918, the country suffered severely in the economic field, although they admit obvious benefits in other spheres of life.

[8] L'. Lipták, *Slovensko v 20. storočí* (Slovakia in the 20th Century), Bratislava, 1968, p. 13.

Thus Professor Kočtúch of the Bratislava School of Economics argues that during the period of Hapsburg rule the Austrian and Hungarian bourgeoisie actually hindered the development of processing industries in Slovakia (though not, of course, heavy industry), while in the First Republic the Czech bourgeoisie 'not only refused to support the industrial development of Slovakia, but on the contrary eliminated existing heavy industry and hindered the development of processing industries. Between 1918–32 about 260 firms employing 28,000 workers were closed down, and in the years 1933–9 a total of 425 industrial firms were put out of operation in Slovakia.'[9]

The Slovak liberal journal, *Prúdy*, explained this by pointing out that a large part of Slovak industry had grown too rapidly and artificially under Hungarian government supervision, while industries in the Czech lands had developed more naturally over a longer period 'and as a result of enterprising efforts under conditions of strong competition'.[10]

These facts and figures constitute a serious indictment of the economic policy of the Prague government, or, using Kočtúch's terminology, of the Czech bourgeoisie. For example, while in February 1921 in Slovakia 127,000 workers were employed in industry, in 1926, Slovak industry employed only 83,429 workers. The number of employees in the machine building industry decreased in comparison with 1910 by 28 per cent. In 1924 the production of iron reached only 41.1 per cent of the 1913 level and production of pig iron only 6.7 per cent.[11] Kočtúch complains that the iron works at Vítkovice in the Czech lands imported iron ore from Sweden at the same time, 'ignoring large deposits of iron in Slovakia, where mining was forbidden'.[12] He omits, however, to add that the modern iron works at Vítkovice probably preferred high quality iron ore from Sweden to the low quality raw material in the Slovak mines which were already depleted.

Kočtúch quotes with bitterness one typical representative of the Czech capitalist class, Dr J. Preiss, the director of Živnobanka, one of the biggest banks in pre-war Czechoslovakia: 'In the economic development there is no room for sentimentalism.'[13] Presumably this also excluded possible anti-Slovak sentiments, which even Preiss would not have cherished to the detriment of the economic interests of his class.

[9] Hvezdoň Kočtúch. *The Economic and Social Development of Slovakia*, Bratislava, 1968, p. 40. This book, written in English, was issued in duplicated form and circulated more or less privately.

[10] *Prúdy*, Bratislava, 1923, pp. 162–3.   [11] H. Kočtúch, *ibid.* p. 40.

[12] *Ibid.*, p. 40   [13] *Ibid.*, p. 39.

Under liberal capitalist production there is a tendency for the strong to gain at the expense of the weak. Professor Kočtúch, as a competent economist, is perfectly aware of this fact. But in his indignation at the over-nationalistic, businesslike behaviour of the Czech capitalists he almost completely overlooks the role played by the new Slovak bourgeoisie which was rapidly rising and competing for positions of influence. There is no reason to doubt the validity of the statistical data used by Kočtúch, but his conclusions amount in practice to the suggestion that one should be sentimental in economic matters. There is indeed some justification for the view that not merely economic considerations should be taken into account, but also other aspects of human life, such as social, ethical, political, or for that matter, Slovak national interests and values.

The Communist shared the belief of the Hungarian rulers in the past in economic progress as a panacea which would make the Slovaks forget their national aspirations and frustrations. However, a closer analysis suggests that the Slovak problem was a matter more complex than can be explained, or solved, by one single cause.

2 THE FIRST CZECHOSLOVAK REPUBLIC

The First Czechoslovak Republic[1] was a multi-national state, formed by the 'Czechoslovak' nation, as set out in the Constitution adopted in 1920. According to the 1930 census which was the first complete one carried out in the Republic, the Czechs numbered 7,400,000 and the Slovaks just under three million. There was a large German minority numbering 3,300,000, mostly living in the border region of the Sudetenland, and 572,000 Hungarians were living in southern and eastern Slovakia. There were also smaller minorities such as the 120,000 Ruthenians in Sub-Carpathian Ukraine, and about 100,000 Poles in Czech Silesia and northern Slovakia.

The concept of a single 'Czechoslovak nation' forming the nucleus of the state was maintained, almost as an axiom, by the three main founders of the new Republic, the Moravian Masaryk, the Czech Beneš and the Slovak Štefánik. The rights of the minorities were laid down in the 1920 Constitution, which embodied all the liberal and democratic principles of the new era. Even in practice the policy of the Prague government towards the minorities gave little cause for complaint. They had their own schools and the Germans had their own university in Prague and a college of technology at Brno. (But a similar Slovak school of technology was founded only in 1939, during the existence of the Slovak State.) The German and Hungarian minorities were provided with a number of secondary schools. In Sub-Carpathian Ukraine the national problem was complicated by a protracted debate over whether teaching should be done in the Russian or Ukrainian language. In most places there the problem was solved by introducing Czech as the official language in schools and offices.

Although they were outnumbered by the Germans, the Slovaks were classified as a minority neither legally nor constitutionally. From most points of view Slovakia was treated as one of the regions

---

[1] Proclaimed in Prague by the Czechoslovak National Council on 28 October 1918. Its frontiers were subsequently established by the Treaty of Versailles in June 1919 and the Treaty of St Germain-en-Laye in November 1919 in relation to Germany and Austria. The Treaty of Trianon in June 1920 dealt with the frontier with Hungary.

of the state: Bohemia, Moravia, Silesia – which semi-officially were called the 'historical regions' – and Slovakia, which was not included in this category. Because for centuries the Slovaks had not shared a common history with the Czechs, they were supposed to be a region without history. In its practical implications this circumstance led to a superior, or at best, a patronizing attitude towards this newly gained, or regained, Slovak branch of the one united nation. The Slovak population on the whole welcomed the separation from Hungary and adherence of the territory to the new Czechoslovak state. There is no conclusive evidence that at least in the beginning there was much desire for Slovakia to become an autonomous region.

One of the important documents relating to the creation of the new Czechoslovak state, as far as Slovakia was concerned, was the so-called Martin Declaration, issued two days after 28 October 1918 when the Republic was officially established in Prague. It explicitly refutes the 'right of the Hungarian government to speak in the name of a people which it oppressed for centuries' and declares: 'The Slovak people are a linguistic and cultural-historical part of a united Czechoslovak nation. The Slovak branch participated in all cultural struggles which the Czech people fought.' There was no mention in this document of an autonomous status for Slovakia. It based its demands on the principle of self-determination for the Czechoslovak nation. The Slovaks were referred to as a 'branch of the Czechoslovak people'.

The Martin Declaration issued at a meeting 'representing all Slovak parties' obviously did not help the Slovak autonomists. On the contrary, politicians who stood for Czechoslovakism used it as an argument against them. The autonomists therefore based their claims on another document, drafted on 30 May 1918 in Pittsburgh in the presence of the Chairman of the Czecho-Slovak National Council, Professor Tomáš G. Masaryk, and representatives of Slovak and Czech organizations in the United States. In the Pittsburgh Declaration, whatever its legal validity, it is explicitly stated that 'Slovakia will have its own administration, its own parliament and courts of justice.' The last paragraph adds cautiously that 'detailed decisions on the structure of the Czecho-Slovak state are to be worked out by the liberated Czechs and Slovaks, and their lawful representatives at home'.

Another document signed by Slovak and Czech organizations as early as 25 October 1915 in Cleveland was much more explicit on the Slovak national cause. It called for 'independence of the Czech lands and Slovakia'. In its second paragraph it demanded 'the unity of the Czech and Slovak nation in a federal state with total national autonomy for Slovakia, with its own parliament, state administration, complete cultural freedom, the full use of the Slovak language'.

Although these were not legally binding acts, they serve to illustrate the ideas forming in the minds of Czechs and Slovaks in the United States, who could not claim to represent their peoples at home but were free to express views which amounted to high treason against the Austro-Hungarian fatherland. Slovak deputies in the Budapest parliament, as the Czech deputies in Vienna, would not have dared to express similar views, especially during the war. The idea of an independent Czechoslovakia was mentioned by a Slovak deputy, Ferdiš Juriga, only in March 1918. It was pursued mainly by men like Masaryk, Beneš and Štefáník, who during the war worked abroad for the realization of this idea and helped to organize military units, and whose contribution to the cause of the Triple Entente and to the creation of Czechoslovakia was more than merely symbolic. They stuck to 'Czechoslovakism' not only on theoretical, scientific grounds – they were following very real and practical aims. In the first place their concept made the nucleus of the new state larger by three million Slovaks and by raising the Slovaks to equal status there was no need to grant them any minority rights, not even cultural autonomy since, according to this view, there was no need for it. Slovak was recognized as one of the official languages; in Slovakia it was practically the only language used in schools and offices. Often it was taught by Czech teachers who came in thousands to Slovakia at this time when Slovakia really needed them. At first they were genuinely welcomed by most of the Slovaks, for in the first years after the war there was an acute shortage of Slovak teachers, as there was of a Slovak professional class generally. Up till then Bratislava had had no university except for a fairly small law school and fragments of a medical school. Therefore when in 1919 the Comenius University was founded, no Slovak, however nationalistic, could resent the presence of Czech professors at the new university. Most of them were men of high academic and scientific standing. They were dedicated teachers who helped to educate a whole new generation of Slovaks to become teachers, lawyers, doctors, and scientists. Some of the Czech university professors in Bratislava lectured in Slovak, which they mastered well enough, although for a Czech, however intelligent, it seems somehow more difficult to learn Slovak than for a less intelligent Slovak to learn Czech.

In secondary schools, too, there were large numbers of Czech teachers who taught their Slovak pupils literary Slovak with skill and competence. This was especially appreciated in a country which under Hungarian rule had had only three Slovak secondary schools and only a few elementary schools. Not surprisingly, in 1910 the Hungarian census officers found only 57.66 per cent Slovaks in the Slovak region. This figure does not include those Slovaks who lived outside this compact region and were scattered in various parts of Hungary, around Békes-Csaba, in Vojvodina, now Yugoslav, and of course in Budapest, where many thousands of workers and professionals of Slovak origin lived. There only a small percentage of Slovaks declared their original nationality in the census.

The Slovaks were reasonably satisfied by the arrangements in the new Czechoslovak state. For the first time in their history they had the opportunity to live their own national life or, and perhaps more important still, they had all the democratic means and opportunities to fight for it.

A few weeks before the creation of the Republic in 1918 Dr Beneš had promised the Slovaks four seats in the government after a Slovak delegation had visited him in Geneva. Dr Šrobár came to Slovakia in the early weeks of the Republic as Minister Plenipotentiary responsible for the administration of the region, which was in political chaos. Bratislava was far from being firmly in Prague's hands. It was not even certain whether this, the largest city in the territory, which had been ascribed by international peacemakers to the new Republic, was going to be the capital of Slovakia. Dr Šrobár came first to the west Slovak township of Skalica to 'establish law and order' with the help of the Czechoslovak legions who had returned from various fronts in Russia, France, Italy and Serbia. (They were former prisoners of war who had joined the armies of the Triple Entente.) The French hurriedly sent staff officers, headed by Marshal Foch, to secure the Slovak region for the new state.

Dr Milan Rastislav Štefánik, a French general of Slovak origin,[2] was to be the second Slovak member of the government, as Minister of War, although there was already a Czech National Socialist Dr Klofáč holding the portfolio of defence – a circumstance which is rather strange and still not quite explained. Šrobár knew that Štefánik was arriving from Italy on 4 May 1919 but made no preparations for his official welcome. He seemed to have had much more important things to do in his 'capital' at Skalica. He issued orders to the Bratis-

[2] Štefánik went to France as a young science graduate, became a well-known astronomer, acquired French citizenship, and after the outbreak of the First World War was conscripted into the army. In a conspicuously short time he became General of the Air Force.

lava garrison not to shoot at a foreign plane, which was expected at about 11.00 am on that day. The plane flew over Bratislava almost on time, but crashed before landing. Investigations were carried out as to the circumstances of this tragic incident.

The Slovak's never abandoned their suspicion that Štefánik's death might have been arranged to provide a solution to the problem of what to do with this ambitious young Slovak. The most probable explanation of his death seems to be that the plane, with its Italian green, white and red tricolour, might have been mistaken for one of the Hungarian Communist planes which were frequently flying over Slovak territory regarded as its own by the Hungarian workers' and peasants' state. (The Hungarian colours are the same as the Italians', only in horizontal layers.) The Slovak Communist historian Holotík comments, that Štefánik thus became the victim of the anti-communist hysteria prevailing in those days amongst the politicians and soldiers who ruled the country. This explantion, however plausible, is not generally accepted by most ordinary Slovaks. Some historians suggest that Štefáník's death was the result of a conspiracy of those who wanted to get rid of this serious rival.

Although Štefánik happened to be the most outspoken advocate of the fiction of one 'Czechoslovak nation' – a circumstance which more than embarrassed contemporary Slovak nationalists – he has now been fully accepted as a legendary hero of the Slovak people. (The name of Štefánik played a great role fifty years later when, after the fall of Novotný, the Slovaks saw in him a symbol of their national pride. However, his new and old admirers did not consider it politically wise to point out how very 'Czechoslovak' and how little 'Slovak' Štefánik actually was.)

The political system of the new state was characterized by a multitude of parties, based on various ideologies, political and national, and various economic and social interests. The working class was represented by the Social Democrats and Communists, the farming population by the Agrarian Party, one of the most powerful of the political parties. During the twenty years of the pre-war Republic this party provided the government with most of its prime ministers. In the years just before Munich and during the Munich crisis the leader of the Slovak section of the Agrarian Party, Dr Milan Hodža, was made Prime Minister; as an avowed Czechoslovak centralist he was to counter-balance the growing strength of the Slovak autonomists. Most of the political parties in Czechoslovakia were centralist, but not all participated in the Prague government. Although it remained constantly in opposition to the 'bourgeois' government in Prague, as far as the national question was concerned the Czechoslovak Communist Party tended to be centralist rather than autonomist. It was called officially the 'Communist Party of Czechoslovakia' and it had one Central Committee in Prague and a regional structure like most centralist or 'Czechoslovakist' parties.

Among the least sensitive to the Slovak national problem were the Social Democrats. An influential Czech representative of this party, F. V. Krejčí, wrote in August 1930 in the daily *Právo Lidu* 'It would be ridiculous and harmful for a race politically so backward to separate off from the stronger brother and boast of having its own national identity.'[3] The Slovak Social Democrat, Dr Ivan Dérer, for many years Minister of Justice and later Minister of Education in the Prague coalition government, argued consistently that the Czechs and Slovaks constituted one nation and he maintains this view to the present day. A pamphlet published by the Executive of the Social Democratic Party for the English-speaking world[4] states: 'On the nationality problems of Czechoslovakia much incorrect information has been spread abroad ... The Slovaks do not form a nation in the real sense of the word, but are a branch of the Czechoslovak nation whose language differs from that spoken in Bohemia less than, for instance, Edinburgh speech differs from London speech.' The pamphlet admits that 'certain differences in the ways of thinking and habit are caused by the fact that the Slovaks, under Hungarian rule, were prevented from living in common with the Czech nation for a thousand years'. It concludes: 'These differences will disappear as soon as a generation has grown up which has been educated in the same schools and lived in the same state.'

How wrong this social democratic prophet was! The exact opposite happened. It was precisely this generation which used those 'certain differences in the ways of thinking and of habit' to develop a definite consciousness of nationhood. The fact that it did not enjoy the full rights to which a nation is entitled, or which it claims, only strengthened its national consciousness.

The National Socialist Party was perhaps the most centralist of all coalition parties. Unlike its German namesake this party was a liberal and democratic one, although it was the most Czech from a nationalist point of view and therefore had only a very small following in Slovakia, mostly among the Czechs who lived there. Its spiritual leaders were Tomáš G. Masaryk and Edvard Beneš, although the former as head of state kept more aloof than the latter from political

[3] *Právo Lidu* (daily), Prague, 17 August 1930.
[4] *Czechoslovakia*, Prague, 1924, p. 28.

parties and their more down-to-earth activities. Beneš was for most of the time Minister for Foreign Affairs, until 1937 when he became the second President of the Republic. Although a liberal democrat, he was a staunch fighter for centralist concepts in political life in general and on the national question in particular.

In Slovakia the only party which from the beginning had a clearly nationalist character was the Slovak People's Party.[5] The slogan 'For God and the People' expressed in a very eloquent way the two main aims and the ideological pattern of its political platform. Its followers were Roman Catholics, the largest religious group in Slovakia forming 80 per cent of the population and in politics it preached outright Slovak nationalism. The clumsy, insensitive way in which the Czechoslovak centralist parties handled the national question contributed more to the spread of Slovak nationalism than the cleverest propaganda of the Hlinka autonomists. This movement had no ready-made political philosophy. It consisted of various groups, united by the desire to find a common cause with other immediate neighbours of Slovakia. It was not a clear-cut separatist movement propagating the creation of an independent Slovak state. There was a pro-Czech group, a pro-Polish one, and a third one favouring the old affiliation with Hungary. The autonomists had no prominent ideologists who could have worked out a comprehensive programme for Slovakia, although this was not a necessary prerequisite for the political success of the movement, either in the short or in the long run. Instead the Hlinka Party confined its campaign tactics to well chosen slogans like, 'Slovakia for the Slovaks', or 'In Slovakia speak Slovak', which were directed not only against the thousands of Czech civil servants in Slovakia, but also against hundreds of thousands of Hungarians who remained in the country. Autonomy itself was a loosely conceived programme, which had not been clearly defined. It was rather a mystique, and was not a practical proposition in everyday politics.

When in 1925 the official daily of the Hlinka Party tried to lay down its Declaration of Intent, it was addressed to the Czechs more as an appeal than as a straightforward positive programme.[6] Besides high-sounding, emotional phrases such as 'Slovakia has been eliminated from the map of Czechoslovakia' (which was not true because the territory had been recognized as a distinct region with clearly

---

[5] Founded in 1913 by the Roman Catholic priest, Andrej Hlinka, a Slovak nationalist who in 1907 received a prison sentence because he was held responsible for the events in Černová, his parish, where 15 people were killed by the Hungarian gendarmerie.

[6] *Slovák* (daily), Bratislava, 20 October 1925.

defined borders and enjoying full Slovak cultural rights), the programme stressed the 'gradual return of Slovakia to Slovak hands', as
if Slovakia had ever been ruled by the Slovaks themselves, at least
during the thousand years since the dissolution of the Great Moravian
Empire. The declaration contained passages about exploitation and
the depression of Slovak industries in favour of their Czech equiva-
lents. The only concrete point was the need to secure for the younger
generation of Slovak intellectuals jobs in schools and offices, since
'even seven years after the foundation of the Republic we have a lack
of Slovak professors, officers, actors, and instead of support, artificial
obstacles are thrown in our way'. This was a genuine Slovak
grievance.

In such appeals to the Czechs no mention was made of the under-
lying hostility of the Slovak Catholic clergy to the Protestant, Hus-
site, and even atheist, Czechs. The Catholics feared that their presence
in Slovakia and the general influence of Prague might prove con-
tagious to the God-fearing Slovaks. This was a factor which most
historians analysing the relationship between Czechs and Slovaks
tend to under-estimate in their strenuous efforts to find more rational
and tangible explanations of the relations between the Czechs and
Slovaks which, with the exception of the first years of the Republic,
have been strained, to say the least. Nevertheless, even though
almost all the political parties except the small National Party (the
Protestant autonomist equivalent of the Hlinka People's Party)
seemed uninterested in the national problem, it is significant that in
the twenty years of democratic rule, the Hlinka Party never gained
a clear majority in the parliamentary elections.

It is illuminating to compare the results of the parliamentary elections in Slovakia in 1920, 1925, 1929 and in 1935, when the last
parliamentary elections before Munich were held (see Table 1).[7]

These figures represent the broad political spectrum until 1938
when, mainly as a result of the international situation, the trends
radically changed.

The biggest political parties in Slovakia were those which had been
politically active in one way or another even before the founding of
the Republic with the possible exception of the Social Democrats, who
had a longer tradition dating from the last two or three decades of
the nineteenth century. They entered the new political situation
with a very modified programme. The Agrarian Party too, had its
roots in the past, mainly in the activities of the few Slovak members

[7] L'. Lipták, *Slovensko v 20. storočí* (Slovakia in the 20th Century), Bratislava,
1968, p. 104.

of the Hungarian parliament who sometimes voiced their views on behalf of the Slovak national cause.

Table 1

Political party	1920	1925	1929	1935
No. of votes cast	1,341,100	1,425,288	1,428,035	1,625,558
Agrarian Party	242,000	247,741	278,979	286,739
Hlinka People's Party	235,300	489,027	403,683	498,641
Czechoslovak Social Democrats	510,300	60,000	135,505	184,389
National Socialists	29,000	37,163	43,968	51,924
Communists	–	198,010	152,242	272,785
German and Hungarian Social Democrats	108,500	5,600	4,824	5,409
Czechoslovak Populists	–	18,173	36,548	37,515
Craftsmen and Small Businessmen Party	–	11,602	30,134	41,996
National Democrats	–	24,957	53,745	25,490
National Party	–	–	35,435	–
National Fascists	–	–	–	32,609
Hungarian national parties	–	–	226,917	230,713
Karpathendeutsche Partei	–	–	13,703	27,561

In the first years after the First World War, before the split with the Communists in 1921, the Social Democrats were by far the biggest party. More than half the electorate cast their vote for the socialists, most of them villagers, for the industrial proletariat was still numerically small. In 1920 the Hlinka People's Party gained fewer votes than the Agrarians, but the situation was reversed in 1925 when they became the largest party in Slovakia. In opposition to Prague the Hlinka Party stood for Slovak autonomy and gained many supporters, especially among the peasant smallholders. After the split with the Social Democrats the Communists became the strongest rank-and-file working-class party, although most of the Social Democrat *deputies* from Slovakia remained with the old party (17 out of 23).

The loss of votes for Hlinka in 1929 can be accounted for by the participation of the autonomists in the coalition in Prague. They had two ministers, one of whom, Dr Jozef Tiso, became president of the so-called independent Slovak State in March 1939. Their followers were disappointed by their efforts, or lack of them, in the interests of Slovak autonomy, for which they were supposed to fight inside the government. Their electoral gains in 1935 were due to the fact that the Hlinka Party went into the elections together with the Protestant autonomist National Party, led by the well-known and respected Slovak poet and priest, Martin Rázus. Analysis of the election figures shows that the Hlinka populists, although after 1925 the largest single party in Slovakia, never attained an absolute majority of all the votes cast there.

A study of the relationship of the Slovak parties to the coalition government in Prague leads to a conclusion with a different emphasis With the exception of the years 1927–9, when the Hlinka autonomists joined the government, the Slovak branches of the centralist parties, and their deputies in the Prague parliament, were always in a minority in Slovakia. The majority of the Slovak voters – whether they gave their support to the Hlinka Party, to the Protestant Rázus Party, to the Communists, to the nationalist Hungarian parties, or to the Slovak branch of Henlein's Sudeten German Party (the notoriously pro-Hitler Karpathendeutsche Partei) – were obviously opposed to the policy of the coalition government. They were motivated either by their nationalist attitudes or, in the case of Communists, by their Marxist belief in the class struggle. They may have somehow modified their tactics but they did not basically alter their stand. At times the combined opposition votes in Slovakia reached 70 per cent and at all times they were more than 50 per cent. In the Czech lands the situation was reversed. There the government coalition was almost continuously composed of the Agrarians, Social Democrats, National Socialists and the Czechoslovak People's Party (a Catholic centralist party which had little following in Slovakia).

The ruling coalition parties strongly supported the idea of political Czechoslovakism. They refused to grant political autonomy to Slovakia. Although most of them recognized the usefulness of treating Slovakia as a region with special problems, they were not aware that the population of this region wanted to be treated as a nation, as a separate ethnic group. Unfortunately, only the Roman Catholic Hlinka Party and the Protestant Rázus Party seemed to understand fully the national aspirations of the Slovak people; most of the other prominent Slovak politicians were opposed to autonomy.

3 SLOVAKIA: 1918-38

Few Slovaks, whatever their political creed or patriotic fervour would deny that Slovakia benefited from the first Czechoslovak Republic, despite all its shortcomings and deficiencies. Its leading statesmen were liberal democrats, learned men who introduced their political philosophy with a fair degree of success into the life of the country. Although the indirect influence of the Russian revolution must be taken into account, the situation in Czechoslovakia in the first months of its existence, with all the initial turmoil and disorganization after the collapse of the Austro-Hungarian empire, was not ripe for a socialist revolution of the Russian kind.

The first concern of the Czechs and Slovaks was national independence and political freedom. Internationalism and socialism as preached by the Marxists were only of secondary importance. The national, patriotic anti-Austrian and anti-Hungarian sentiment prevailed above all others. In those days there was very little anti-Czech feeling in Slovakia. That was one of the reasons why by the end of 1919 Hungarian attempts to regain Slovakia had been successfully resisted, and this part of the Republic could settle down and look forward to a new life in a new state.

The Republic inherited about 75 per cent of the industrial equipment of the old Empire, 24 per cent of its population and 21 per cent of its territories. It was a rich inheritance, providing a good material basis on which to build. Even Slovakia inherited a large proportion of pre-war Hungarian industry because most of the plants were situated in the northern region – the most industrialized after Budapest and its surroundings.

Slovak economists now argue that Czech businessmen were not very interested in the future industrial development of Slovakia. It is true that the free play of natural economic laws worked in a way which eventually caused a 'de-industrialization' of Slovakia. From the point of view of an industrially highly-developed Bohemia, Slovakia was more suitable for agricultural development and offered an abundant source of cheap labour and raw materials. Yet those who see in these tendencies an expression of Czech imperialism, and a

desire to reduce Slovakia to a colonial status, are vastly over-simplify-
ing the problem.

For one thing, tens of thousands of previously landless Slovak
villagers became, as a result of a far-reaching policy of agrarian reforms, owners of their own plots of land, which they soon learned to
cultivate and manage with the help of loans from the state and from
private agricultural banks. This fairly large section of the Slovak
population had a vested interest in the strength of the Agrarian
Party which even in Slovakia had a considerable following. For this
reason to the very end of the First Republic the opposition Hlinka
Party never gained complete control among the peasants. The autonomists amongst the Slovak bourgeoisie realized this and therefore tried
to establish their own banks, but in competition with the solidly
established agrarian banks which had strong capital support from
Prague, they made little headway.

Hundreds of new schools were opened. Each year thousands of
young Slovaks matriculated from secondary schools, and this was a
decisive factor in social mobility. The final examination from a secondary school, 'maturita', opened the doors to middle-class status, even
when the school leaver did not go on to university. The young intelligentsia had excellent opportunities for advancement in the first
decade of the Republic.

Admission to the new Comenius University in Bratislava was
simple; it was open to every holder of a secondary school certificate.
The student could choose any faculty and had hardly any fees to
pay. There was a good system of state scholarships, providing those
who matriculated and later studied with distinction with grants and
thus supporting students who came from the poorer classes during
their five or six years at the university. Slovak students were free
to go to Prague to the ancient Charles University and a considerable
number did so. There were other reasons for the small proportion of
working-class students at the universities. They wanted to become
wage-earners as soon as possible and 'maturita' provided a sufficient
qualification for most junior posts in the growing civil service and for
executive jobs in private business and industry.

For many young boys, mostly of peasant origin, the secondary
school also provided the opportunity to enter one of the numerous
schools of theology, attached to each bishop's see. The schools trained
hundreds of Roman Catholic priests as did the Theological Faculty of
Comenius University, which awarded the degree of Doctor of
Theology to the more accomplished ones. But for most of the Roman
Catholic clergy a four-year course at a bishop's seminary secured a

safe position with good prospects of advancement in the church hierarchy. Although by its nature the Roman Catholic Church is supposed to be cosmopolitan and universalist, in fact it became the breeding ground of Slovak nationalism. Its important religious function was to save Slovakia from traditional Czech protestantism – the Czech Hussites were not very popular with the Slovak Catholic clergy.

The priesthood was the cheapest and easiest avenue to high position in Slovak society. The bishop's boarding schools on a secondary level, and the seminaries on a university level, provided free board and lodging. Priesthood offered the poorest peasant boy an excellent opportunity to become a highly respected member of the community. He did not fear unemployment which was particularly important during the economic depression of the early thirties when job opportunities were diminishing even for university-trained Slovaks. The depression was an additional reason for the increased Czech–Slovak rivalry and hostility, in teaching, the civil service, business, the army and the gendarmerie, during this period. The competition for jobs became the main cause for national friction in these social strata. The new Slovak intelligentsia became jealous and envious of the positions held by Czechs who had overstayed their welcome. Although the Slovaks thought that the presence of Czech officials and men of the professional class had already become unnecessary, the latter were not prepared to return home because unemployment had also become a serious problem in the Czech lands.

In 1933 the total unemployed in Czechoslovakia rose to 700,000. The working classes in Slovakia were hit harder by the depression than their Czech counterparts. They were traditionally inclined towards the socialist parties, and to a lesser extent to the Communist Party. The latter was aware of the importance of the national question, but based its policy on the assumption that the answer to nationalism lay in internationalism. That is one of the reasons why the Slovak Communists could not benefit politically from the situation that had developed in Slovakia, especially among the intelligentsia. Nevertheless, a small group of Slovak writers and young intellectuals associated with the periodical *Dav* were converted to the Communist cause. They believed that Communism would solve the Slovak national problem, just as they thought that it had fulfilled the aspirations of all the nations comprised in the Soviet Union.

Statistics show clearly how deplorable the situation of the Slovak white-collar workers and lower professional class was in this later period and how unjust their treatment at the hands of the Czechs.

The most significant figures are those showing the participation of Slovaks in the central administration in Prague, although the argument that in the Prague government the percentage of Slovak ministers was less than that of the Slovak population in the country is misleading, for the simple reason that most of the Slovak parties chose to be in opposition to the government. Even if not quite of their own will, they were forced into opposition by circumstances which made it politically more expedient for them to stay outside the coalition. They thought that they could fight for the Slovak cause more effectively in this way. More revealing would be the proportion of Slovak deputies in parliament, which was relatively smaller than that of the Czechs. But the ratio was so close to the actual composition of the voting population in the Czech lands and in Slovakia that even this argument is not conclusive.

The participation of the Slovaks in the central government administration in Prague is a different matter. For example in the Ministry of Education in the year 1930 out of 417 civil servants of all ranks there were only four Slovaks. The situation in this respect was slightly better in the Slovak department of this ministry in Bratislava, where out of 162 employees there were ninety-four Czechs and sixty-eight Slovaks.[1] If the Czechs argued that the negligible percentage of Slovaks in the Ministry of Education and other departments was due to the fact that Slovaks preferred to stay in Slovakia, which was true in those days and is still true today, this explanation was inadequate for Bratislava, the regional capital of Slovakia, which during the First Republic naturally attracted thousands of Slovak white-collar workers. They felt quite at home there, although before 1939 the city was not nearly as Slovak as it is now. Slovaks would gladly have taken jobs in the Slovak department of the Ministry of Education, if they had been given the opportunity.

The Slovaks are not a militaristic nation. They do not appear to be greatly interested in army careers. Still, this national trait does not account for the fact that in the late thirties in the Ministry of Defence in Prague, out of 1,300 civil servants only six were Slovaks. The Czechoslovak Army had 139 active generals, but only one of them was a Slovak. Amongst 436 colonels there was not one Slovak. Out of 20,800 professional officers and non-commissioned officers only 830 were of Slovak nationality. That represents 3.9 per cent.[2]

These figures are quoted from sources revealed during the so-called independent Slovak State, but their validity is not doubted by contemporary Slovak historians. Most Czech historians accept them too,

[1] *Slovenská Vlastiveda III*, Bratislava, 1944, p. 338.   [2] *Ibid.*, p. 338.

without making any serious attempt to justify them or explain them away. One of the first Slovak sociologists, Professor Štefánek, pointed out that in the Slovak section of the nationalized railways in 1924, the ratio of Czechs and Slovaks was: in the administrative category 2,916 Czechs to 2,436 Slovaks; in the semi-clerical 3,216 Czechs to 10,735 Slovaks; amongst qualified workers there were 123 Czechs to 4,494 Slovaks; amongst the unskilled 17 Czechs to 1,073 Slovaks.[3] In this branch of industry the situation for the Slovaks was not too bad, but even here there were interesting trends.

If growing Slovak nationalism and the influence of the autonomist Hlinka Party is to be explained by economic factors at all, this applies especially to the new social group of white-collar workers. But economic considerations were only part of the cause. The availability of jobs in the state administration from the highest to the lowest level as a rule depended on affiliation to some coalition party. In most government departments jobs were only offered to and kept by members of the political party to which the minister belonged. Most government departments during the two decades of the First Republic remained in the hands of the same political party if not of the same minister. For example, the state railways were run by the Ministry of Transport, the head of which was traditionally a Social Democrat. Hence most, if not all, the employees on the railways held Social Democrat membership cards. The Ministry of Agriculture was in the hands of an Agrarian, the Ministry of Foreign Affairs under Beneš preferred members of the National Socialist Party. This influenced not only the numerical strength of the coalition parties, but affected election results. Most of the holders of membership cards and their families tended to vote for their party. They had vested interests in the strength and stability of their employer. It was quite conceivable that a man who in his heart was an autonomist, a Slovak nationalist resenting the presence of the Czechs in his country, should as a member of the Agrarian Party actually vote against his real convictions (against autonomy for Slovakia) and for 'Czechoslovakism'.

Contemporary Slovak economists tend to forget that Slovakia was a backward country compared with the Czech lands. They argue that it was not as backward as the Czech centralists of yesterday and today have tried to prove. But it seems illogical that the Czech bourgeoisie are accused of having used Slovakia only as an agricultural appendix to their more highly developed industrial region and at the same time of having acted in a way which was destructive to Slovak agriculture,

[3] *Ibid.*, p. 338.

as for example Professor Kočtúch claims.[4] He illustrates his case by pointing out that in the period 1926–30 the annual income of a farm worker equalled 3,105 Kč in Bohemia, 2,267 Kč in Moravia, and only 1,689 Kč in Slovakia. There is no reason to doubt the reliability of these figures. But are we to conclude from them that it was a deliberate policy on the part of the Prague centralists to bring about this situation? More likely it was a relic of the past which could not have been removed in the comparatively short period of the existence of the First Republic. Still, the centralists would find it difficult to justify and explain the fact that taxes were actually higher in Slovakia than in the Czech lands or the fact that the state purchasing prices of corn and other products were lower in Slovakia. This difference was supposed to compensate for higher transportation costs. But the conclusion of the anti-centralists that this transport policy was intended to hinder the development of Slovak agriculture would appear to be farfetched. It would assume a rather unusual attitude on the part of the Czech capitalists who, as with most capitalists, were not acting deliberately against their own economic interests.

Modern Slovak economists claim that Slovakia was to become the supplier of raw materials and cheap labour for Czech industry and agriculture. During the First Republic about 15,000 seasonal workers, migrated annually from Slovakia to Czech parts of the country.[5] While deploring the fact that between 1918 and 1937 more than 202,000 Slovaks emigrated abroad, which certainly was not symptomatic of a healthy economic situation, this should not be regarded as a completely negative phenomenon. To claim as a highly positive factor that during the socialist republic there was no emigration abroad, as official party and government statements do, is very misleading in a state which makes legal emigration of this kind virtually impossible. Slovaks who could not emigrate abroad had to go to the Czech lands. About half a million did actually do so and settled there permanently. In addition to these, tens of thousands of Slovaks commute, to this very day, hundreds of kilometres a week between their places of work in Bohemia and their homes in Slovakia. Slovak politicians and economists deplore this as a serious loss for Slovakia generally, and for the Slovak economy in particular.

However, it was not Slovak nationalism which brought about the

[4] H. Kočtúch, *The Economic and Social Development of Slovakia*, Bratislava, 1968, pp. 73–5.
[5] This trend increased considerably during the socialist republic, especially in the first years after 1945 under the scheme of repopulating the former border regions from which more than two million of Sudeten Germans were expelled.

fall of the first Republic. Naturally Czech centralism on the one hand and Slovak, German and Hungarian nationalism on the other, did not help to unify the Republic or to improve its image in the eyes of the world – especially among those who were eagerly looking for internal Czechoslovak reasons as a justification for a policy of appeasing Hitler and his allies. They thought that they had found such a justification in the dissatisfaction of the Slovaks, and more seriously in the hostile attitude of the majority of the Sudeten Germans who wanted to join Hitler's Reich; in the latter case, unfortunately, they were right. In the former case, they were wrong.

4 AFTER MUNICH

There were politicians in Czechoslovakia who welcomed the Munich solution and eagerly looked forward to an alliance with Hitler. There were men of anti-democratic, openly pro-fascist views, not only in Slovakia but in the Czech lands as well. The fact that in the end Bohemia and Moravia became only a 'Protectorate of the Third Reich', whereas Slovakia became theoretically independent, does not necessarily prove that Hitler trusted the Slovaks more than he did the Czechs. At a time when the Slovaks were supposed to be jubilant about having their own state at last, few of them had illusions about their real independence. Most Slovaks realized that with Hitler as an ally and protector, they would have little real opportunity to live a full national life in their new state.

After the September 1938 Munich Agreement, during the so-called Second Republic, which lasted from October 1938 until the middle of March 1939, Slovakia managed to achieve a fairly high degree of autonomy. This period in Slovakia was marked by anti-Hungarian resentment because Budapest had exploited the international situation to deprive Slovakia of the most fertile southern parts of the country.

Horthy's Hungary had always been on very friendly terms with Mussolini's Italy. When Horthy saw that a large piece of the Czech territory had been carved out for Hitler under the terms of the Munich agreement, he hoped that Mussolini would help him to achieve similar gains at the expense of Slovakia. Immediately after Munich the Hungarian government asked for a plebiscite in that region of Slovakia which they claimed, threatening military occupation if the Slovak autonomous government headed by Dr Tiso did not comply with this demand. There was much diplomatic wrangling between Prague, Bratislava and Budapest. In the end the question of the handing over of Slovak territories to Hungary was left to be decided by the four powers which signed the Munich agreement. But Britain and France had by now lost interest in this part of the world, and the final decision rested in the hands of the Italian and German Foreign Ministers, Count Ciano and von Ribbentrop. Germany did not fully accept the Hungarian claims, Mussolini supported them because his aim was to eliminate Slovakia completely from the map of Europe, to achieve a common Hungarian–Polish frontier, and thus create a bloc which would help to counter-balance the influence of Hitler in this region. Precisely these considerations led Hitler to give partial support to the Slovak position. Ribbentrop's compromise plan was adopted and an agreement was signed in Vienna on 2 November 1938. What kind of compromise it was is indicated by the fact that the Hungarians had to renounce their claim to Bratislava, the capital of Slovakia, and to the historic town of Nitra, the national shrine of the Slovaks where the first Christian church had been built in 833. This achievement was hailed by the Slovak autonomists as a victory resulting from their good relationship with the Germans and – as they suggested – the clever handling of the situation by the Slovak foreign experts.

The autonomous Slovak government claimed to have saved these territories from Hungarian occupation. But when they settled down to govern under new political conditions and a new state structure (the hyphen in the new official name of the state, 'Czecho-Slovakia', was not only of symbolical importance, but had practical significance) the ruling Hlinka Party amalgamated all political parties except the Communists, whose legal activities were suppressed on 9 October 1938. Soon afterwards the Social Democrats suffered the same fate. All the non-socialist parties were amalgamated into the new Slovak National Unity Party. A one-party system was established on the fascist model, the only ruling party in the autonomous region without an opposition. In December 1938 this 'united' party held elections for a new Slovak regional parliament. The new régime got 97.5 per cent of the votes. It is interesting that only three years earlier, in 1935, the Slovak autonomist block (the Catholic Hlinka Party and the smaller Protestant Rázus Party) had barely managed to scrape together 36 per cent of the votes. Now, in an autonomous Slovak parliament, out of sixty-three deputies there were fifty Hlinka populists. The Slovak Agrarians who before Munich had had twelve deputies in the central parliament in Prague, were now given only four; the remaining new partners got only a token number of one each.

The situation in the Czech part of the Second Republic did not differ much. There too, the Communists were outlawed and the remainder of the former parties joined a close coalition which had a structure similar to the new party in Slovakia. The Czech politicians of the Second Republic, mostly former Agrarians and National Democrats, were continually reassuring Hitler that the new Czecho-Slovakia would change its foreign policy. The new Minister of Foreign Affairs, Chvalkovský, assured Ribbentrop on 13 October 1938: 'From now on we intend to pursue a policy of close collaboration with Germany.'[1] He even went so far as to promise the Nazis that he would solve the 'Jewish question'. But in those days soon after Munich, there is evidence that the Slovak autonomists were even more eager to please the Germans.

Pro-Nazi enthusiasm was voiced first by Slovak fascist extremists. One of them, Dr Vojtech Tuka, who had spent many years in prison because of his anti-state activities, was released only shortly before Munich and later became Slovak Minister of Foreign Affairs, informed the German consul in Bratislava that the leader of the Hlinka Party, Dr Josef Tiso, was favourably inclined to the idea of total separation from Prague, but would carry it out at a later stage in the autumn of 1939.[2] Whoever inspired Tuka to express such views, it was a foregone conclusion that the Slovak autonomists 'would grasp their historical chance' as Ribbentrop expressed it, when, in the middle of March 1939, Hitler decided to put an end to the post-Munich Republic. In February, in his opening speech to the Slovak autonomist parliament, Tiso did not mention Czecho-Slovakia at all. The '*gleichgeschaltete*' Slovak press indicated, weeks before March 1939, that 'things in the world are on the move', and that 'the Slovak people must be prepared to face the situation with great confidence.'[3] There was no need to use too much pressure on people like Tuka, Ďurčanský, Mach and the leader of the Slovak 'Karpathendeutsche Partei', Karmasin, to induce them to welcome Hitler's offer of an independent Slovak state after he had taken final steps to 'correct the Czechs'.

The central government in Prague under the Czech politician Beran, a prominent member of the former Agrarian Party, who was known before Munich for his pro-German sympathies and for his reorientation of the foreign policy of Czechoslovakia away from the Soviet Union, was not fully aware of the secret dealings of men like Tuka with Berlin. Nevertheless, suspicions were growing in Prague that separatist tendencies were gaining ground in Bratislava and that they had reached the point of becoming practical possibilities. Prague tried to counter-balance these trends by promising the Slovaks

---

[1] *Geschichte des Zweiten Weltkrieges in Dokumeneten*, I, Freiburg–München, Doc. no. 125, p. 293.

[2] L'. Lipták, *Slovensko v 20. storočí* (Slovakia in the 20th Century), Bratislava, 1968, p. 169.

[3] *Slovák* (daily), Bratislava, 22 February 1939.

more autonomy within the framework of the Republic. Hitler's Czech partners who emerged after Munich must have accepted the re-assurance of the German envoy in Prague that he did not know any-thing about his government's encouraging Slovak separatism. In Prague they came to the conclusion that Hitler did not support the idea of an independent Slovak state. On the night of 9 March 1939, Beran sent military and police units to Bratislava and removed Tiso from his office of Slovak Prime Minister. The radicals who did not manage to flee to Vienna were interned, and the Prague government placed Slovakia under military rule. They installed in Tiso's place a less radical autonomist, Karol Sidor.

The situation was very confused. The Prague government obviously misjudged the state of affairs before and after this ill-conceived act. Anyhow, it was too late to act firmly. When Prague realized that Berlin and the local Slovak Germans did, after all, fully support the radical separatists, the soldiers withdrew to their barracks. En-couraged by this, Slovak extremists urged Sidor to declare an indepen-dent Slovak state, but he refused. Tiso re-emerged and accepted an invitation from Hitler to come to Berlin on 13 March. The result of this visit was the new Slovak State which was unanimously pro-claimed by the autonomous Slovak parliament. There is enough historical evidence to show that Tiso acted under extreme pressure, under the conditions of Ribbentrop's ultimatum which actually mentioned 12.00 of 14 March as the deadline for the declaration of a separate Slovak state. Ribbentrop did not omit to use the old threat that otherwise the Hungarians might annex Slovakia, a possibility that not only the autonomists, but all Slovaks, dreaded most of all.

After the declaration of Slovak independence, Sub-Carpathian Ukraine, in the easternmost part of Czechoslovakia, which had also gained an autonomous status after Munich, became completely isolated from Prague. This region fell prey to the Hungarians, who occupied it, obviously with Hitler's consent. Bohemia and Moravia went directly to Germany. A few hours after Tiso's visit to Hitler the Czecho-Slovak president, Hácha, was invited to Berlin. On 15 March 1939 he 'agreed' to German occupation.

It is difficult to assess with any measure of accuracy the degree of active sympathy felt by the Slovak people for the new Slovak State. But there can be no doubt whatsoever that the sympathy of Hitler towards the Slovaks was not a manifestation of his affection for small nations. He did not single out the Slovaks for favourable treat-ment out of any feelings of real friendship. He merely exploited the genuine grievances of the Slovak people and was grateful to those of its leaders who made it easier for him to destroy his Czechoslovak neighbour as a further step in his much more ambitious scheme to become the master of Europe. The willingness of the separatist radicals, and in the end of Tiso and even Sidor himself, to collaborate with Hitler, however hard they tried to justify their action, amounted in fact to a betrayal of the Czechoslovak Republic, and served the immediate and future interests of the Slovak people very little. Their main motive, which they frequently stressed in order to soothe their feelings of guilt, was that by giving in to Hitler they had saved Slovakia from Hungarian, and for that matter German, occupation. They told the Slovak people to consider themselves lucky to have escaped the fate of the less reasonable and less realistic Czechs, who were now under total German occupation.

Hitler's collaborators in Bratislava could boast not only of formal recognition by Germany and her close allies like Italy, and of other new facist puppet states like Croatia, but also by the Soviet Union. This was the cause of much confusion, especially in the minds of the quite considerable number of Slovaks who until recently had been members and sympathizers of the Communist Party and had pro-Soviet leanings. The Soviet Union had complete control of the policy of the clandestine Communist Party, which changed with an astonishing elasticity according to the daily requirements of Soviet diplomacy and disregarded the needs and mentality of the Slovak people.

The Slovak Communist historian Falt'an claims that 'populist clerico-fascism deeply discredited the healthy patriotic and nationalist feeling of the Slovaks'.[4] This view is reasonably acceptable. Less convincing is the argument that the clerico-fascists during the Slovak State derived their popular support only from the previous period, and that they gradually lost the sympathy of the people when they tried to build on the foundations of their past a 'new reactionary and foreign fascist ideology of Slovak statehood'. According to this view the Slovak leaders were supported only by the 'very aggressive young intelligentsia and a part of the petit-bourgeoisie'. For a Marxist, however nationalistically minded, it would be difficult to accept that the working class and the small peasantry could have in any way favoured the new régime.

The views of Falt'an, who was a colleague of Husák in the Department of History of the Slovak Academy of Sciences and who fully supported the latter in 1968 and 1969, are typical of the attitude of

[4] Samo Falt'an, *Slovenská otázka v Československu* (The Slovak Question in Czechoslovakia), Bratislava, 1968, p. 105.

most contemporary Slovak historians, including Husák himself, to the Slovak State. Naturally they do not view the Slovak State as a great achievement of the national movement for political and social liberation. But Falt'an admits that he is not certain either that the creation of the State contradicted Slovak national interests especially when twenty years of the existence of the Republic, 'juridical arrangement between the Czechs and Slovaks has not succeeded.'[5] Falt'an complained that 'after all the Republic did not manage to put up a defensive fight for its existence and anyhow after the Munich capitulation its hours were numbered'. He argues that 'statehood as an exercise of national freedom must not be rejected and regarded as a betrayal of the nation'. That sounds convincing enough, but his further reasoning, used in 1968 a few months before the Russian invasion, which he could not have anticipated, seems now most strange. 'It would be treason if equal and democratic coexistence with another nation or nations were to be replaced by a status of satellite subordination to another nation.'[6]

Most modern Slovak historians, although officially condemning the Slovak State, admit, as Falt'an puts it, that 'there were tremendous developments in national life during that period, despite economic subordination and dependence'. Bearing in mind this mitigating circumstance they do not seem to condemn the fact that 'Germany had an interest in, and actually gained, the first right to the mineral wealth of the country, and that Slovak industry served German war aims and became part of the German monopolies.'[7] The labour potential of Slovakia, especially the labour reserve, was integrated into German industry and agriculture, and the commercial contacts of the Slovak Republic with other states were subject to certain restraints. German capital participation in Slovak industry increased from 4 per cent in 1938 to 51.6 per cent in 1942. At the same time, as a result of appropriating Jewish property and of a wartime boom, the Slovak bourgeoisie increased its participation in industrial enterprises. Production was being increased especially in the food processing, textile and chemical industries, and in the building materials, wood and paper industries.

The Slovak Ministry of Economy issued licences for the establishment of 250 new enterprises and for the further development of 80 enterprises. The figures given by Slovak Marxist students of the economy of the Slovak State are generally very impressive. However

---

[5] *Ibid.*, p. 106.   [6] *Ibid.*, p. 106.
[7] L'. Lipták, *Ovládnutie slovenského priemyslu nemeckým kapitálom* (The Takeover of Slovak Industry by German Capital), Bratislava, 1960, p. 60.

hard they try to explain them away and point out the ill-effects of all this for Slovakia, because the greater part of these represented war investments ordered by the Germans, they recognized that 'useful work was done for the Slovak community as well', out of which 'the [Hlinka] regimists made a good deal of propaganda capital'.[8]

On the growth of culture and the position of the intelligentsia generally in comparison with the former Czechoslovak Republic, 'when the Slovak intelligentsia held only subordinate functions in the state and social system and was forced to collaborate with the centralist great-Czech ideology of Czechoslovakism',[9] Falt'an comes to the conclusion that its position and participation considerably improved during the existence of the Slovak State. However, this statement in no way amounts to approval. Falt'an rejects clerico-fascism with its reactionary and even perverted nationalism, which amounted to ideological, political and national subordination to German Nazism.

[8] S. Falt'an, *Slovenská otázka v Československu* (The Slovak Question in Czechoslovakia), Bratislava, 1968, p. 109.

[9] *Ibid.*, p. 109.

5 THE NATIONAL POLICY OF THE CZECHOSLOVAK COMMUNIST PARTY

After the 1917 Russian revolution, new Communist Parties were formed from splinter groups which broke with the old social democratic parties, and in some places, as in Bavaria and Hungary, were instrumental in setting up short-lived workers' and peasants' socialist republics. These new parties accepted the idea of Moscow as the centre of world Communism quite naturally, even before the creation of the Comintern. This recognition was a genuine expression of proletarian internationalism. Moscow, if it did not actually dictate, at least very clearly directed the activities of all the individual Communist Parties of the world. Not that the Bolsheviks in Moscow and the foreign professional revolutionaries in the Comintern totally disregarded specific problems facing individual Communist Parties. But generally most Communists believed that the interests of the Soviet Union would not clash with the specific interests of the workers and peasants and working intelligentsia in their own countries.

The Czechoslovak Communist Party was founded in 1921, splitting from the right wing of the old Social Democratic Party. The mood in the new state was not revolutionary in the Bolshevik sense. But the working class showed strong socialist tendencies. This fact was reflected in the election results during the first years of the Republic. The socialist block gained in strength, but since most of the Social Democratic leaders were willing to cooperate with the bourgeois parties in the coalition and were satisfied with a programme of social and political reforms within the framework of a democratic state, the left wing formed its own party and joined the Communist International (Comintern).

From the very beginning the Czechoslovak Communist Party, although recognizing the principle of self-determination to the point of secession as proclaimed in Moscow, constituted itself as a highly centralized and centralist party, disregarding the national complexity of the new Republic. There was not only Slovakia as a territory and the Slovaks as a nation, but also more than three million Sudeten Germans, most of them workers, who in those days were rather more inclined to socialist and Marxist ideas than were most Czechs and Slovaks. The Hungarians and Sub-Carpathian Ukrainians represented other, not insignificant, national groups with their own specific problems. But national interests were not the first concern of the Czechoslovak Communist Party. On the contrary, in this age of upsurging internationalism the Communists tended to treat them as bourgeois prejudices.

Nevertheless, in their approach to the national question the Communists were more subtle and sophisticated than the old Social Democrats and the Czech National Socialists who stood for a unified Czechoslovak nation. For example, in 1921 the Communist leader Šmeral put forward in parliament general proposals for the recognition of the existence of a Slovak nation. He did not offer any concrete plans for implementing these in practical political terms. The Communists had no programme for an autonomous status for Slovakia or for some other form of a federal state even on the Soviet model. Following the recommendation of the Comintern in 1924, the Czechoslovak Communist Party adhered to and declared the principle of the existence of a Slovak nation but again it did not make this an important issue in its political platform.

One of the explanations for this lukewarm attitude of the Communists to the question of Slovak national rights was perhaps the fact that by then Slovak nationalism had become the main political programme of the right-wing Hlinka Party. Further, the Communists had to look for political support not only from the Czech and Slovak working classes, but also from the substantial German, Hungarian and Ruthenian minorities.

As far as the Czech working class was concerned, it had been imbued by the Czech Social Democrats not only with a socialist and democratic spirit, but also with an anti-Austrian Czech patriotism, Czech national self-confidence and pride. Šmeral, at the first Congress of the Czechoslovak Communist Party, chided the Czech working class for being too nationalistic and too patriotic. He criticized Czech workers for carrying out their revolution only against Austria, and not against their own bourgeoisie. He complained that since 28 October 1918, the date of the foundation of the Republic, 'social patriotism has had a much more solid basis in our country than anywhere else in post-war Central Europe'.[1] Šmeral added that 'while the German bourgeoisie in Germany and Austria-Hungary was discredited by the defeat in the war, the Czech bourgeoisie strengthened its position by leading the fight for national liberation. That is why the situation in our country is substantially different, although the socio-economic structure is similar.'

[1] K. Pomaizl, *Vznik ČSR 1918* (The Creation of CSR), Prague, 1965, pp. 83–4.

The Russian working class's first concern – if it had a say in the matter at all – was not to grant real independence and freedom to the various nationalities living under Tsarist oppression. Similarly the Czech workers who joined forces with their bourgeoisie in a truly national-democratic revolution did not encourage the Slovaks to fight for their national rights, even had they been convinced, which they were not, that they were a separate nation. After all, most of the Slovak leaders of those times, including the legendary Slovak general Štefánik, believed in the existence of one Czechoslovak nation. In any case the Czech Communists no doubt believed in the self-healing effect of Communism which would automatically solve all problems, including the national one.

Slovak historians in the 1960s criticized not only the Czech Communists but also the Slovak Communist leaders for under-estimating Slovak patriotism, claiming that it 'was their duty to implement the principle of self-determination and to work with more conviction for the recognition of the Slovak nation. Autonomy for Slovakia was the minimum demand that the Communists should have put into their programme in the interest of Czechoslovakia's unity, of coexistence, and, of course, to achieve revolutionary political aims.'[2]

But there were occasions when the Czech Communists found the right psychological approach to the Slovaks. For example, Václav Kopecký, a young Czech Communist journalist and politician who after the Communist takeover in February 1948 became one of the most outspoken centralists, maintained at the Congress of young Slovaks in Trenčianske Teplice in 1932 that:

> The revolutionary proletariat of Czechoslovakia never acquiesced in the fact that the Slovaks were forced into a position of a nation with unequal rights. We always condemned this as imperialist oppression. We always repudiated and repudiate now all the privileges of the Czech nation against the Slovaks and we claim for the Slovak nation the right to determine its destiny freely and fully. We are resolved to support this right by all means at our disposal...Revolt in the name...of a nation which wants to live.[3]

These words – more high-sounding than sincere – were calculated to please many young non-Communist Slovaks present at that Congress. But the Communists did not succeed in clambering on to the

---

[2] Samo Falťan, *Slovenská otázka v Československu* (The Slovak Question in Czechoslovakia), Bratislava, 1968, p. 85.
[3] *Tvorba* (weekly), Prague, no. 28, 14 July 1932.

nationalist bandwagon. By 1932 many young Slovaks had already joined the party which gave first priority to the Slovak national cause, the Hlinka autonomists. As nationalists they were trusted more than the Communists, who so far had not even paid sufficient lip-service to Slovak aspirations.

Among the organizers of the Trenčianske Teplice Congress was a group of Slovak intellectuals with definite Marxist leanings, some of them members of the Communist Party. They included the well-known political writer Dr Vladimír Clementis, the poets Laco Novomeský, Ján Poničan and called themselves Davists, after the review *Dav* (The Crowd), which they published. Although they fully supported Communist policy they suggested that the official representatives of the party underestimated the national question. They did not go as far as to advocate Slovak autonomy as a practical political issue, but preferred to discuss the theoretical side of the problem. They too seemed to believe in the omnipotence of Marxism, including its internationalist substance, but they were more sensitive to the national needs of the country. Although they did not share the anti-Czech sentiments which the Slovak autonomists fomented in the people, they were particularly conscious of the unequal opportunities of the Slovak intelligentsia in relation to the Czechs.

It is no coincidence that Slovak Communists like Clementis and Novomenský and the younger Husák were among the first victims of the Stalinist purges in the 1950s, soon after the Czech Communists like Kopecký, who was regarded as an intellectual, and Gottwald, who never claimed to be one, came to power in February 1948. These Slovak Communist intellectuals, who heard such encouraging and actually nationalistic inflammatory words from the Czech Communist Kopecký in 1932, were now suddenly denounced as Slovak bourgeois nationalists. 'Bourgeois nationalism' represented the worst kind of deviation from the party line after Stalin had seen what more independent Marxist thinking led to, especially in matters concerning nationalism, in Yugoslavia.

While the Slovak nationalists, or 'clerico-fascists' as the Communists called them, looked for support from similar movements and ideologies abroad, and sympathized with forces like Hitlerism that were hostile to the Republic, the Communist Party in the last two years of the Republic became one of the staunchest defenders of Czechoslovak democracy. Confronted with the serious threat posed by German Nazism, the Party was inclined to stress the common danger which faced Czechoslovakia as a whole. Consequently the specific problems of Slovakia were not in the forefront of its interests.

The position of the Communist Party had been strengthened by the conclusion of the Czechoslovak–Soviet pact of mutual assistance in 1936. At the time of Munich the population was convinced that the Soviet Union would have come to help Czechoslovakia if asked to do so, even if France refused. But under the terms of the pact Soviet military action was conditional upon simultaneous French intervention. The Communists nevertheless opposed the acceptance of the Munich *Diktat* and became bitter critics of President Beneš. They condemned his capitulation, even accusing him of treason.

When in March 1939 Hitler tore up the Munich agreement and helped Slovakia achieve 'independence', the Communists did not receive his new creation with enthusiasm. In the circumstances they had every reason to reject the Slovak State, but, despite this, the Soviet Union, shortly after the German–Soviet Pact in August 1939, accorded it *de jure* recognition. Under these new conditions the Slovak Communists, in their clandestine struggle against 'Slovak clerico-fascism', did not advocate the restoration of the pre-Munich Czechoslovak Republic. After the outbreak of the Second World War the Slovak Communists actually repudiated the slogan 'For a free Slovakia in a free Czechoslovakia' which the now illegal Central Committee of the Czechoslovak Party had adopted in Prague. The Slovak Communists thought that this policy lacked realism and would find no symapthy in the country. At this stage, however, they were not opposed to the Slovak state as such, but only to its clerico-fascist character and its active collaboration with Nazi Germany.

In the middle of March 1940 the Moscow leadership of the Czechoslovak Communist Party under Gottwald, who had emigrated to the Soviet Union soon after Munich, took account of the new situation. In a coded cable Gottwald instructed the clandestine Slovak Party:

> It is necessary to change our pre-war slogans. The idea of 'restoration of Czechoslovakia' today is an expression of imperialist and anti-Soviet plans. The national question today is different. It is reduced to the problem of Czechs and Slovaks. We emphasize explicitly that the principle of complete right of self-determination is binding for our Party. This means the right to an independent state existence. For the Czechs it means fighting for the restoration of a national and state existence. In fighting for the right of self-determination our road differs from the road of world imperialism and Beneš.[4]

[4] Beer, Benčík and others, *Dejinná križovatka* (On the Crossroads of History), Bratislava, 1964, p. 59.

This new policy reflected the political interests and diplomatic considerations motivating the Soviet Union in its recognition of the 'clerico-fascist' Slovak state.

At this stage of the war Beneš and his group were already organizing the struggle for the liberation of Czechoslovakia on the side of the Anglo-French alliance. He had in mind pre-war Czechoslovakia and refused to recognize an independent Slovakia. Gottwald however advised the Communists at home that, 'Slovak separatism has a different role to play now... The Slovak State represents a basis for the fight for complete freedom of the Slovaks.'[5] This implies that the Czech and Slovak Communists in Moscow at this stage of the Hitler–Stalin honeymoon accepted the existence of the Slovak State. Nor was there any reference to the idea of the restoration of the Czechoslovak Republic in the clandestine materials of the Slovak Communists at home. They accepted 'the reality of the Slovak State'. Certainly it was more realistic than the concept advocated at that time by the Central Committee of the Slovak Communist Party, of a Slovak Soviet Republic, although they did not exclude 'the possibility of another solution on a federal basis or other form of coexistence with the fraternal Czech people'.

In this tragic period both the Czech and Slovak Communists proved how insincere, or at least how confused, were their views on the national question. The slogan of 'Soviet Slovakia' had fallen on barren ground. It was only a manifestation of a faulty evaluation of the international scene and of the internal composition of Slovak political forces, including the wishes of the Slovak working class. Moreover, Gottwald's instruction that 'the perspective of the Party is to show that it is possible by internal struggle and in cooperation with the German working class to preserve...not only the remaining national rights and gain new concessions, but to put realistically the question of complete freedom', must have sounded like a cruel joke to the Czechs living under Nazi occupation. It was as well for Gottwald and his comrades that these optimistic words of advice failed to reach many of his followers at home. Otherwise Gottwald's complete about-turn when Hitler invaded the Soviet Union in June 1941, and his new instructions to the Czech and Slovak Communists to become good patriots again, and recognize Beneš as a democratic leader, might have seriously damaged his reputation.

After June 1941 the Czech and Slovak Communists abroad who had refused to join the army of Beneš in France and, after the col-

[5] *Příspěvky k dějinám KSČ* (Contributions to the History of CPCz), Prague, 1967, no. 3, pp. 411–13.

lapse of France, in Britain (most of them preferring internment to military service), now became enthusiastic soldiers in the Czechoslovak Army. Many hundreds of them had had useful experience on the battlefield in the Spanish Civil War.

The Communist leaders in Moscow and London, if not in Slovakia, returned to their pre-war anti-Munich patriotic policy of defending the democratic Czechoslovak Republic. Old grievances against Beneš and his 'capitalist clique' were now forgotten, or laid tactically aside. Once more, they were ready to form a fighting coalition with the democratic bourgeois representatives of the Czech and Slovak people abroad. Though they were not included in the exile government in London, Czech and Slovak Communists did have members in the State Council, a kind of provisional legislative body, and in its various commissions which consisted of experts who helped the Council, in an advisory capacity, but who were not actually members of it. On the whole the Communists were very cooperative and obstructed the policy of Beneš very little.

6 THE STRUGGLE IN EXILE

At the time of the Munich agreement of September 1938 Beneš was forced into accepting a *Diktat* which he knew to be a dire threat to the survival of the Czechoslovak state. He was not a capitulationist as the Communists branded him. Being told in no uncertain terms by his Western allies, that he could not count on their help, and not trusting the Russian offer of help, he gave in. His resignation and departure from Czechoslovakia immediately after the Munich agreement was not an act of cowardice. From the moment he went abroad he began to organize the struggle for the liberation of his country.

Although he understood better perhaps than any other man the real circumstances and implications of Munich, he was nevertheless convinced that the Hlinka Party and through it the Slovak people were at least morally responsible for the collapse of the Republic in March 1939. He seems to have had more sympathy for President Hácha, who succeeded him on Hradčany, the presidential castle, after Munich and remained formal head of the Protectorate of Bohemia and Moravia after the occupation by Hitler, than for the Slovak President Tiso and his colleagues who agreed to Hitler's plans for creating an independent Slovak state. His old views and a new bitterness determined his attitude towards the Slovaks. He never made any secret of his centralist, Czechoslovak, political convictions. They were quite genuine and not motivated by the desire of a Czech bourgeois representative to dominate the Slovak people, as the Communists, especially the Slovak ones, suggested.

In exile almost all the Czech politicians joined Beneš in his cause. They recognized him as their constitutional leader. However, the more prominent Slovak politicians in exile were not as united certainly not under Beneš and not on his terms. He managed to gain the support of Slovak politicians of minor importance like the Agrarian Lichner and the Social Democrat Bečko. In the best tradition of his party the latter was an ardent advocate of 'Czechoslovakism' and, although he was a man of very small political stature, he became minister in the London exile government. However, Beneš' relations with the really outstanding Slovak personalities abroad, like the former Czechoslovak Prime Minister Dr Milan Hodža and the ambassador in Paris, Dr Štefan Osuský, were not as cordial. In fact, they were non-existent. These men, perhaps with an eye on their own personal careers in a future Czechoslovakia or even a Slovakia in a quite different post-war setting, for example in a federalized Central Europe, completely abandoned their centralist concept of a unified Czechoslovak nation and now accepted the existence of a separate Slovak nation, though not of the so-called independent Slovak State under Hitler. That was their basic quarrel with Beneš. For him 'Czechoslovakism' was a fundamental issue on which he could not yield. He gradually eliminated these first-rate Slovak statesmen in exile from Czechoslovak political life abroad, which came to be centred around his personality.

After Munich and even during the first months of the war, Beneš was not completely hostile to the idea of a federation or confederation in Central Europe. He discussed all kinds of combinations and possibilities, especially with the Poles. He even included the Hungarians and admitted the possibility of a readjustment of pre-war frontiers within the new political framework. In this connection he wrote in one of his messages home, 'We have no interest in spoiling our relationship with the Hungarians, especially in view of the way the Slovaks have behaved and still do behave.'[1] It is quite conceivable that the purpose of these messages was to frighten or put pressure on the Slovaks, who were always afraid of Hungarian aspirations. But Beneš would not and in fact did not go so far as to sacrifice Slovak territory, which was after all also Czechoslovak, to the Hungarians. However, he definitely repudiated the idea entertained by Hodža that Slovakia should be an equal partner in a future federation. He complained openly that, 'Hodža is trying to impose himself as the political representative of Slovakia and he wants to be recognized unconditionally as the leader and main representative of the Slovaks.'[2] Beneš liked to point out that in France and England people took an unfavourable view of the Slovaks and viewed 'with misgivings their discord, rivalry, personal ambitions, and lack of unity'.[3]

When the leaders of the Slovak State decided to participate on Hitler's side in the war against the Soviet Union, the future problem of Slovakia seemed to be simplified for Beneš. He was convinced that the Slovaks would discredit themselves completely in the eyes of the Allies. He showed his antipathy for the Slovaks in a conversation with his favourite Slovak, Lichner. He told him, 'First they stabbed

---

[1] *Dokumenty z historie československé politiky 1939–1943* (Documents on the History of Czechoslovak Politics 1939–1943), Prague, 1966, Doc. no. 80.
[2] *Ibid.*, Doc. no. 46.   [3] *Ibid.*, Doc. no. 46.

a knife in our back, then they went into war against the Poles. . .
Today they are marching against the Russians. It is horrible.'[4] It was
indeed horrible from all points of view. The behaviour of the leaders
of the Slovak State was inexcusable; it amounted to open treason
against the Czechoslovak Republic, and in its consequences it was
also against the interests of the Slovak people, who, one can safely
assume, did not go to war against Russia with the same fervour and
expectations as did the Germans. Nevertheless even allowing that
statesmen, like everyone else, are capable of adopting irrational and
emotional attitudes, the extent of Beneš' wrath is surprising. In his
conversation with Lichner he pointed out: 'I must remind the
Slovaks of this all the time. I shall tell them this at home. Our
journalists will have to write about it. It is high time to stop pam-
pering them so that one day they will stop behaving in such a
swinish way.'[5]

Similar outbursts against the Slovaks were often heard in his
circles in London. They were not only secretly whispered in intimate
conversations, but were openly expressed and found their way into
official documents. Unfortunately, such attitudes influenced the
general policy towards the Slovaks in the restored post-war Republic,
when Beneš returned home with his government. Not surprisingly, in
Slovakia the people learned of the feelings and views of Beneš and
had no illusions about the centralist tendencies of his government.
The separatists exploited this in their propaganda against the otherwise just cause for which Beneš was fighting abroad.

Meanwhile the Communists in both parts of occupied Czechoslovakia had again completely changed their tactics. They expressed
their disagreement with the declaration of the Czechoslovak government of 30 June 1943 which again stressed the idea of a united
Czechoslovak nation. They thought that it could only have a negative effect in Slovakia, where it was very well known from repeated
BBC broadcasts.

The Communists in the London State Council criticized the government, saying that neither the Council nor the Legal Commission was
informed of the content of this important document. The Czech
Communist Nosek complained:

> The declaration is based on the idea of a single sovereign
> Czechoslovak people. It creates a precendent and is prejudicial
> to what should happen to Slovakia after the war. In my view
> there is no sovereign Czechoslovak people, but only a sovereign

[4] *Ibid.*, Doc. no. 205.   [5] *Ibid.*, Doc. no. 205.

Czechoslovak Republic, which represents the Czechs and the Slovaks. They are two nations whose existence, economy, culture, language and destiny predetermine that they shall coexist closely in a united Czechoslovak state.[6]

Against criticism of this kind, which did not come only from Communists, Beneš argued that the question of the future of Slovakia could not be settled in exile without the participation of their political representatives at home. This argument sounded plausible enough, but there is enough circumstantial evidence to suggest that he was merely trying to evade the issue, especially when in other no less important matters Beneš was quite ready to establish binding principles.

He was supported by most Slovak members of the State Council, such as the Minister of the Interior, the Agrarian Dr Slávik, the anti-Hlinka Slovak Catholic priest Macháček who, although admitting that the relationship between the Czechs and Slovaks was 'not sufficiently understood', inclined to the view that 'after all, the Czechoslovaks are by nature one nation, predestined to live, in good and bad days together, in harmony and mutual understanding and unity'. Macháček did not see 'why we should in the present dangerous times talk about two nations and two languages'.[7] Slávik and Macháček were not Slovak politicians of Hodža's or of Osuský's calibre, but their arguments must have pleased Beneš and the Czech centralists.

In Slovakia the non-Communist opponents of the Slovak State – the number of which grew as chances of German victory diminished – had no clear views on the Czech and Slovak issue. Beneš must have appreciated a memorandum of 10 February 1943 which was brought to London by a former secretary of the Agrarian Party in Slovakia. It praised the pre-war Republic as a model of social justice and national and religious tolerance. In June 1943 a group of Slovak Social Democrats sent a message to London in which it was suggested that the pre-war Czechoslovak Republic was beyond criticism. In this message Beneš was informed that the Slovak Communists at home were divided into two groups: the intellectuals like Husák and Novomeský who stood for Slovak independence, and the second group, not mentioned by name but described as people with a working-class background who advocated absorption into the Soviet Union.

A more significant non-Communist group, headed by the old and

[6] *Nové Československo* (The New Czechoslovakia), London, 24 July 1943.
[7] *Archive of the Institute of History of the Communist Party of Czechoslovakia*, File 40 – State Council, quoted by S. Falt'an.

experienced politician Dr Vavro Šrobár, a prominent anti-separatist who in the first years of the Republic had been Minister Plenipotentiary for Slovakia, expressed fears of a possible revolution at the end of the war and proposed to Beneš the formation of a Slovak National Council. The group's memorandum suggested that under favourable circumstances the Slovak parliament could abolish the Slovak State and declare Slovakia a part of the Czechoslovak Republic. Šrobár's group declared its full confidence in the London government, 'because your plans and ours are identical'. They stood for 'unity of the state without reservations, without political separatism'. They only claimed 'complete equality with their Czech brothers and nothing else'.[8] It is significant that the well-known Slovak autonomist leader and Chairman of the Slovak parliament, Dr Martin Sokol, was one of the co-authors of this memorandum. He personally guaranteed the readiness of the Slovak parliament to abolish the Slovak State at 'an appropriate moment', which naturally could not be defined in exact terms. Sokol's attitude shows that the top Slovak autonomists did not form a monolithic group, especially in September 1943 when their feeling of security in an alliance with Hitler must have been shaken by the changing fortunes of the war.

Beneš was naturally pleased with this memorandum, but he had certain misgivings about the suggested Slovak National Council. He agreed with the idea, but only as a temporary arrangement and under the sovereignty of the government. The Council could be the highest political organ in Slovakia until the time when the united Czechoslovak government at home would function again. Beneš was not inclined to commit himself on the delicate issue of a Slovak National Council: not even Šrobár's safe anti-autonomist record was a sufficient guarantee against suspected Slovak separatism. As a shrewd tactician Beneš could not ignore the possibilty of revising the Czechoslovak constitution so as to recognize the existence of a Slovak nation. But at the same time, he strongly recommended that the other alternative, the existence of a united Czechoslovak nation, should be taken into consideration. As a temporary arrangement he suggested three regional parliaments, one for Bohemia, one for Moravia, and one for Slovakia and Sub-Carpathian Ukraine. This scheme was not based on national boundaries but on old historical regions, giving two parliaments to the Czechs in Bohemia and Moravia. (The Moravians never seriously claimed that they were a separate nation from the Czechs.) On the other hand, Slovakia and

---

[8] *Slovenské národné povstanie – Dokumenty* (The Slovak National Uprising – Documents), Bratislava, 1965, p. 91.

Sub-Carpathian Ukraine, a much more heterogenous region containing Slovaks, Hungarians, Germans, Poles and Ruthenes, was offered only one regional parliament.

Beneš did not totally reject the concept of decentralization, but he would not consider it on a national basis. He was quite adamant in this respect when he negotiated with Czech and Slovak Communist leaders in Moscow in December 1943. He said:

> You will never get me to recognize the Slovak nation. That is my conviction, and I am not going to change it. You as Communists are entitled to defend your attitude, I have no objection to that. But I am of the firm conviction that the Slovaks are Czechs and the Slovak language is only one of the dialects of the Czech language, like other Czech dialects – for example, that spoken in Haná.[9] I cannot stop anybody from calling himself a Slovak, but I shall not agree with a declaration that a Slovak nation exists. Anyway, this question will be decided only after the war.[10]

It is astonishing that an intelligent and experienced man like Beneš, a genuine democrat and liberal thinker, should have taken such an intransigent stand over the Slovak question. His attitude was, of course, encouraged by some centralist-minded Slovak politicians of minor importance at home and abroad and he was not alone. Not one Czech politician, with the exception of the Communists, and they only when it suited Moscow, accepted the idea that Slovakia was a national unit and not merely an administrative region.

In Slovakia the non-Communist anti-fascists were at first unwilling to cooperate with the Communists. They could not find a common political platform, particularly in the period before the Soviet Union was forced into the war by Hitler. In this period, although they could not boast of military victories, the prestige of the Western participants in the alliance was much higher than that of the Soviet Union which until June 1941 had adopted an attitude of benevolent neutrality towards Nazi Germany. But when after Stalingrad the Soviet armies began to drive out the Germans, the respectability and political importance of the Slovak Communists rose. The non-Communist democratic activists began to see no reason why they should not cooperate with the Communists when Britain and the United States were marching together with Soviet Russia towards the by now almost certain victory over Hitler and his unholy alliance.

---

[9] A district in Central Moravia.
[10] *Cesta ke květnu* (The Road to May), Prague, 1965, pp. 53–4.

In January 1943 the Praesidium of the Executive of the Communist International in Moscow accepted a resolution entitled 'On the Political Line and Most Urgent Tasks of the Communist Party of Czechoslovakia'. It stressed the character of the anti-fascist war as one of national liberation, aimed at creating a Czechoslovakia in which 'the people will have all rights and freedom to decide the form of their government and its policy'.[11] If previously the Slovak Communists had been ready to cooperate with the bourgeois anti-fascists only in order to work for the Slovak National Uprising, now the Comintern provided them with a broad but clear guideline on what tactics to apply.

A revealing document concerning the attitude of the Slovak Communists to the Slovak State and to the future of Slovakia was published in the Bratislava weekly *Nové Slovo* in 1969.[12] The document had been kept hidden in Party Archives until that time. It is a report which the Fifth Illegal Central Committee of the Slovak Communist Party[13] sent through Šmidke to Gottwald in Moscow and it was compiled in July 1944 a few weeks before the Uprising. The introductory paragraph of the report stresses that 'those who have been living in exile for a long time, unable to follow developments [in the Slovak State] are unable to evaluate conditions properly and cannot understand the mood and thoughts of the Slovak people'. This is a clear hint that even Czech and Slovak Communists living in exile in Moscow were not the best judges of the policy to be adopted in Slovakia, although in the following sections of the report the main criticism is directed against the Beneš government in London. The report evaluates various stages of the Slovak State which actually came into existence in October 1938, very soon after Munich, when for all practical purposes a dual republic was created. The only political group which was being persecuted was the Communist Party. Of the national groups, the Czechs were removed from all leading positions in the state and in industry; and, of course, the Jews' property was confiscated and about 60,000 out of 87,000 Jews were forcibly evacuated to Poland. The report repudiates the views held in London that from the beginning only the Protestants were opposed to the régime and that only they were the courageous standard-bearers of freedom. 'This is nonsense because opposition thinking does not

---

11 Beer, Benčík and others, *Dejinná križovatka*, p. 176.
12 *Nové Slovo*, Bratislava, nos. 33 and 34, 14 and 21 August 1969.
13 So-called because the previous four illegal Central Committees were arrested. Members were Novomeský, Husák and Šmidke.

have its origin in religion but is motivated by political and social causes. It is true that the Protestant clergy have discredited themselves less than the Catholics, but this does not imply that they did not discredit themselves at all. And this goes for secular circles, too.'

Mentioning only in passing that in fact only the Protestant clergy voiced misgivings against the evacuation of Jews, the report analyses the economic and social conditions in the state. It says:

> The régime managed to solve economic problems to the surprise even of those who were favourably inclined to the régime. There is a reasonable supply of consumer goods. Compared with neighbouring countries (Bohemia, Hungary, Germany, Poland) the situation in Slovakia is better from the point of view both of real wages and of the supply of goods. Wages have frequently been increased, the factories enjoy all kinds of privileges. The Slovak crown is the best currency in the commercial world of Europe...The German mark is a valueless piece of paper and, although the official rate of exchange is 11.65 crowns to the mark, the black market value is only 1–2 crowns...The workers are dissatisfied more on political than on social grounds, but despite that one may assume that after political changes have been made the workers and peasants will come out with their social demands.

Summing up the chapter on the economic situation the report states: 'Generally speaking after the experience of six years, Slovakia is capable of an independent economic and financial existence. It is in a position to stand on its own feet and has sufficient resources (even technical ones) and production potential to face international competition.'

Turning to the national question, the report warns that

> after the war only those prepared to adopt a firm position on this matter can hope to receive support from the population – those who can be relied upon not to take from the Slovaks what they have already achieved and for which even the Hlinka populists can claim credit. In this respect there is a difference between us and the Czech lands. The Czechs have lost not only political freedom but their national freedom as well. The Slovaks are politically worse off than during the Czechoslovak Republic, but from the national point of view the Slovaks and Slovakia have gained.

On the question of a separate Slovak state the authors of the report wrote to Gottwald:

The exiles, especially in London, are either misinformed about the situation or else deliberately misconstrue it. The fact remains that this state is independent in a way which is possible for a small nation during a war. There is no doubt that the state came into existence by grace of Hitler and it still exists by his grace. A thousand times panic-mongers have spread rumours that the Germans would occupy Slovakia but so far this has not happened. The régime directs its internal affairs independently. The economy is in the hands of the native people. The legislature, the schools etc. are run by native people. The German influence is strong but not to the extent that independence is only a façade. For instance, during the last five years the Gestapo have not arrested one single Slovak citizen. Vilo Široký[14] who was taken to Brno from his Bratislava prison to be confronted by some witness, has been returned, although the Germans would have liked to liquidate him. German pressure is exercised through interstate negotiations, both political and economic, but is not felt by the man in the street...Hitler so far respects independence and the Germans from the Reich have behaved, especially in the last few months, in an exemplary way.

The authors of the report express their awareness that this situation could be changed overnight and that 'independence could be buried in a few hours, as has happened to far larger states'.

This eventuality, which the report mentions but does not take very seriously, did in fact come about shortly afterwards, when the German divisions came to save the Tiso régime in August 1944. They remained in occupation of Slovakia after the defeat of the Uprising until they were finally driven out by the liberating Soviet armies and General Svoboda's Czechoslovak regiments.

When *Nové Slovo* published this document in 1969, it not did not state why it had hitherto been kept secret, although during the Fifties it could have been used by the prosecutors as evidence against Husák, Novomeský and Šmidke, proving their almost positive attitude towards the Slovak State; they clearly stood for Slovak separatism. The report concluded:

> If this state had a different political structure and were ruled by another régime, to say nothing about a change in its alliance with other states (having in mind the Soviet ally in the first place), there would be no objections to independence from a Slovak point of view. Not surprisingly, many honest people are

[14] A leading Slovak Communist whose role and profile are described in the following chapters.

seriously considering and participating in movements whose aim is to change the régime, to give the state a different substance, but to keep its independence.

Knowing to whom these words were addressed and knowing that the Czech Communist Gottwald in Moscow, not to mention Stalin, might have different plans for the future of Slovakia, the report ends: 'When this state collapses, together with its régime, nobody will be sorry, assuming that what will come will not take anything away from the Slovaks, but will improve their situation. This improvement is being looked forward to by the Slovak people.'

In Moscow Gottwald must have read this document with very mixed feelings. However, soon after he arrived with the report in Moscow, Šmidke was sent back to Slovakia to restore the illegal party organizations, badly hit by frequent arrests.[15] He returned to Slovakia with instructions to prepare a national uprising together with the anti-fascist democrats, and was promised Soviet help.

In looking for partners the Communists even considered such autonomist leaders as Karol Sidor, who as Slovak ambassador to the Vatican had connections with the Czechoslovak movement abroad, and also the previously-mentioned Dr Martin Sokol, Chairman of the Slovak parliament, who showed willingness to use the parliament in a process of liquidation of the Slovak State by quasi-legal methods, as Šrobár had suggested to Beneš a few months previously. But since the London exiles were not too enthusiastic about cooperating with such well-known Hlinka populists, the Communists themselves became worried lest the support of these men should discredit them. Moreover, if such men had the opportunity to participate in the anti-fascist coalition, their influence, which was growing as the chances of extremist pro-German collaborators like Tuka, Mach, and Tiso himself deteriorated, could grow into a considerable force outweighing the Communists. In the coalition they would naturally become allies of the non-Communist anti-fascists. So the idea of bringing these autonomists into the coalition was dropped altogether. The former Agrarians and members of the Rázus Protestant Autonomist Party were adopted as more acceptable allies. They held

---

[15] Husák and Novomeský, two of the three members of the illegal Firth Central Committee, stayed at home throughout the war. They were not arrested although they were well-known Communists. Husák was legal adviser to an international transport firm. Novomeský worked first at the Soviet Legation in Bratislava and, after it was closed down, he continued undisturbed in his literary activities. This was probably due to their personal connections with fellow-intellectuals who had influence in the highest quarters, such as the powerful Minister of the Interior, Šaňo Mach.

important positions in the state apparatus; most of them had remained genuinely anti-fascist and could be very helpful in the preparation of the Uprising.

With these bourgeois anti-fascists the Communists, on the basis of the so-called Christmas agreement, created the Slovak National Council at the end of 1943. The programme of this body represented a compromise arrangement between the Communists and their partners. Its aim was neither a proletarian nor a bourgeois national revolution. The task of the Slovak National Council 'was to guide the struggle of the Slovak people and at an appropriate moment to take over power and transfer it to the elected representatives of the people'.[16] The Slovak National Council declared itself in favour of restoring the Czechoslovak Republic, in which the Czechs and Slovaks would live together on an equal basis. The future Republic would be a democratic state which in its foreign policy would co-operate mainly with Slav countries, especially with the Soviet Union. The programme envisaged economic reforms and the elimination of the churches from political life of the country. This was a broad political platform on which all anti-fascist forces could unite and join in the main immediate task – the organization of the Slovak National Uprising.

The Slovak National Council recognized the leadership of Eduard Beneš in the struggle of the Czech and Slovak people, despite the fact that it disagreed with his concept of the restored Republic, particularly that aspect concerning the constitutional position of Slovakia. Beneš was reluctant to recognize this body. The Czechoslovak Communist leaders in Moscow, on the other hand, did so at once. A week before the Uprising, on 23 August 1944, they gave the Slovak National Council full recognition not only as an instrument for carrying out the revolution but also as a future national organ representing the Slovak people. This in itself had no immediate practical bearing on the Uprising, but it strengthened the moral support and political standing of the Communists. In the eyes of the nation they could now present themselves as true patriots and even nationalists. The Moscow document recognizing the Slovak National Council states that the solution of the Slovak problem 'will be achieved in a united Republic in a fraternal settlement with the Czech nation on the basis of equality and the wishes of the Slovak nation'.[17] The Slovaks regarded this as a clearer pledge than the

---

[16] G. Husák, *Svedectvo o slovenskom národnon povstaní* (Testimony on the Slovak National Uprising), Bratislava, 1964, pp. 47–8.

[17] *Slovenské národné povstanie – Dokumenty*, p. 312.

vague promises of President Beneš who consistently prevaricated, arguing all the time that it was for the people at home to decide. He refused to acknowledge the fact that the Slovak people had already made up their minds – at home.

President Beneš is on record as stating that he knew of each step in the organization of the Uprising; he agreed with it principally because he realized that it would strengthen his position with the Allies. This attitude implied rather mixed feelings. In a sense the Slovak fight at home was competing with his struggle abroad. This conflict often arises in movements of this kind and in Poland and Yugoslavia, it brought disastrous results for the emigré representatives of the struggle for national liberation. In the case of Czechoslovakia, as a result of the undoubted statesmanship of Beneš and his undisputed standing with the Allies, this problem was not so acute in the first years after the war.

The broadcasts from Czechoslovak government in London made no mention of the Slovak National Council during the first months of its existence. The Slovak Communists allege that this was on Beneš' own instructions. It is possible that he did not consider it opportune to openly support an organization which from the point of view of the government in Bratislava was illegal and had therefore to act underground. Those Slovak historians who tend to treat Beneš as a ruthless hard-liner on the Slovak question – and who themselves adopted a rather hard-line attitude towards him – maintain that, when the Uprising took place, Beneš did not behave in accordance with the expressed wishes of the Slovak leaders at home. They do not admit that he was right to refuse the rather Quixotic Communist claim that he should have issued an appeal to the Czech people to do the same as the Slovaks and they forget that the situation in the Protectorate was manifestly different from that in Slovakia.

In Slovakia, unlike the Czech lands, the complete restoration of pre-Munich Czechoslovakia was not a self-evident goal for the resistance fighters even though they recognized the benefits of a common state with the Czechs. The Slovaks had no illusions about the Slovak State created in March 1939. They knew it was Hitler's puppet. Its existence was absolutely dependent on the fortunes of its Nazi masters and when it became clear that Hitler was losing the war, a sense of self-preservation made many Slovak politicians dissociate themselves from the protector who could not even protect himself.

The various groups in the gradually emerging anti-fascist, anti–German alliance were united in believing that resistance at home had to rely on help from abroad. They recognized allegiance to Beneš' exiled government in London, although the Communists naturally looked to Moscow and to the Party leaders headed by Gottwald who lived there during the war for guidance. The bourgeois resistance groups in Slovakia were inclined to accept the view that a military putsch based on an influential section of the Slovak Army, with which they had good contacts, would be the best way of defeating the Slovak State. This action would coincide with the last stages of Germany's military defeat. The Communists, although not rejecting this idea, believed, in accordance with their doctrine that a 'continuous open struggle of the masses' was a pre-condition of liberation, if possible with the help of the Red Army.

The Communists tried hard to keep their Party cells working. After the German invasion of the Soviet Union they attempted to organize workers' guards. Their impact however was negligible. Their existence only laid the Party open to increased persecution. In the spring of 1943 the whole Party organization in Slovakia and by then, the fourth, illegal Central Committee was liquidated by the Slovak secret police, so that the Czechoslovak Communist leaders in Moscow had no contact with their followers in Slovakia. Beneš was more in touch with Slovak non-Communist politicians at home than Gottwald with the Slovak Communists. An additional reason for the isolation of Slovak Communists was mistrust for Communist intellectuals like Husák and Novomeský. Unlike Communist leaders of working-class origin who languished in jails they were more or less free citizens. In Moscow it must have been known that these men were using their comparative freedom to promote Communist policies, although it was rather difficult to catch up with the frequent and rapid changes these were undergoing.

At the end of July 1943 Moscow sent Karol Šmidke, a leading Czech Communist official, to Slovakia where he had worked for a long time before the war. He was a deputy in the National Assembly in Prague representing a Slovak constituency. Šmidke restored the Party organisation and formed a new, the fifth, illegal Central Committee with Husák and Novomeský as its members. The Party adopted new methods of work, less spectacular and risky than before. Instead of actions calculated for immediate effect, the Party's main aim was to prepare for an Uprising in collaboration with all the anti-fascist forces.

Beneš was well informed about the various groups hostile to the Slovak State. He relied on a comparatively few 'Czechoslovakist' hardliners, mostly Czechs who still managed to stay in Slovakia and survive the clerico-fascist state. More important for him, however, was a small group of Slovaks led by Šrobár who had good contacts with high-ranking officers of the Slovak Army.

Beneš had virtually no supporters amongst the most influential bourgeois anti-fascists, members of the radical wing of the former Agrarian Party and of the Rázus Protestant Autonomist Party. They held strong positions in the Slovak civil service and the higher echelons of Slovak industry and finance, which proved to be of great importance in the preparation of the Uprising. They were the closest partners of the Communists in the Slovak National Council, particularly of Husák and Novomeský.

Outside these groups, the Slovak Minister of Defence, General Čatloš, played his own special game. Inspired perhaps by the French Admiral Darlan who in 1942 deserted Pétain and became a supporter of the Americans when they landed in North Africa, but more probably having learnt a lesson from recent events in Rumania and Bulgaria, Čatloš approached the Russians in 1944. He offered to transfer the whole Slovak Army to them. His plan did not materialize. Beneš rejected it because Čatloš' aim was to secure an independent Slovak State, something which for different reasons neither the Russians nor Beneš wanted.

In the meantime the Partisan movement in Slovakia had grown in size and strength. Since the establishment of the Slovak National Council, the Partisans did not only enjoy the active support of the

Communists. Now they could rely for actual help on local national councils on which both Communists and Democrats were sitting as partners in a coalition. The first major group of Partisans was formed by Ľudovít Kukorelli in eastern Slovakia. In the Turiec region Karol Žingor organized so-called Partisan camps in conjunction with Ján Repta who started a similar movement in the hills of Western Slovakia. In central Slovakia the most famous Partisan groups were 'Sitno' and 'Vtáčnik'.

The Partisans were still regarded as a specifically Communist army. The democratic anti-fascists therefore increased their efforts to gain ground among the officers of the Slovak Army. One of them, Lieutenant-Colonel Ján Golián, the commanding officer of an infantry regiment in Banská Bystrica established direct contact with Beneš. On 23 March news reached the Slovak National Council that Golián had formed the so-called Military Resistance Centre and had been appointed Commander-in-chief of this body by Beneš. The Slovak National Council was taken by surprise. Later Golián was joined by General Viest whom Beneš had sent from London. Viest was one of the few Slovak officers of the former Czechoslovak Army to go into exile, a particular embarassment to the Slovak State as he had also been the only Slovak General before Munich.

The activities initiated by Beneš caused some confusion and friction amongst the resistance fighters in Slovakia. Under conditions of illegality mutual suspicions and doubts about the aims of the movement, personal ambitions, coupled with lack of regular communication, generally give rise to situations difficult to disentangle. In Slovakia this aspect of the resistance struggle was evident.

Communist attempts to establish contact with the rank and file of the Slovak Army were not successful even though the Army was conscripted. The bulk of the Partisans was in fact recruited from Army deserters. The Germans were aware of the deficiencies of Slovak soldiers. Those sent to the Eastern front were not known to be enthusiastic fighters, and Slovaks could not even be used as occupation forces in the Ukraine where originally they were presented as Slavs preferring the Germans to the Russians, thus setting an example for other Slav nations under Russian rule.

The Slovak Army had little experience of active combat. In March 1939 it fought to save part of Slovak territory from the Hungarians, during the German invasion of Poland on the other hand they proved to be rather difficult allies. There were rebellions in the Slovak garrison towns of Ružomberok and Kremnica; a whole unit of Slovak pilots fled from Piešťany airport to join the Poles; later desertions to the Partisans in the Soviet Union were so frequent that Slovak soldiers had to be withdrawn from the front; and after the Allied landings in Italy many Slovaks joined the Partisans there.

Slovak officers too found common cause with the anti-fascists. However they remained with their units in the legal Army on the advice of the resistance movement. In April 1944 after Šrobár's intervention the Military Resistance Centre headed by Golián, agreed to become a constituent part of the Slovak National Council. It was a compromise solution which allowed Golián to recognize first allegiance to Beneš who still could not make up his mind about the Slovak National Council.

In June 1944 the Military Resistance Centre together with the Slovak National Council prepared a plan for the Uprising. A delegation was to be sent to the Soviet Union to discuss joint military moves with the Red Army. On the night of 9 July 1944 Šmidke and two non-Communist officers, General Jurech and First Lieutenant Hanus, were to fly to Moscow but the flight had to be cancelled because of alleged technical difficulties. Despite suspicions arising out of this incident, discussions continued in the course of which two alternatives for the beginning of the Uprising were worked out. According to the first plan, which was obviously more advantageous, the date was to be fixed by the Slovak National Council after consultations with the Soviet military command. The alternative was actually an emergency measure: the Uprising would start as a defensive movement in the event of a German occupation of Slovakia.

The Slovak Minister of Defence General Čatloš, did not participate directly in these discussions. He was busy preparing and trying to sell his own plan. But at least some of the leading persons of the resistance movement had knowledge of the Minister's intentions.

On 2 August Lieutenant Korecký, a delegate of Golián's military Resistance Centre, helped by a radio link with the Czechoslovak military headquarters in Britain, reached Moscow by plane. He handed over the plans of the Uprising to General Pika, head of the Czechoslovak military mission in Moscow and Beneš' representative. Two days later, Šmidke, the Communist, and Colonel Ferienčik, the non-Communist, both official delegates of the Slovak National Council, succeeded in leaving the military aerodrome near Banská Bystricia, which was still held by the Slovak air-force. This flight was piloted by major Lysický acting on orders from Čatloš. Lysický was expected to negotiate on behalf of Čatloš with the Soviet authorities. Although Lysický enjoyed the confidence of the Slovak National Council, the fact that Šmidke arrived in Moscow with the help of the Minister of

Defence of the Slovak State, caused many complications. The Soviets thought it advisable to keep his mission secret: after all, their official partners were Beneš supporters, men like General Pika who worked out an ambitious plan based on information brought from Slovakia by Korecký. This promised the Soviets a far-reaching strategic success. The Czechoslovak resistance would open the frontiers in the Carpathian Mountains to the Red Army. Within twenty-four hours the front would have advanced three hundred kilometres to the west, and the Soviets would rapidly occupy the whole of Slovakia.

Military leaders in Moscow were not too hasty with their reply. The Red Army still stood on the Vistula. According to Pika's plan, military action in Slovakia would begin when the Russians reached Cracow. In fact, on 15 August the commander of the Fourth Ukrainian Front ordered his troops to be ready for an offensive in the Carpathians. This might have given the impression that the Soviets had accepted the Czechoslovak plan but, events in Rumania which took place at the same time caused them to change their mind. On 26 August preparations for the offensive in the Carpathians were called off. Moscow thought that Rumania was much more important, offered better possibilities and more immediate results.

In Pika's plan a major role was allotted to the two Slovak divisions, stationed along the Carpathians, which were supposed to open the way to the Red Army. The Germans, acting either on their own information or generally mistrusting the Slovaks in such an exposed position, decided to disarm those two divisions and the order was carried out on 29 August, the very day the Uprising was officially proclaimed by Golián. Just before that he had to suppress an attempt by a group of Slovak officers in Banská Bystrica to capture the town in the name of General Čatloš. Before noon on 30 August the Free Slovak Radio Banská Bystrica broadcast a proclamation of the Central Revolutionary Council headed by Šrobár, urging revolt against the Slovak State and the German armies occupying Slovakia. Golián and Šrobár adopted the second alternative for the beginning of the Uprising. The moment was not chosen by them but forced upon them by the Germans. President Tiso and, strangely enough, Čatloš called on the Slovak soldiers to resist the Communist rebels and traitors to the very end. This attitude was to be expected in Tiso's case; it was natural for the President of the Slovak State to give his blessing to the Germans. Čatloš' motives were more complicated. Was it the tactical move of a man playing a double role, or an expression of resentment against those who were reluctant to believe him?

The Germans' action resulted from their distrust of the Slovak

Army either with Čatloš or without him. However, even if they did still suspect the Minister of Defence of their model puppet state, it was tactically sensible to use him now to spread confusion among the Slovak soldiers whom they feared might join the rebels.

At least in its initial stages the Uprising looked more like a spontaneous movement than a coordinated action by either Golián, Šrobár and their Central Revolutionary National Council, or by the Slovak National Council. The central body for the Partisans was the Ukrainian Command of the Partisan Movement. But it was characteristic of the confusion of those days that when the Command decided to postpone any open clash with the Germans in Slovakia, the orders reached the Partisans too late. By then the Partisan unit 'M.R. Štefánik' named after the legendary Slovak hero of the First World War, had blown up the railway tunnels near Strečno and Král'ovany, thus damaging the most important link between eastern and western Slovakia, and the tunnel near Handlová, which stopped German supply lines to the Turiec region in central Slovakia. This happened on the night of 23 August. The same Partisan unit appeared in Martin, which was occupied on 25 August by the Slovak Army under the pretext of protecting the town against the Partisans. In fact the officers and rank and file of the Army came to Martin to save the town from German occupation and hand it over to the Partisans.

In Brezno, north-east of Banská Bystrica, the military commander of the town, waited only for his old friends the Partisans to come. When on 25 August they arrived and arrested the local fascist leader together with a German officer who was in possession of important documents, they met with no resistance. On the same day the workers in the nearby iron works at Podbrezová downed tools and expelled the German managers. With the help of the Partisans they occupied the plant and marched into Brezno with their comrades from the engineering works in Piesok to join the Partisans. The town of Ružomberok, a former clerico-fascist stronghold (the birth-place of Andrej Hlinka, founder of the People's Party), was occupied by the Partisans and the Slovak Army on 26 August. They opened the gates of the regional prison and released the political prisoners held there.

On 27 August Slovak soldiers in Martin intercepted the German military mission headed by General Otto as it returned from Rumania under the pretext of protecting them from Partisans in the region. Actually the German officers were arrested and when they refused to hand in their weapons and attempted to resist they were shot in the barrack courtyard. Meanwhile local national councils in the surrounding towns and villages seized power, organized new Partisan units and arranged for the Slovak Army to provide them with weapons.

The instruction to postpone direct action issued to the Partisans by the Ukrainian Command was a result of negotiations by Šmidke and his colleague Ferienčik on 24 August with the Czechoslovak Ambassador in Moscow Zdeněk Fierlinger. The meeting was attended by members of the State Council based in London and now sent to Moscow to maintain contact with the Soviet authorities and keep an eye on Czech and Slovak Communists. Beneš still tried hard to discredit Šmidke's mission and thus the Slovak National Council. He argued skilfully that Čatloš had helped them to come to Moscow and that they had actually brought with them the so-called 'Čatloš Memorandum' in which the Slovak Minister of Defence had outlined his plan.

The Communists in Slovakia and their coalition partners in the Slovak National Council thought they should wait for the completion of Šmidke's mission and his return to Slovakia. However, individual Partisan leaders who were either not informed of the tactics of the Slovak National Council, or were dissatisfied with the slow course of events, began to act on their own. They were assisted by the local garrisons of the Slovak Army and by the population who joined the rebellion unreservedly.

In the days immediately before the official proclamation of the Uprising by Golián and Šrobár the enthusiasm of ordinary people seemed to be more typical than the 'coordinating' activities of the leaders in Bratislava, London and Moscow. It was a real 'people's movement'. Slovak partisans, soldiers, workers, peasants and intellectuals, wherever they had the chance, went into action virtually without their new national leaders. The latter joined the people only after they had seen what was happening and realised they could not stop the course of events.

Dr Husák, one of the creators of the Slovak National Council, was still in Bratislava on 30 August when, after Golián seized power in Banská Bystrica, one of Šrobár's men read the Proclamation of the Central Revolutionary National Council on the rebel radio. Husák obviously was waiting for Šmidke. When he heard about events in Banská Bystrica he hurried there with two democratic members of the Slovak National Council, Lettrich and Josko. They came not to stop the Uprising but to counteract Šrobár's attempt to exploit the situation for his own political purposes although Šrobár pretended to be a devoted member of the Slovak National Council which he helped to establish.

Husák and his more trusted democratic colleagues drew up their own Declaration of the Slovak National Council and published it in Banská Bystrica on 1 September. Full support for the Slovak National Council was given by the three Partisan brigades which arrived in Banská Bystrica on the night of 29 August: they were quick to realize the implications of the conflict between various politicians and officers aspiring for leadership.

Šrobár's Revolutionary Council was dismissed but Šrobár came out of the wrangle unharmed. The rule of the Slovak National Council, as the only legitimate executive and legislative organ was established. The Slovak State ceased to exist where now the writ of the Slovak National Council was running. Soon normal life came to the liberated territories which covered the whole of central and some adjoining parts of eastern and western Slovakia. A good transport system was functioning, factories were manufacturing goods, peasants were bringing in their produce, shops offered an abundance of supplies thanks to many friendly and sympathetic Slovak officials in the state administration and industry. They took good care that food and other consumer items arrived in time to the territory in which they expected the Uprising to take place. The Director-General of the Slovak State Bank, a former Professor of Economics at the Comenius University in Bratislava, Dr Imrich Karvaš, was mainly responsible for an adequate supply of Slovak currency in the liberated territories. Some of the Slovak officials stayed in Bratislava with the consent of the organizers of the Uprising to safeguard help and ensure a flow of supplies from the capital.

In the meantime Šmidke and Ferienčik returned from Moscow to Banská Bystrica. On 5 September they informed the Plenary Session of the Slovak National Council of the results of their negotiations in Moscow. The chief aim, as they put it, had been to coordinate the Uprising with the general policy of the Red Army. In the event this goal has not been achieved. Nevertheless Šmidke helped Husák to strengthen the position of the Slovak National Council and above all, brought for his own Party members strict instructions to cooperate with all democratic forces for the success of the Uprising.

When on 28 August the Germans began to reoccupy Slovakia they did not realize it would take them two months to suppress a movement with which the majority of Slovaks sympathized. Eventually they did reestablish the revengeful rule of their desperate henchmen in Bratislava. Golián and Viest were taken prisoners and executed by the Germans.

The Uprising as such was liquidated but the Germans failed in their attempt to finish off the Partisans who retreated to the mountains and forests. From there they continued to harrass the Germans until in the early months of 1945 they were joined by the Red Army and the Czechoslovak brigade under General Svoboda. The Germans and the Hlinka Guards destroyed tens of villages and burned them to the ground. They killed hundred and thousands of men, women and children in their senseless rage at defeat in a region where a few years ago they had been so certain of victory. These reprisals only proved the Germans' bitter disappointment and their deep resentment towards a people which, despite the ambiguous attitudes of its leaders, had risen against the Slovak State because although it was their first 'national state', it was fascist: they had rebelled against the primitive nationalism which their fascist leaders had for so long been propagating.

Beneš intended to send a government delegation to the territory ruled by the Slovak National Council. The original function of such a delegation was to take over civilian rule in the steps of the Soviet armies gradually liberating Czechoslovakia. The Soviet and Czechoslovak governments agreed to this in May 1944. However the Slovak National Council refused to accept the government delegation. It considered this would be prejudicial to its future competence and status as the real government of Slovakia. When the Slovak leaders eventually agreed to receive the Czechoslovak government delegate, they made it clear that they did not recognize him as superior to the Slovak National Council but only as a liaison officer with the representatives of the Czechoslovak government abroad. In its declaration of 16 October 1944 the Council stressed again that it was 'the supreme organ of the struggle at home and assumed full legal and executive power in the liberated territories'. It stated that many of the principles of the Constitution of 1920 had been overtaken by the course of events and they shrewdly pointed out that even the government organization abroad had deviated from these principles in more than one respect. 'Therefore we are of the opinion that this Constitution cannot at this time form the foundation of the internal political structure of Czechoslovakia', the declaration concluded.[1]

Whatever the makeshift arrangements of the Czechoslovak government in London, handicapped by the very fact of being abroad, Beneš maintained his belief that in all respects the Constitution of 1920 remained valid. Two Czech ministers in London, Šrámek and Ripka,

---

[1] J. Lettrich, *O slovenskej národnej rade* (On the Slovak National Council). Bratislava, 1945, pp. 36–7.

stressed this as an essential point in their message of 20 September 1944 to the Slovak National Council, and emphasized: 'Now it is particularly important that everybody should know that there is complete agreement between us and you.'[2] The Beneš government tended to treat the Slovak National Council as a kind of regional administrative body, a regional parliament as permitted by the 1920 Constitution, and they therefore refused to accept it as a national organ with full legislative and executive powers.

This interpretation was partly made possible by the somewhat ambiguous attitude of the Moscow Communists (mostly Czech) who, unlike the Slovak Communist leaders at home, were not too explicit on the question of the competence of the Slovak National Council. Indeed, at this stage it seemed that on the national issue the Slovak Communists were in closer agreement with their non-Communist colleagues on the Council than with their Czech comrades in Moscow. The latter recognized the present status of this Slovak organ, but, as to the future, their attitude in the above-mentioned document of 23 August 1944 declared only that 'the all-Slovak congress of the national councils will express the will and wishes of the Slovak nation, and the new Slovak National Council will be entrusted with the function of temporary responsibility for public administration of the Slovak territory in agreement with the Czechoslovak government, represented by its delegate in the liberated territory'.[3] This was close to Beneš' own view.

When one of the high-ranking officials of the Czechoslovak government in London reported on the attitude of the Czech Communists in Moscow, with whom he had discussed the position of the government delegate in the territory held by the Slovak rebels, he wrote that he felt that the delegate should represent the authority of the central government. There is no reason to doubt that this was a faithful account of the views of the Czech Communists in Moscow. When Gottwald, the Czech Communist leader in Moscow, informed the Soviet Minister of Foreign Affairs of the character of the Uprising and its political platform, he spoke of 'a democratic Czechoslovak Republic based on equal rights for the Czech and Slovak nations'. Gottwald did not exclude the federative principle, but he did not emphasize it. In this and other statements he probably did not want to prejudice the question of the constitutional position of the Slovak National Council.

In September 1944 the Slovak Communists and Social Democrats

[2] *Slovenské národné povstanie, Dokumenty*, p. 537.
[3] *Ibid.*, p. 312.

held a joint congress at Banská Bystrica at which both parties were merged into a single Communist Party of Slovakia. The final document of this congress declared:

> The Slovak nation as a member of the family of Slav nations has defined the governmental, economic and social form in which it intends to realize its ideals. We want the new Czecho-Slovakia [notice the hyphen] to be a state of three Slav nations: the Slovaks, the Czechs and the Sub-Carpathian Ukrainians. These three nations have to decide forms of mutual co-existence on a basis of equality. We are firmly convinced that this agreement will be reached and that nobody will claim any special rights which would force our nation to turn in the direction of other nations. The friendlier and more settled the relations between the Slovaks and the Czechs, the firmer will be the new Czecho-Slovak Republic.[4]

This statement clearly indicated the will of the Slovak Communists, now fused with the Social Democrats, to live with the Czechs in one state; but the statement also included a warning, if not an open threat, that the Slovaks might consider other possibilities if the Czechs were not willing to accept their solution to the national question. The Slovak Communists could scarcely have had in mind the Poles, known for their anti-communist and anti-Russian sentiments, or the Hungarians, who were neither Slavs nor any less anti-communist. Rather the idea of a Soviet Slovakia as a part of the Union of Soviet Socialist Republics was still lingering in the minds of the Slovak Communists, although the slogan had been abandoned, or at least buried, for the time being. However, it would not have fallen on fertile ground in Moscow: Beneš was well aware of the interests of Soviet diplomacy and it is therefore unlikely that this possibility seriously concerned him. Nor is it likely to have perturbed Gottwald who, although paying more lip-service to the rights of the Slovaks and allowing certain high-sounding principles to be laid down in his Constitution of May 1948, when he took over absolute power, was even less inclined to concede Slovak national demands than his non-Communist 'Czechoslovakist' predecessor.

Despite all his reservations, Beneš could not but welcome the Slovak Uprising: his government's propaganda stressed the principle of unity and the heroic deeds of the Slovak people. However he himself only mentioned the Slovak National Council in public in a speech in the middle of September 1944 and he emphasized his own role

---

[4] *Pravda*, Banská Bystrica, 17 September 1944.

in the preparation of the Uprising, the way in which 'our allies in the West and in the East' were being kept informed,[5] their knowledge and his own of what the Slovaks wanted and what they were preparing.

Dr Vladimír Clementis, the Slovak Communist intellectual, who was out of favour with the Communist Party[6] and who, as a member of the legal commission of the State Council, did not officially represent the Party, saw the Slovak Uprising from a different point of view, much closer to that of his old friends Husák and Novomeský and their democratic partners in the Slovak National Council. He wrote in the Czechoslovak weekly published in London that 'Slovaks have proved beyond doubt, and against strong odds, that they are capable of waging a revolutionary national struggle.' He seemed to be worried about the eventual outcome of this struggle but 'whatever happens after these first two weeks of battles and heavy sacrifices, nobody and nothing can rob Slovakia of this victory'.[7]

Finally, after the national question had been discussed with a delegation from the Slovak National Council consisting of the Democrat Ursíny and the Communist Novomeský, who had come to London to negotiate with Beneš on the oustanding issues, the government in exile agreed to drop its hitherto uncompromisingly 'Czechoslovakist' principle. It was not, however, a case of genuine conversion, rather an attitude forced upon it by the course of events. The extraordinary session of the Czechoslovak government in London on 23 October 1944 accepted the viewpoint taken by the Slovak National Council:

> We stand for a Czechoslovak Republic as an independent and common state of Czechs, Slovaks and Carpathian Ukrainians on the principle of equality. The definitive constitutional arrangements will be made by the legitimate representatives of these three nations...The government, as long as it is abroad, does not intend to, and must not, interfere in these matters...The government is firmly convinced that this view is in agreement with the political intentions of the Slovak National Council.[8]

This document is of the utmost importance. In it, for the first time the Slovaks were recognized as a nation and the Slovak National

[5] *Čechoslovák* (weekly), London, 15 September 1944.
[6] The Party had suspended Clementis from membership for the duration of the war because of the deviationist views which he held in France, where he had emigrated after the fall of Czechoslovakia. He opposed the Soviet policy in the first stage of the war, and joined Czechoslovak Forces abroad.
[7] *Ibid.*
[8] *Slovenské národné povstanie, Dokumenty*, p. 748.

Council as their national organ. Beneš himself was forced to change his stand on the function of the government delegate in Slovakia and declared that 'the administration of Slovakia should be the concern of the Slovak National Council'.[9]

The change in Beneš' political tactics had been brought about by the very firm stand taken by the Slovak delegates. In an interview with an emigré journal published in Moscow, Novomeský declared self-confidently: 'We did not go to the exiles to get some kind of a majority to recognize the existence of the Slovak nation. . .There is no question of voting on the issue of whether a nation exists or not; the Slovaks would be a nation even if another nation refused to recognize their independent national existence.'[10] Here lies the crux of the whole matter; Novomeský was right in suggesting that the essential and final criterion is the will of a people to be considered as a nation, especially when that will is based on objective factors, such as territory, language and a common heritage.

The devoutly patriotic attitudes taken by Communists like Novomeský were the real cause of the personal tragedy of these and many other Slovak intellectuals soon after the Communists took over the Czechoslovak Republic in February 1948. Husák was another Communist of this kind. He too was soon to be criticized for his 'bourgeois nationalist' views. Among other accusations hurled at them by Gottwald in Prague and Široký in Bratislava were their activities during the Slovak Uprising. First, party critics and, later, secret police investigators and Gottwald's prosecutors in the people's courts of 'justice' reminded them of the nationalist stand they had taken. This perhaps was the only thing which was not invented in the charges against them. It was however put in a different and quite distorting light by being linked with absurd accusations that they were agents of western imperialism and, of course, of Tito's Yugoslavia.

Not that nationalism was altogther foreign to Communists of a different type, like Viliam Široký, a pre-war member of parliament from Bratislava, a man of working-class background. As he was of uncertain national origin in a country like Slovakia with large Hungarian and other minorities, the Party found it useful to present him as an internationally-minded leader. He was intelligent and a good platform speaker. After the fall of France, to which he had emigrated in 1939, he had managed to get to the Soviet Union for a short time. He returned home to organize clandestine Party activities but was

9 *Cesta ke květnu* (The Road to May), Prague, 1965, p. 298.
10 *Československé listy*, Moscow, 1 January 1945.

soon arrested, like most of the working-class Communist leaders. Non-intellectual Communist leaders seemed to be regarded as more dangerous by the Slovak clerico-fascist authorities and were imprisoned together with hundreds of ordinary Party members, particularly if they were Jews.

Široký kept sending out written instructions from his prison, always faithfully reflecting the prevailing official Party line. More than two years before the Slovak Uprising he stressed in these instructions the right of the Slovaks to self-determination, even the right to have their own state. He called for a 'fearless application of the national spirit, of the national idea in our politics'. He expressed himself in favour of Slovak state independence and at the domestic policy level against all forms of nazification introduced by Tuka and Mach. 'To fight for state and national independence means that the whole national liberation front must have a national character. The aim is to finish with the shameful situation in which the Slovak army is fighting against the fraternal Russian and Ukrainian peoples, in which it is waging war against it own fundamental national interests.[11] It must be remembered that this was the policy of the Party before the Soviet Union concluded a new treaty of alliance with the Beneš government in December 1943. Široký's quoted instructions are indicative, not only of Communist policy, often changed so frequently as to be meaningless, but of the mentality of the Slovak people whose favour they sought to gain by expressing such views.

When in 1949, as Chairman of the Slovak Communist Party and Vice-Premier of the Czechoslovak government in Prague, Široký became prominent in the witch-hunt against the 'bourgeois nationalists' who had expressed far less vehemently nationalist views during the Slovak State than he had, he considered his instructions from prison an embarrassment both for him and for the Party. He therefore ordered Miloš Gosiorovský, who was at that time the official historian of the Party, not only to omit the compromising passages from all quotations, but, as Professor Gosiorovský disclosed later,[12] to falsify his original hand-written manuscripts.

After the liberation of Czechoslovakia in 1945 and especially after February 1948, Gottwald, and later Novotný, also came to regard the Slovak Uprising, the policy of the Slovak National Council and that

---

[11] *Archive of the Historical Institute of the Slovak Communist Party*, Doc. 1/64, quoted by S. Falt'an.

[12] In 1963 at Party meetings and statements to the Central Committee, which were not published.

of the Slovak Communists at that time, as a dangerous and embarrassing episode, despite the fact that he had informally accepted its general outline in Moscow. Historical evidence now seems to indicate that the Allies intended Czechoslovakia and other neighbouring countries to be included in the Soviet sphere of influence after the war. This is one of the reasons why the Soviet Union had a free hand in directing the political actions of the Communist Parties in these countries.

In fact at certain stages during the war even the Soviet Union did not appear to object to the implementation of the federal principle. At the end of December 1944 Dimitrov, one of the most influential leaders of the world Communist movement, perhaps second only to Stalin himself, voiced positive views on federalism when discussing the subject with leaders of the Czechoslovak Communist Party, including Laco Novomeský as representative of the Slovak National Council. Dimitrov mentioned that the complete separation of the Slovaks from the Czechs would be against the interests of the Slovaks themselves. However, he thought that the best solution in liberated Czechoslovakia would be for the Czechs and Slovaks to enjoy a position of equality. There would be a Czech government in the Czech lands, a Slovak government in Slovakia and a common federal Czechoslovak government and parliament.[13]

Whatever the views of most Slovaks at this stage, a complete return to the pre-war Republic was unthinkable. For the Slovak Communists, even incorporation into the Soviet Union would have been a better alternative. Thus Gustáv Husák wrote in a weekly published during the Uprising:

> Six years of the existence of the Slovak State have weakened the will of the Slovak nation to live in one state with the Czech nation. The separatist propaganda, like the rather unfortunate formulation of our internal problems by the Czechoslovak government in London, have by no means contributed to the popularity of the future Czechoslovak Republic among the Slovak population. The Slovak working masses have in recent years moved politically and nationally in the direction of the Soviet Union and the call for the incorporation of Slovakia into the Soviet Union has frequently been heard.[14]

Nevertheless the Slovak National Uprising did have the effect of crystallizing the generally accepted idea of a new Czechoslovak

[13] *Cesta ke květnu*, I/2, p. 519.
[14] *Nové Slovo* (weekly), Banská Bystrica, 15 October 1944.

Republic in which the Slovak nation would find sufficient scope and means, guaranteed by precise constitutional and other legal norms, to live a free life as a nation. Although smaller than the Czechs, and in some respects less advanced they would be accorded full equality of opportunity.

The Slovaks had not been prepared to wait for liberation to be brought to them from abroad. At a time when even in Moscow it was thought to be premature to fight, the Slovaks had taken up arms. From a purely military point of view, the Uprising might have started too early. The original plan, for the Slovak Army to come over *en bloc* and open the Carpathian Mountains to the advancing Red Army had not succeeded. The Soviet leaders diverted their divisions to Rumania where issues for them more important were at stake. Hungary could easily be reached from there and the Soviets wanted to be in the Balkans before their Western Allies.

But judged even from military aspects, the Uprising was by no means a failure. It caused great damage to the Germans although they still had sufficient forces to suppress it. By the end of October they had recaptured Banská Bystrica but the rebels cut essential supply lines to the south-eastern front. The Germans lost the support of thousands of Slovak soldiers and their mistrust of the whole Slovak Army including its highest command, was proved more than justified.

Politically and morally, the Uprising showed that the Slovaks were prepared to bring the highest sacrifice in order to gain national freedom. It was a great moment in the troubled history of the nation. However much the Slovaks had been blamed for the events of 1848 when they turned against the Hungarian anti-Hapsburg revolution, or for 1938 when their leaders competed with their Czech counterparts for Hitler's favours, whatever Czech democrats and liberals have thought of them, there can be no doubt that the Slovaks had shown their real mettle. The rebels fully realized the price they would have to pay, even if the Uprising proved successful, and what the consequences would be if they were defeated. Therefore it would be unjust to dismiss the Uprising as only a minor episode in the great struggle which mankind waged against fascism. It would also serve no purpose to point out that it happened too late anyway, that at that stage of the war the Slovaks could already predict the outcome, and acted not just to save face but to save their skin.

It is only fair to acknowledge that no serious student of Czechoslovak history has attempted to give such an interpretation. Still the rather scant treatment of the subject outside Czechoslovakia, suggests

that the great Slovak rebellion is being regarded as much less relevant to the final outcome of the war than it actually was. The Warsaw Uprising, or the dramatic events in Rumania and Bulgaria, where
governments and kings changed sides in the war and enemies of yesterday suddenly became allies of today, have naturally attracted more
attention. It is equally natural that in Czechoslovakia, both Communist and non-Communist historians are much more concerned
with the Slovak Uprising. It has always been a burning issue in post-
war Slovak, or for that matter, Czechoslovak politics. One's attitude
towards the Uprising became the touchstone of one's political out-
look. This was especially evident in the Sixties and in the period
immediately before the fall of Novotný. By that time all the Slovak
and most Czech historians helped to remove thick layers of lies
surrounding the Uprising. Their efforts made it possible to tell the
true story.

8   AFTER THE LIBERATION

The Slovak Communists were somewhat disappointed by their Czech comrades in the discussions with Beneš on the future of liberated Czechoslovakia and had to compromise on the status of Slovakia. On this issue Husák again made explicit references to a common and united federative state at the first conference of the Slovak Communists, held from 28 February to 1 March 1945. The conference then accepted a Manifesto, in which the federative principle was implied, though not explicitly stated. The Manifesto demanded that in the armed forces, for example, there should be national Slovak units on Slovak territory, with Slovak officers and Slovak as a language of command, under a common Czechoslovak central general staff in which Slovak officers would be proportionally represented. But the main proviso of the Manifesto was the recognition of the Slovak National Council in the sense claimed and used during the Uprising, as the supreme representative, legislative and executive organ of Slovakia.

The Slovak National Council − a coalition between the Communists and Democrats − fully endorsed the contents of the Slovak Communists' Manifesto, at least as far as the national programme was concerned, at its plenary session on 2 March 1945. These moves were intended to influence the negotiations between Beneš, then still in Moscow, and the Communists. Actually, the so-called Košice Programme adopted on 5 April 1945 in the east Slovak capital, the first seat of the Beneš government on its return from exile, was the outcome of long discussions, in which the non-Communists and the Communists vehemently defended their respective views. The non-Communist parties believed in the pre-war concept of a centralized Czechoslovakia: they stood for private ownership of the means of production and parliamentary democracy. The Communist Party, in principle, supported the platform of the Slovak National Council, and of course took a Marxist view on economic matters. All political parties in the Czech lands and in Slovakia joined to form the National Front. This constituted the coalition government of Czechoslovakia. Immediately after the war this government was concerned more with the reconstruction of industry than with its nationalisation.[1]

The first Prime Minister of liberated Czechoslovakia was Zdeněk Fierlinger, a former Czechoslovak ambassador in Moscow with social-democratic sympathies. It was he who presented the policy of his government in Košice, with the exception of the sixth point of the Programme, relating to the position of Slovakia, which was read by Gottwald, who became Vice-Premier. (Whoever conceived this idea did not lack political astuteness.) It was Gottwald who called it the Magna Carta of the Slovak nation. Husák was not particularly impressed by this analogy; he did not like the expression because, as he wrote later, 'Magna' was an overstatement and 'Carta' implied something that 'feudal overlords used to grant their subjects'. His view was that the solution of the Slovak question, even as formulated in the Košice Programme, had been achieved through the struggles of the Slovak nation. 'It was nobody's present to the Slovaks',[2] he commented. Although Husák wrote this many years later, it is quite probable that this was what he and his colleagues actually felt at the time for although the Programme broadly accepted the rights of the Slovak nation it carefully omitted the term 'federation'. From then on the very word, and indeed any mention of the federative principle was studiously avoided in political debate in Czechoslovakia. Nevertheless the Slovaks, including the Communists, regarded the Košice Programme,[3] in comparison with the pre-war Constitution, as a great achievement. Its main advantage lay in the recognition of the Slovak National Council. The central government of the Republic would exercise common state functions in the closest cooperation with this Slovak organ. The Board of Commissioners was to be the executive body of the Council, the virtual government of Slovakia, although not explicitly so called. The Slovaks were guaranteed equal representation in central government offices, institutions and economic organizations.

The Programme did not fully accept the idea of purely Slovak army units with Slovak officers only, as proposed in the Slovak Communists' Manifesto. But it went more than half way towards it by stating that in 'the framework of the newly-built united Czecho slovak defence forces and united service regulations, national Slovak units (regiments, divisions, etc.) will be formed which will have a

---

[1] The first nationalization decrees were introduced on 28 October 1945, but affected only heavy industry, large enterprises and banks.

[2] G. Husák, *Svedectvo o slovenskom národnon povstaní*, p. 595.

[3] Košický vládny program (The Košice Government Programme), Košice, 1945.

majority of men, non-commissioned officers and officers of Slovak nationality, with Slovak as the language of command'. Officers and non-commissioned officers of the former Slovak army, 'as far as they have not sinned against the Slovak national honour' and were not liable to criminal prosecution for their activities during the former régime, were taken into the Czechoslovak army in their present ranks.

Gottwald, obviously to pacify the Slovaks, characterized the Košice Programme thus: 'I cannot imagine a new government which could tell the Slovaks less and give them less than this.' The Communists regarded the Programme as a minimum, while the non-Communists saw it as the maximum, and, as so often happens in such compromises, there was ample scope for subsequent conflicting interpretations.

Husák and Novomeský accepted the Košice Programme as good and disciplined Communists, hoping that the immediate future would soon give them the chance to promote an interpretation and political application closer to their original concepts. They seemed to regard the national question as more important than any other point of the Programme. The degree to which these nationally-minded Slovak Communists had to retreat reflected the range of disagreement between them and the official Communist line taken by the Czechoslovak Communist leader Gottwald in his compromise with Beneš. This was the root of the quarrel a few years later, a quarrel in which Gottwald represented a fairly united body of Czech Communist opinion against a divided group of Slovak Communists. In this quarrel Gottwald found allies in Slovak Communists like Široký, Bacílek and D'uriš.[4]

One of the conditions Husák and Novomeský insisted upon was the rehabilitation of their spiritual leader, Dr Vlado Clementis, whose party membership had been suspended during his exile in France and Britain on account of his deviationist views at the beginning of the war. In this they were successful. In 1945 Clementis became Secretary of State in the Ministry of Foreign Affairs and deputy to Jan Masaryk, following the then agreed policy that Slovak State secretaries should be appointed in ministries headed by non-Slovaks, and *vice versa*. However, Clementis, partly because he was fully occupied in his new job, but more probably because he was still not completely trusted by Gottwald and Široký, played only a minor role in the political life of Slovakia after the war.

After the liberation of the whole of Czechoslovakia by the Soviet

---

[4] For many years Julius D'uriš was Minister of Finance under Antonin Novotný but in 1963 he was removed from the government because of his frequent clashes with the Party leader.

and US armies on 9 May 1945, the practical implementation of the Košice Programme was the main test of the sincerity of President Beneš, of his government and of individual members of the coalition, in their attitude to the Slovaks. In fact, its main principles were incorporated into the new Constitution. But there remained problems of implementation and these were to account for certain differences in the development of the Czech lands and of Slovakia.

While in Bohemia and Moravia the Communist Party was the strongest in membership, the non-Communist parties, which formed the coalition government with the Communists, kept their own politically autonomous position within the framework of the National Front. All parties and other social and cultural organizations had to belong to it. The Government thus resembled a genuine national coalition with no party in opposition, as happened, for example, in Britain during the war. Before February 1948, the individual parties in the National Front, such as the Czech Social Democrats (before their fusion with the Communists), the Czechoslovak Catholic People's Party, and in particular the Czech Socialists, exercised a high degree of influence in the political life of the country as real, although not quite equal, partners of the Communists.

In Slovakia on the other hand the Communist Party had to deal with a numerically stronger coalition partner although its membership was twenty times higher than it had been in 1938. The Slovak Democratic Party in the last free parliamentary elections in May 1946 received 999,622 votes (62%), the Slovak Communist Party only 485,596 (30.4%).[5] At the beginning of 1948, immediately before the Communist takeover in February, the Communist Party in Slovakia had 180,000 members, the Democratic Party 257,000.[6] But unlike the non-Communist parties in the Czech lands the Democratic Party in Slovakia had no solid organizational basis. It was an amalgamation of all kinds of people and interests, including many former members of the Hlinka Party (though not those who had been discredited by their activities during the Slovak State). The Communists were not too particular either about receiving into their ranks former 'ordinary' Hlinka Party members. Indeed, some of the worst types (mainly of working class and peasant origin) from the infamous Hlinka Guards, the Slovak counterpart of Hitler's SS, managed to find their way into even the highest posts of the Party apparatus and survived the Stalinist purges, unlike many reputable old Party members.

[5] L'. Lipták, *Slovensko v 20. storočí* (Slovakia in the 20th Century), Bratislava, 1968, p. 265.   [6] *Ibid.*

Moreover, not only were the Slovak Communists better organized than the Democrats, but the other two Slovak parties, the Labour Party (which for a time thought that it might continue as an independent party despite the fusion of the Slovak Social Democrats with the Communists during the Uprising), and the Catholic Freedom Party, were only very poor counterparts to the non-Communist parties in the Czech lands. In addition, the Slovak Communist Party could rely on the support of the Czech Communists in most matters, certainly more than the Democratic Party could on the Czech non-Communists.

As far as the national question was concerned, a paradoxical situation developed in Slovakia. The Slovak National Council, as suggested by the Košice Programme, became the national organ in Slovakia with a Board of Commissioners as its executive body, acting under the supremacy of the central government in Prague. But as a result of the elections in May 1946 the Democratic Party had a clear majority in Slovakia. On the other hand in the Czech lands the Communists obtained 41 per cent of the votes in these elections. Although they lacked an overall majority, they were clearly the strongest party. As was to be expected, their Communist colleagues in Slovakia were consequently less inclined than was the Slovak Democratic Party to emancipate Slovakia from the central organs in Prague and to emphasize the autonomist elements of the Košice Programme. When the Slovak Communists wished to curb the power and influence of their stronger partner in the Slovak national organs, they had in practice to look to the central government in Prague for support and understanding. This was the case not only in important matters of economic and social policy, but even in matters which would ultimately represent an obstacle to the autonomy of Slovakia, even though it was for such autonomy that the Communists had earlier fought. In the end the decision of the central government and Czechoslovak National Front in Prague to limit the powers of the Slovak National Council and the Board of Commissioners was accepted by the Slovak Communists.

Thus until February 1948 the Slovak Communists did not directly oppose the limitation of Slovak autonomous rights even those guaranteed in the Košice Programme, and the increased influence of the central bodies in Prague. It helped them to introduce economic and political measures which they and their Czech comrades considered progressive: a more consistent policy concerning the confiscation of German, Hungarian and collaborators' property, and stricter punishment of the leaders of the former Slovak State (a matter in which the Slovak Democrats seemed to show more leniency, because they expected mass support from that section of the population which was still predominantly Catholic and even anti-socialist).

The Slovak Communists in fact contributed to the limitation which later led to the almost total liquidation of the powers of the Slovak national organs when in February 1948 the Communists in Prague became the sole rulers of the country and the new non-Communist partners in the 'renovated' National Front became mere puppets.

Until February 1948, the Slovak Communists, at least those at the highest level, such as their chairman Široký and the General Secretary, Bašťovanský, had ceased to regard the central government in Prague as the main source of danger. Instead they turned against their coalition partner, the Democratic Party, which they saw as the new nucleus of Slovak reaction. Široký, analysing the circumstances of the Democratic victory in the elections of May 1946, maintained that one of the main reasons for it was that Communists in Slovakia had trusted the Democrats too much and had not been sufficiently aware of the potential danger they represented. He himself had not taken part in the Uprising in August 1944: he had been in prison and since 1945 he had spent most of his time in Prague in various government posts, so the criticism was indirectly meant for Husák and the other Communist leaders in Slovakia. They were blamed for not having emphasized sufficiently the anti-fascist and popular character of the movement and also for concentrating too much on its national aspect. Now Široký blamed the Party for underemphasizing the principle that the main solution to national as well as to all other problems lay in the field of economics. 'The industrialization of Slovakia', he said, 'will be the main proof of the new relationship between the Czechs and Slovaks.'[7] He did not attempt to describe in detail what this new relationship should be.

Široký's words, even at this early stage, sounded ominous for the Slovak national cause as conceived by Husák and Novomeský and their non-Communist partners. Certainly the industrialization of Slovakia was an important issue, perhaps the most important one. After the war Slovakia was in a desolate and desperate state. The war had hit this part of the Republic much more heavily than the western regions where only the final battles against the retreating Germans were fought. Most of the towns in Slovakia were badly damaged; whole villages were destroyed and transport and industry completely disrupted. In the Czech lands most of the towns, includ-

[7] *Pravda* (daily), Bratislava, 1 August 1946.

ing Prague, and most of the industrial plants remained intact. The difference between the industrial potential of the Czech lands and that of Slovakia increased alarmingly.

The emphasis of the first Two Year Plan, starting in the New Year 1947, was therefore on reconstruction. Its aim was to reach at least the pre-war level of production. This applied mainly to Slovakia, which received substantial help from the central government in Prague and the Board of Commissioners in Bratislava. In Slovakia the Two Year Plan had the special additional task of raising industrial production to 10 per cent above the pre-war level. The trend in the first years of the pre-war Czechoslovak Republic, during which many Slovak factories had been closed down as superfluous, was now reversed. Plans were made not only for the reconstruction of old plants, but also for the construction of many new ones. Some industrial plants in the Sudeten border region were moved to Slovakia following the expulsion of the German population.

The Slovak Democratic Party, which was in favour of strengthening the private sector of industry, thus gained little credit for the benefits Slovakia reaped from the undoubted growth of the public sector; even the peasants became more sympathetic to the Communists, who were also more insistent and consistent in implementing the laws on agrarian reform than the Democrats. It was in this period that the Slovak Democrats thought it expedient to raise once more the national question. The Communists, under the leadership of Široký, and effectively directed by Gottwald in Prague, no longer attached any importance to this question. They argued that the situation in Prague had changed, that the Czech bourgeoisie was no longer in sole command of political and economic power, that on the contrary its influence was diminishing and would diminish even more rapidly in the future. 'There is nothing to fear from the Czech working class', the Slovak workers and the nation were told by Široký.

9 THE ROAD TO FEBRUARY

A political crisis in Bratislava in the autumn of 1947 preceded the upheaval which was to come a few months later in Prague. The Communists in Slovakia consolidated their position despite their disappointing results in the parliamentary elections. The Democratic Party had gone too far in its efforts to gain the favour of former members of the Hlinka Party and the Communists exploited this factor to the full. It was well-known that the Democrats had made strenuous efforts to save the leaders of the fascist Slovak State from execution. They publicly proclaimed their aim to save Tiso, the Roman Catholic priest who, in 1939, despite the Vatican's alleged lack of enthusiasm became President of the Slovak State. Although at his trial his main line of defence was that he had only been trying to make the best of a bad job, he had in fact been Hitler's willing puppet. Among other crimes he had handed over to the Germans, at their demand, the Slovak Jews, most of whom perished in concentration camps.

The Communists were well aware that the Democrats' attempt to save Tiso would receive considerable support from the Roman Catholic clergy. Still, the influence of truly reactionary elements was not strong enough to take effective action when Tiso and Tuka were eventually executed. When the long-delayed date of execution was announced, there were no visible signs of protest. Nevertheless, in the autumn of 1947 the state security organs, which though dominated by Communists, were actually headed by a non-Communist General Fierenčik, started to investigate contacts between the leaders of the Democratic Party and Hlinka underground exiles like D'určanský and Sidor. Some discrediting material was allegedly found, presented and cleverly used in Communist propaganda. But that was only one of the factors which precipitated the crisis. Bad weather made the 1947 harvest a disastrous one and the situation was worsened by the political mood in the villages and farms; this increased radical feeling in the country. The trade unions blamed black marketeers and owners of small businesses, either shop-keepers or small industrial entrepreneurs, who supported the Democratic Party. They were in fact partly responsible for disorganizing whatever the state tried to organize. Despite the radical monetary reform of 1945, which left nobody in the country with more than 500 crowns, private entrepreneurs managed to become relatively rich in a comparatively short time. It is difficult to be certain of the truth of the Communist claim that by autumn 1947 there were 35,000 new millionaires in Czechoslovakia but it was probably not without substance. The Communists accordingly recommended the imposition of a 'millionaires tax'.

Czechoslovakia, with Slovakia as a useful springboard, started to move quickly along the road which most of the People's Democracies had trodden with such monotonous similarity – a road which led internally to the total usurpation of power by the Communists and externally to their integration into the power-structure of the Soviet Union. Whether this process was accelerated by the Cold War, or whether the Cold War was a result of it, the international situation was certainly affected by Czechoslovakia's final conversion to Communism. In the autumn of 1947 a meeting of nine Communist Parties in Warsaw (including the French and Italian Parties which by that time had lost their positions in the post-war coalition governments, but had not ceased to play a leading role in the political life of their countries) established the so-called Information Bureau of the Communist Parties, better known as the Cominform, to succeed the old Comintern, which had been dissolved in 1943.

In October 1947 the Central Committee of the Slovak Communist Party, on the recommendation of Široký, initiated a campaign to change the political structure of Slovakia, the composition of the Board of Commissioners and other organs of the people's power. On 30 October 1947, faithfully following this policy, the Slovak Congress of Trade Unions and Employees Councils insisted on the solution of the political crisis by fundamental changes in the Board of Commissioners. They proclaimed that the new Board should consist of men who 'enjoy the confidence of the Slovak people and would guarantee that Slovakia will be ruled in the spirit of the Slovak National Uprising' carefully adding the modifying statement, 'and the reconstruction programme of the Gottwald government'.[1]

The Communist members of the Board resigned with the intention of bringing the political crisis to a head. The Czech non-Communist parties found it difficult to save their Democratic colleagues in Slovakia, especially when they had been portrayed by the Communists as supporters of Hlinka-fascist elements and as they did

[1] O. Jaroš and V. Jarošová, *Slovenské robotníctvo v boji o moc* (The Slovak Workers in their Fight for Power), Bratislava, 1965, pp. 256–7.

actually profess a more nationalist and anti-centralist programme than did the Slovak Communists. Thus the Slovak Democrats received no support from Prague and the Communists in Bratislava, supported by the Czech Communists, achieved their aim. A new Board of Commissioners was formed – with a Communist majority. Dr Husák, who had been Commissioner for Transport up till then, became its head. The Democrats did retain their majority in the Slovak National Council. Nevertheless the fact that the Democratic Party was openly wooing former Hlinka Party members and that they had actually concluded a pact with the clergy concerning the numerical participation of Roman Catholics in important positions in the Party and in the state, where they exercised considerable influence, greatly strengthened the Communists' hand. Dr Husák skilfully combined legal and constitutional methods with organized pressure groups from below, in order to outmanoeuvre the Democratic Party successfully.

Events in Slovakia showed that the Communists did not have to rely on parliamentary majorities and activities to achieve their aims. The Communists enjoyed the support of a fairly large section of the population, not only in Slovakia but also, and to an even greater extent, in the rest of Czechoslovakia. In this, the situation was somewhat different from that of other People's Democracies, although the methods of the final takeover were essentially the same. In Czechoslovakia the working classes were genuinely convinced that socialism as preached by the Communists could solve the economic, social and political problems of the country.

The immediate cause of the February events in 1948 was the resignation of twelve non-Communist ministers from the Prague coalition government (all except the non-party Minister of Foreign Affairs, Jan Masaryk and the Minister of Defence, Ludvík Svoboda). They did so in protest against the Communist Minister of the Interior who, without consulting his coalition partners, had promoted his men to the highest ranks in the police force. The non-Communists expected President Beneš to refuse to accept their resignation; they also expected him to force the Communists to revoke their tactics. But in the end Beneš had to give in to the Communist Prime Minister, Gottwald, who insisted that the 'rebellious' ministers be replaced by new men from the reconstituted non-Communist parties. Gottwald did not confine himself to the constitutional methods of cabinet politics; he knew that he could count on the support of powerful trade unions and other mass organizations of the National Front such as the Youth movement, all under strong Communist influence. By dramatizing the whole issue the Communists managed to convince the working classes that the reactionary remnants of the Czech and Slovak bourgeoisie were preparing a *putsch* to restore the pre-Munich capitalist system and to rob them of their socialist achievements, in much the same way as the French and Italian Communists had been manipulated out of the post-war coalition governments a few months earlier.

The subsequent events are well known. Suffice it to say here that the non-Communist Democratic members of the Board of Commissioners in Slovakia refused to follow the example of their opposite numbers in the central government in Prague and declined to resign. Dr Husák, although hitherto very jealous of the independent and autonomous position of the Board in relation to the central government, seemed now to be quite willing to recognize the subordination of the Board of Commissioners to Prague. He argued that the Board had no choice but to resign because the Prague government was practically non-existent. It was not a bad legal point although Husák, a trained lawyer, did not always confine himself to legal arguments when it suited him to use other less constitutional ones. The Democratic Commissioners were dismissed, and a new Board established shortly after the Prague government had purged itself of 'reactionary elements'. Just as in Prague Gottwald seemed to have no difficulties in finding his Plojhars,[2] so in Bratislava Husák solved the February crisis by reconstituting the Board of Commissioners and the Slovak National Front and accepting as collaborators relatively obscure men from non-Communist parties.

The course of events in Slovakia in February was less dramatic than in Prague, partly because of the outcome of the Slovak political crisis a few months earlier. Even at the lower levels of the administration, despite the smaller numerical strength of the Communists as compared with the Czech lands, the takeover was smoother and in many ways more complete. The Democratic Party had already been thoroughly weakened and shaken when Dr Husák became Chairman of the Board of Commissioners in the autumn of 1947. After the February events the Democratic Party ceased to exist even in name, unlike the situation in Prague where the Czech Socialist Party and Catholic People's Party retained some vestige of their former organizations and their names and daily newspapers. In Slovakia the widely read Democratic daily *Čas* (Time) stopped publication altogether. The new daily *L'ud* (The People), representing the new Party of Slovak

[2] Plojhar, a Roman Catholic priest who was a member of the Czech People's Party and became Minister of Health in the new Gottwald Government.

Reconstruction, became only a badly-disguised Communist propaganda sheet with a circulation of about two thousand. The only reason for its existence and costly maintenance was to prove that after February Slovakia too retained a multi-party system within the reconstructed National Front, and the Communists had a total monopoly of the press.

Despite the radical change in the political structure of Slovakia, Husák and his intellectual colleagues soon realized that their power had little base in reality. The real rulers of the country did not reside in Bratislava, nor in the Central Committee of the Slovak Communist Party, nor in the Slovak National Council, now headed by the Communist Šmidke after the Democratic chairman Lettrich had been dismissed (he eventually emigrated), nor in the Board of Commissioners. Later events have shown that February sealed not only the fate of the 'reactionary' bourgeois parties in Bohemia and Slovakia, but also the fate of the Slovak Communist Party and the Slovak national organs. Once the Communists in Prague had established themselves in power, they showed their real attitude towards the Slovaks. It became obvious that their hitherto active support of Slovak national rights had been merely tactical and that their stance was continually adapted to the political exigencies of the day and inspired primarily by what suited their own interests or those of the Soviet Union.

Still, the February events in Czechoslovakia had a special character of their own, despite the similarities with events which had led in other People's Democracies to the liquidation of genuine coalition governments. The Communist take-over in Czechoslovakia took place in the physical absence of the Soviet Army; her divisions had left in the summer of 1946, as had been agreed by the Allies. The Americans too had evacuated the western and southern part of Bohemia, including the big industrial city of Plzeň (Pilsen) with its famous Škoda works. In the case of Czechoslovakia, the Soviet Union could afford to act in such a gentlemanly way because it knew the strength of its Communist Party, and it was justified in assuming a genuine feeling of gratitude on the part of the Czechs and Slovaks whom it had liberated from German oppression. Soviet leaders were inclined to trust even Beneš, who had concluded a treaty of alliance with them in 1936 and renewed it during the war on 12 December 1943 in Moscow. Indeed, Czechoslovakia was the least troublesome People's Democracy from their point of view.

Despite all this, it would be naïve to think that the Czech Communists would have succeeded so easily if it had not been for their political opponents' fear that the Soviet Union might intervene if the chances of a Communist victory in February had appeared to diminish. This probably paralysed the non-Communists into a passive acceptance of the inevitable, an attitude which the Czechs, and for that matter the Slovaks, have so often adopted in their troubled history and which characterizes their behaviour to this very day.

February had another, perhaps more far-reaching effect. It meant the end of Czechoslovakia's separate road to socialism which had hitherto so often been stressed even by Gottwald himself. The Soviet Union regarded this country as too important to allow it to experiment in socialism. It might even have remained a parliamentary democracy with a multi-party system. Moreover, as a multinational state with its basic conception of two 'state-forming' nations, as the rather clumsy phrase incorporated in the Constitution emphasized, Czechoslovakia could not be permitted to look for ways which would actually solve the problem of nationalities in a different, perhaps even more satisfactory, way than the Soviet Union had managed.

The Soviet Union claims to be a voluntary federation of socialist republics with various autonomous regions within them. As in many other matters, the words of the Soviet constitutions, including the one introduced by Stalin in December 1936, read well – in many respects very well, especially where they deal with the position of the nationalities. The right of secession is laid down as a fundamental right of each of the family of socialist nations. But woe to those who mistake the written word for reality and who attempt to exercise this right. This is one of the reasons why Stalin and his successors (although they had allowed discussion of the subject of federation at a certain stage during the war as a model for other Central and East European nations), stopped all speculation about federal systems outside the Soviet Union. This applied equally to the Balkan Federation, tentatively suggested by the Bulgarian Communist leader Dimitrov and the Yugoslav Communist Tito, or to a Czechoslovak–Polish Federation, which seemed to Stalin even more risky because it could have involved the non-Communist Czechoslovakia of Beneš and the non-Communist Poland of Mikołajczyk. The main reason why Stalin was opposed to similar groupings outside the Soviet Union and to federations of any kind, even socialist ones, was his concern that they might represent larger and stronger political units, which would be more difficult to deal with.

In the case of an existing multi-national state, i.e. Czechoslovakia, the Soviet Union supported those who in the end decided against a federal Republic of Czechs and Slovaks. Only Yugoslavia managed to imitate and in certain respects improve upon the Soviet model. After the liberation it established itself as a federal republic with a high degree of political autonomy for the various nationalities. Strangely enough, in this respect, the Soviet Union found allies in staunch 'Czechoslovakists' like Beneš and almost all the Czech politicians. But in Soviet eyes Beneš' 'good behaviour' in this matter was far outweighed by his unwillingness to concede their general concept of the political structure of Czechoslovakia. Because it became clear to them that he would not willingly accept a Communist monopoly of power in the state, they must have sighed with relief, when, a few months later, on 5 June 1948 Beneš resigned. He died in September of the same year. The Communists were safer guarantors of Soviet interests in this important country. Under their rule the Soviet model of socialism was subsequently adopted in all spheres of Czechoslovak life.

The split with Yugoslavia in June 1948 must have been anticipated in the inner circles of the top Communist leadership. With the existence of the Cominform since October 1947 it is probable that, when the Yugoslav heresy came into the open, it did not come as a complete surprise to Gottwald in Prague, Rákosi in Budapest, or to other leaders of the People's Democracies. The Yugoslav disease had to be eradicated. In the first place, it was spread by the dangerous and highly infectious virus of nationalism. In most other respects Tito, at least at that time, seemed to be a good Marxist and Leninist, and even Stalinist. He had in fact been less willing than Stalin to cooperate with the imperialists. Tito's more 'Marxist' Marxism could not however have endeared him to Stalin. It was a deviation from the Russian line, a sign of an independent approach; it smacked of efforts to look at things primarily from a Yugoslav angle. It was a nationalist attitude, and 'bourgeois nationalism' was one of the main crimes of which Tito was accused. There was perhaps more than a grain of truth in this accusation if the adjective 'bourgeois' is omitted.

The Soviet attitude was that of a great power whose aims were basically little different from those of the former Tsarist Empire, which had also subjugated other nations. The Tsars too had to fight the nationalism of the smaller nations in order to satisfy their own Russian nationalism. In their writings on the national question Lenin and Stalin often alluded to 'great-Russian chauvinism', as opposed to true proletarian internationalism. They would never have admitted that the latter expression might simply be a cover for Soviet imperialism.[3] Anyway Stalin was more concerned with 'bourgeois nationalism' in the Soviet Union than with 'great-Russian chauvinism'. Asked which of the deviations was the more dangerous he stated, with a typical show of sophistry: 'The one we are not fighting at the moment.' Stalin in fact did little to counter great Russian chauvinism, whereas he never ceased to fight 'bourgeois nationalism' —a policy which had catastrophic consequences for some of the nationalities in the Soviet Union.

The Stalins of history have always been more popish than the Pope, more royal than the King. In his complicated, if not psychopathic, mentality Stalin was constantly trying to prove that he was at least as good as any Russian in Moscow. He was a man with a profound inferiority complex, as a Georgian in relation to the Russians, as a semi-intellectual in relation to the real intellectuals (whom he hated most of all), and perhaps as a frustrated orthodox Christian cleric in relation to the Jews, although like most anti-semites he kept one or two in his entourage as close associates who would help him carry out his paranoiac ideas.

Stalin's dread lest his satellites should catch the Yugoslav disease was one of the primary motivations for the purges he ordered in the People's Democracies. His radical methods of treatment were soon applied in Czechoslovakia, and especially in Slovakia. Stalin was concerned with Czechoslovak nationalism and the 'Czechoslovak road to socialism'. But the Czech Stalinists regarded the problem of nationalism as a solely Slovak affair. The Czechoslovak Republic suffered from the same direction for both Czechs and Slovaks, but for the Slovaks the effects were more deadly.

As I have already shown, until 1948 the Slovak Communist Party had had a certain amount of autonomy and influence in Slovak politics, although it continually had had to counter Czech centralism, which until then had come mainly from Beneš. After 1948 this role was taken over by the Czech Communists.

The Slovak Communist Party had been separately represented in the pre-February Prague coalition. But on 26 July 1948 the Praesidium of the Czechoslovak Communist Party decided that 'the working class and the toiling masses of Czechoslovakia had to have one political leadership in the form of a united Communist Party'.[4] It

---

[3] Marx used the term 'imperialism' only when referring to a style of government, as for instance that existing under Louis Napoleon. Thus Marx's and Lenin's views on imperialism were far from identical.

[4] K. Kaplan. *Utváření generální linie socialismu v ČSSR* (The Forming of the General Line of Socialism in the CSSR), Prague, 1966, p. 103.

recommended that the Central Committee of the Slovak Communist Party dissolve the Party as an autonomous body and incorporate itself fully into the Czechoslovak Party. The Praesidium of the CPCz generously allowed the Slovak branch to keep its title as the Communist Party of Slovakia but its Central Committee was to be subordinated to the Central Committee in Prague, and was to respect its instructions and carry out its policy in Slovakia.

In September 1948 the Slovak Communists obediently carried out this recommendation. Although it was a matter of great importance (otherwise the new rulers in Prague would not have insisted on its implementation), they did not deem it necessary to submit these changes to a Party conference or congress. A short session of the Central Committee was sufficient. The traditionally obedient and disciplined Slovak leaders like Široký, Bacílek and Bašťovanský had probably neither scruples nor misgivings. Husák and Novomeský probably had, but this time they kept quiet, silenced no doubt by the recent assaults on Tito for his 'bourgeois nationalism'.

After the actual disappearance of the Slovak Communist Party as an independent political unit, fundamental changes in the state organs of Slovakia were a foregone conclusion. The Slovak National Council and the Board of Commissioners gradually became empty symbols of Slovak nationhood. Instead of dealing with specifically Slovak affairs, their role was confined mainly to the task of implementing all-state laws and instructions. Instead of directly promoting Slovak interests they became one of the many instruments in the hands of the Czech Communists who were intent on fighting 'unhealthy tendencies of local patriotism' – a phrase later used to suggest far more dangerous charges – charges which were to become characteristic of the Stalinist purges and show-trials in the early Fifties.

The first serious hint that even the diluted rights which the Slovaks were guaranteed by the new Constitution of 9 May 1948 might be endangered came at the end of June 1948 when the Praesidium of the Central Committee of the CPCz discussed the implications of the Yugoslav split for Czechoslovakia. There it was almost expressly stated that in Slovakia there was an analogy to the Yugoslav heresy. A more direct attack came in 1950 when Husák, Novomeský and Clementis were forced to engage in self-criticism both at the Ninth Congress of the Slovak Communist Party and at the Ninth Congress of the Czechoslovak Communist Party. They confessed to having harboured bourgeois nationalist tendencies in relation to the Czechs and to the Hungarian minority – at this stage Zionism was not yet a serious crime. Stalin had shortly before recognized the state of Israel and had even given it material support; and the Slovak bourgeois nationalists were in fact criticized for holding anti-semitic views. Gradually they were removed from their offices and Party functions, and they were finally arrested in the first months of 1951.

What were the real grounds behind the accusations brought against these Slovak Communists, mostly intellectuals? The only logical answer can be that they were too concerned about the constitutional position of the Slovak nation. They tended to show a more independent, sensitive and elastic approach to the problem than the Party diehards in Prague and in Bratislava. The interest in the national question shown by Slovak Communist intellectuals such as Clementis, Novomeský and Husák was not an expression of anti-Czech sentiment. Being intelligent and well-educated Communists and knowing the feelings of the Slovak people, their Slovak patriotism was directed only against Prague centralism; they gave unquestioning allegiance to the Soviet Union and even to Stalin's kind of Communism. His theories on nationalism seemed acceptable and even attractive to them. In their view the Soviet Union had achieved an ideal solution to its own national problem, which was much more complicated than Czechoslovakia's. Even if one admits that there might have been a grain of truth in the allegation that, in a sense, they were anti-Prague, there was no foundation whatsoever in the accusation that they were anti-Moscow and the first attacks on them did not refer to anti-Sovietism.

In one respect however their accusers had a semblance of a case. Clementis and Husák had an almost chauvinistic attitude towards the Hungarian minority in Slovakia. As Communist internationalists they were, of course, supposed to be free of such sentiments. The official doctrine of the Party taught them that the Slovak workers and peasants shared common interests with the Hungarian workers and peasants, especially now that Hungary itself was a People's Democracy, an ally of the Soviet Union and therefore an ally of Czechoslovakia. However, Clementis and his friends in the first years after the war until the end of 1947 were perhaps over-zealous in implementing the official policy of the Czechoslovak Communist Party and government. This was, of course, with the consent of Stalin, and, incidentally, at that time, also of the United States and Britain, which had agreed to the deportation of the German and Hungarian minorities from Czechoslovakia. The new state was intended to be the home of two Slav nations only, the Czechs and the Slovaks. Beneš, in the bilateral agreement with Stalin in June 1945, had magnanimously ceded the Sub-Carpathian Ukraine to the Soviet Union although this region had never belonged to Russia. Nevertheless, even after Hungary had returned the areas of southern Slovakia which had been ceded under the post-Munich *Diktat* of Vienna in November 1938, there remained a substantial Hungarian minority in this region.

Clementis, as Secretary of State at the Ministry of Foreign Affairs, was very insistent on the Hungarian issue. At international conferences he fought vehemently for the annexation of three Hungarian villages on the right bank of the Danube, because, he maintained, Czechoslovakia needed a more solid bridge-head on this side of the river where the frontiers of Czechoslovakia, Hungary and Austria converged. It was not Clementis' own personal policy, but on this particular question he went well beyond what would have been required from a strict adherence to state and Party instructions. During the war and in the period immediately following, Stalin himself supported the modern version of the panslav idea. He used it as a propaganda weapon against the Germans who had oppressed almost all the Slav nations during the war. In the last century, young Slovaks of Štúr's generation used to hold meetings in the ruins of the ancient castle of Devín, which stands on a cliff-top facing Austria, at the meeting-point of the rivers Danube and Morava. It is one of the Slovak national shrines, even more venerated, perhaps, than Nitra, where the first Christian church was built, and where King Svätopluk of Great Moravia reigned in the ninth century. For many years, on 5 July, the anniversary of the arrival of the first Slav evangelists, St Constantine and St Methodius, has been celebrated by all-Slav assemblies with official Soviet blessing and participation.[1] Clementis always made a point of being present at these mass gatherings. He made enthusastic speeches of a panslav and naturally pro-Soviet nature, and always with a clear anti-Hungarian and anti-German emphasis. He kept on reminding his audience that for centuries the Slovaks had been oppressed by the Hungarians and Austrians. Slovak Communists, especially those who were intellectual and patriotic, as he was, could not forget recent history, especially the losses to Hungary in 1938.

But unlike the Sudeten-Germans, the Hungarians were not expelled from Czechoslovakia, although some moved to Hungary in exchange for those Slovaks in Hungary who wished to be repatriated and to take part in the process of the 'reslovakization' of the southern part of the country. In addition to these Slovaks, thousands of families came down from the mountains of northern Slovakia to the fertile valleys where they settled permanently. There was some hostility towards the Slovaks repatriated from Hungary; evil tongues whispered that among them were many who had discredited themselves in Hungary during the most violent fascist era of Szallassy.[2] The number of old Slovak settlers who decided to return from Hungary was relatively small. Most stayed where they had lived for many decades. Only a few, more enterprising, people who could claim Slovak origin thought it expedient to move from a defeated Hungary to a country on the side of the victors like Czechoslovakia.

In the period immediately after the war the Slovak Communists tended to over-reach themselves in their anti-Hungarian zeal. Although the fate of the Hungarian minority in Czechoslovakia after the war differed in many ways from that of the Sudeten-Germans, most of whom had joined Hitler's cause long before the end of the First Republic, one can question the measures taken against the Hungarians who had now reverted to Czechoslovak citizenship. After all, many of them had been Communists before the Horthy occupation in 1938 or, as Hungarian peasants, many would in 1938 have preferred to stay in democratic Czechoslovakia rather than

---

[1] In 1950, however, the general drive against all manifestations of nationalism put a stop to these celebrations.
[2] He had become the ruler of Hungary in 1944. His predecessor, Admiral Horthy, had been removed with the help of the Germans because he toyed with the idea of changing sides, as King Michael of Rumania had done.

return to their old feudal fatherland. It was, for example, senseless to rename and thus 'reslovakize' purely Hungarian towns and villages. Thus Párkán became Štúrovo after the nineteenth-century Slovak national leader, who had nothing to do with this town and had probably never been there in his life. The town of O-Gyala (which incidentally had quite a respectable Slovak name – Stará D'ala) was renamed Hurbanovo, after another Slovak leader of the 1848 rebellion. Today Hviezdoslavovo and Bernolákovo, both former Hungarian towns, also have new names commemorating Slovak poets and national heroes. True enough, these 'errors' were primarily the responsibility of the so-called Slovak 'bourgeois nationalists' but they were, if not conceived, definitely approved by Gottwald himself who expressed no objection to this deviation from proletarian internationalism. This is not to question the essential justice of the cause of the Slovaks against the Hungarians, but the Slovak Communists might have been expected to pay more attention to their own Marxist hypothesis that it was not the Hungarian people but only the ruling classes who were responsible for the oppression of the Slovaks.

Early critics also rebuked these Slovak bourgeois nationalists for their anti-semitism. Husák admitted at the Ninth Congress of the Slovak Communist Party that there was some justification for the criticism. However, it was not the most serious part of the attack on 'bourgeois nationalism', and may have been embarrassing to Rudolf Slánský, the second-in-command of the Czechoslovak Communist party, who like most Jewish Communist leaders, was not too happy about his origin, All his life Slánský had been dedicated to the Communist cause and a faithful follower of Stalin in the Soviet Union and of Gottwald in Czechoslovakia. His party record was spotless. There is not the slightest evidence to support the later accusations against him that he had Trotskyite or other treacherous learnings. He was a Moscow-trained Communist and spent most of the war years there except for a short interval during the Slovak Uprising when Gottwald sent him to Slovakia to ensure that the rebellion took its proper Moscow-approved course. Like most of the accusations against the Slovak bourgeois nationalists, the charge of anti-semitism was grossly exaggerated. True, Husák preferred not to surround himself with Jewish Communists, although his personal secretary was a Jew. Husák probably thought that the Party should appeal to the mentality of the Slovak people which is mostly Roman Catholic. He therefore did not consider it expedient to put Communists of Jewish origin into high posts. According to Husák, it would have made the Party appear to be Jew-ridden, providing an easy target for hostile allegations, such as those which had been made earlier by Hlinka Party propaganda. The Slovak Communists knew only too well that anti-semitism had not perished with the Slovak Jews in Hitler's concentration camps. The few surviving Jews although not associating the crimes of the Tiso régime with the Slovak people, did sometimes view the presence of former active Slovak fascists in Party and government functions with misgivings. Husák, as an astute politician, could not ignore the Jewish aspect of the situation in Slovakia, or what remained of it after the war. He was not particularly happy when, for a short time, a Slovak intellectual of Jewish origin, Dr Edo Friš, became General Secretary of the Slovak Communist Party, It is on record that he opposed this appointment. Friš was soon replaced by Bašt'ovanský, a rather obscure former bank clerk who was relatively little known before the war. It was perhaps unfortunate that Jewish Communists did not themselves resist the temptation of being nominated to important posts, and thus incurring the hidden resentment of men like Husák who thought it necessary to draw the Party's attention to this delicate question.

In Prague there were several Jews in the central apparatus of the Party. Slánský, as General Secretary had not chosen them as fellow Jews, and certainly did not do so without Gottwald's approval or initiative. Actually, the principal Czech Communist responsible for cadres was Marie Švermová, the widow of Jan Šverma, a well-known Czech Communist leader who had died during the Slovak Uprising. Švermová was not a Jewess. In her endeavour to fill important posts with reliable and competent men she could not avoid appointing a relatively high number of Jews. Though a good Communist, she was rather bad at understanding human nature. In this respect Husák and Novomeský were, perhaps, better psychologists and possibly that was why they were regarded by Gottwald and Široký as worse Communists.

The tragic irony of the fate of Slánský and other Jewish Communists, who in 1949 and 1950 were instrumental in the witch-hunt against the bourgeois nationalists, was that very soon they themselves became the victims of this same witch-hunt, and in turn suffered fates no less horrible than those which had befallen Clementis, Husák, Novomeský and numerous other Slovak Communists. When Stalin changed his tactics in relation to the Arab world, and Israel became the 'agent of Western imperialism in the Middle-East', he singled out Jewish Communists in the Soviet Union and in the People's Democracies as the main enemies of socialism. He started a ruthless wave of persecution against them. But, claiming to be a Marxist, he could not liquidate them as Jews – they had to be Zionists. He eliminated almost all of them from political life. Perhaps he remembered the type of Bolsheviks he had had to liquidate before the war; a high percentage of them had been Jews and only a minority of the accused were intellectual non-Jewish Communists like Bukharin. Stalin disliked intellectuals and Jews; he doubly hated Jewish intellectuals. After the war, having helped the Communists to seize power in the so-called People's Democracies by removing their bourgeois antifascist allies, Stalin started to purge the Communist Parties. He must have carefully analysed the profiles of the men in Yugoslavia who dared to challenge his omnipotence. They were Communists with a long record of devoted service to the Party, self-confident and proud men like Tito, Kardelj, Djilas and Moshe Pijade. Most of them had fought in the Spanish Civil War, where they had witnessed how little Stalin's Russia had helped the Spanish republican and socialist cause, how the Soviet Union had merely paid lip-service to the antifascist struggle in that country, while Hitler and Mussolini had supplied Franco with modern weapons and regular troops. Stalin had sent only a few 'Soviet experts', who were in fact mostly non-Russian Communists from the Moscow apparatus of the Comintern, whom he had chosen to die on the battlefields of Spain instead of in his own concentration camps. He regarded all Communists who had come into contact with capitalism in any form, even Spanish capitalism against which they fought, with deep distrust. That is why most of those who fought in the International Brigades became victims of Stalin's purges. They were branded as traitors, as Jewish cosmopolitans (like Moshe Pijade), and of course, worst of all, as bourgeois nationalists (like Tito himself).

In all the trials in the People's Democracies, whether it was the Rajk trial in Hungary, the Kostov trial in Bulgaria, Patrascanu in Rumania, Gomulka in Poland, or the Slánský trial in Czechoslovakia in 1952, the main accused was Josip Broz Tito, the first Communist leader outside the Soviet Union who had refused to be an obedient tool of Stalin, perhaps because he took the holy Marxist scripture too seriously, as heretics often do. For this reason alone he was the most dangerous Marxist heretic of them all. Together with Tito as the main accused there stood in the dock the idea of one country's separate road to socialism. This concept was often discussed in socialist countries after the war, before it was perverted into the practice that all People's Democracies must march to socialism along the Soviet road. The only individuality left to the People's Democracies was their name. Basically they were to have the same system as Stalin had introduced in the Soviet Union, with the difference that in most of these countries the semblance of non-Marxist parties remained, whether Catholic or peasant, cemented together into a National Front under the undisputed leadership of the Communist Party. All those who dared to think that the implementation of different methods, corresponding to the specific conditions and needs of each country, was the only reasonable and practical way to achieve socialism, and that it was perhaps a better way than that practised by the Soviet Union, were branded as the enemies of proletarian internationalism. The only proof of a good Communist was his unquestioning and positive attitude to the Soviet Union. The slightest sign of anti-Sovietism became the strongest proof of anti-Communism.

In the Slánský trial, held in Prague in 1952, eleven of the fourteen accused were leading Communists of Jewish origin. The three non-Jews were Joseph Frank, former Deputy Secretary-General of the Communist Party of Czechoslovakia, Karel Šváb, former Deputy Minister of National Security, and the Slovak, Vladimír Clementis, former Minister of Foreign Affairs. All three of them were sentenced to death and executed together with eight Communist Jews. Three Jews, Arthur London, Vavro Hajdu and Eugen Löbl were sentenced to life imprisonment.

The only man whose main crime was alleged to be bourgeois nationalism was Clementis. All the rest were Zionists, cosmopolitan saboteurs and Western agents who, following the example of Tito, had attempted to restore capitalism and to remove Czechoslovakia from the socialist camp. Clementis was arrested in the spring of 1951, almost certainly with the consent of Slánský, who was then still General Secretary of the Party. Most of the accused in this trial were actually arrested on the orders of Šváb who was chief of the secret police until the day of his own arrest. These fourteen men represented a very mixed group of individuals who in their activities either in the Party or in high government office had clashed with each other and, as usual in political life, indulged in joint intrigues. For example, it was generally known that Slánský and Clementis did not see eye to eye. The orthodox Slánský could never forgive Clementis his war-time deviations, although the latter's original heresy later became official Soviet policy. The only real crime Clementis ever committed was that of independent and intelligent thought, and Slovak patriotism which had nothing to do with political nationalism, either with or without the 'bourgeois' prefix. Standing trial together with Slánský and Šváb, he was forced, by all the ruthless means used by

the Prague secret police with the assistance of Soviet experts, to confess to all the crimes mentioned in the indictment. Probably he was
picked out for this trial because he was the most prominent representative of the progressive Slovak intelligentsia. Also perhaps because his younger colleague, Husák, who was imprisoned about the
same time as Clementis, refused to 'help the Party' and the police,
and energetically repudiated all charges. It would have been a risk
to put this stubborn man in the dock. He would have spoiled the
show.[3]

Clementis confessed to bourgeois nationalism thus:

> After my return to Slovakia in 1945 my activities were hostile to
> the People's Democratic Republic because I remained a bourgeois
> nationalist. I must admit that the ideas of the subversive group
> of Slovak bourgeois nationalists were clearly marked by Titoist
> influence. Like the Titoists in Yugoslavia, we in Slovakia propa-
> gated a foreign and hostile ideology of bourgeois nationalism.
> I fully admit my guilt in taking part in this subversive group
> of Slovak bourgeois nationalists, which tried to separate the
> development of Slovakia from the development of the state as a
> whole, thus strengthening reaction and hindering the progress
> of socialism and the development of the people's democratic
> order.[4]

Clementis stood accused together with eleven men, whose Jewish
origin was stressed by the prosecution as a very relevant factor, a
decisive element in the trial. All the evidence points to the fact that
anti-semitism, under the guise of anti-Zionism, had become the official policy of the Party. Gottwald and his Soviet experts obviously
thought that this was the best way of gaining support and sympathy
for the Party, which had become unattractive to the masses. Gottwald was evidently convinced that, by purging the Party of Zionist
and alien elements, the Communists would regain their popularity.

True enough, Slánský, Geminder, and the economists Frejka and
Löbl were not the sort of men likely to be popular with the masses.
Being of Jewish origin they could be used as in the the old Tsarist
and now Stalinist fashion as scapegoats for all the ills and difficulties
that the Party and the new socialist state had encountered. In reality
they were all faithful members of the Communist Party, but being
intelligent and highly educated men, they represented a potential

[3] Husák was eventually tried in the summer of 1954 after the death of Gottwald and Stalin, when Novotný was First Secretary of the Party. He still
did not confess. He was sentenced to life imprisonment.
[4] Eugen Löbl, *Sentenced and Tried*, London, 1969, p. 138.

risk to Stalin and the kind of socialism he stood for. While in the case of Clementis there had been times in his political career when his views could have been construed as heretical, it is very difficult to trace the slightest sign of deviation in the activities of the other accused. What went on in their minds was another matter.

While there might have been some justification for branding Clementis a nationalist because of his deep Slovak patriotism (which he never attempted to hide), Slánský was always first a Communist and then a Czech. Now he was actually accused of being a Jew and therefore an Israeli Zionist agent. In Slánský's case, if there was conflict of loyalties at all, it was between his Czech and his pro-Russian feelings. He was definitely anti-Zionist. But Stalin and Beria treated most Jewish Communists, as Zionists, as pro-Israel agents. So did Gottwald and his Berias – Kopřiva, Bacílek, Barák, Štrougal – men engaged in the macabre game of musical chairs in the Ministry of National Security in Prague. That was their justification for putting so many Jews on show trial. Slánský and his Jewish comrades were always rather embarrassed by the accident of their origin. While Clementis was proud of being a Slovak, Slánský was not proud of being a Jew; and anyway, as a Communist, he did not accept the idea of the Jews as a nation. An atheist, he rejected Judaism as a religion. Now he was accused of Zionism and executed together with the 'bourgeois nationalist' Clementis who, together with Husák and Novomeský, had been accused of anti-semitism a few years earlier.

Whoever was responsible for arranging this trial must have known that Clementis was a popular leader in Slovakia while Slánský and his comrades in the Czech lands were not. Clementis presented a serious danger to Stalin and Gottwald, although after 1945 not a single instance of his deviationist attitudes was known. But because of his past he was a potential revisionist *par excellence*. His Party record during the war was not too good. He had clashed with the official policy of the Soviet and Czechoslovak Communist Parties in August 1939 when he questioned the morality of the Soviet–German pact, and in the winter of 1939–40 when he expressed his disagreement with the Soviet war against Finland. In addition to this he had volunteered for the Czechoslovak Army in France before the 'imperialist' war became a 'just' one following Hitler's invasion of Russia.

Clementis' accusers knew that his execution would not make the Party popular, at least not in Slovakia, where it would be resented as an obviously anti-Slovak act. But if he were to be tried together with so many Jews and presented as their close accomplice, Beria's experts in liquidation hoped that the Slovaks would accept the sacrifice. The blood of Clementis must be diluted by the blood of eight high-ranking Jewish Communists. Only in this way, his executioners thought, would the death of Clementis pass without any serious consequences for the popularity of the Party. That was the paranoiac logic behind the production and direction of this particular show trial.

In the Czech part of the country the majority of Party members appeared to react to the trial as its initiators had anticipated. Many people actually believed that the sentenced men were traitors. Most of the journalists and writers, some of them present at the trial, hailed their execution as a great victory for the people. Those few who had doubts or were convinced that the trial was a fraud, kept silent and fell into a helpless apathy. Anyway a large segment of the non-Communist population of Czechoslovakia was not averse to watching the bloody spectacle of the despised Communist leaders cutting one another's throats.

The organizers of the trial, in their efforts to gain approval for their horrible deed, accused Slánský and his accomplices of dictatorial methods. One of the accused, the former head of the secret police. Šváb, was blamed for 'violating principles of socialist legality' as the phrase went. In many ways this was true. But his prosecutors used even worse methods against him, and so far they have not been punished. In any case Slánský's executioners promised a new spirit in the Party and exhorted the population to look forward to the future with optimism after the removal of the traitors. But the promised change did not take place. The secret police remained the same, first under Kopřiva, and then under Karol Bacílek (who had been called to Prague from Bratislava, where he had been Commissioner of Information).

Slánský and Clementis were arrested during Kopřiva's tenure of office. They were tried and executed under Bacílek. Both Czechoslovak security ministers were acting under the direction of experts from Moscow, as Bacílek later revealed in his clumsy attempt to exculpate himself. He argued that he was not responsible for the trials at all but that he was only carrying out Soviet orders. He actually named his Soviet overlords, but only in the summer of 1968, hoping thus to save his skin. In fact, what Bacílek divulged and the way he defended himself was only a sad and sordid admission of the fact that a minister of a so-called independent and sovereign state was not responsible for what happened in his own government department. Bacílek did not realize that, far from exculpating himself, he was in fact condemning himself as much as his Soviet masters and their system. Bacílek, when he replaced Kopřiva, stated that he was called to office to change the old methods and put an end to Šváb's perversion of justice. A few Communist officials of minor importance were actually released from prison during Bacílek's reign. At the same time he was a more than willing instrument in the murder of high-ranking Communists, some of them former close friends of his. Unless he was a fool he must have known that they were innocent. But he was not a fool, only a political careerist corrupted by power. He obviously enjoyed wearing a general's uniform, to which rank he was promoted, for he had only been a private in the old Austro-Hungarian Army. In his new rank he had to be taught even the most basic of military procedures, including the salute! This rather pathetic old man, a former anarchist Czech worker who after the First World War came to Slovakia to become a Communist official, spoke a strange mixture of bad Czech and bad Slovak; he presented the very caricature of ethnic 'Czechoslovakism'.

Despite the expectations in Gottwald's Prague, the Slovak intellectuals were embittered by the execution of Clementis and the continued imprisonment of prominent Slovak politicians such as Husák, Novomeský, Okáli and Horváth. Most Slovaks were fully aware that it was an attack on the Slovak nation as such, on their hard-won national rights, which were being curtailed from month to month. It was not a campaign against bourgeois nationalism, whatever this phrase implied, but against Slovak patriotism. The Slovak writers, although some tacitly acquiesced because they felt helpless[5] did not believe for a moment that their most esteemed colleague, the greatest living Slovak poet, Laco Novomeský, could be a traitor. They were bewildered by the evidence he gave in the Slánský trial against his friend Vladimír Clementis, at the same time confessing his own crimes as Clementis' accomplice in acts of bourgeois nationalist treason.

After the trial, many Slovak intellectuals were removed from their party and government jobs. The frequent purges which took place in the early Fifties were directed mainly against intellectuals. Some of the best known Slovak writers, like Matuška, Mináč, Tatarka and Chorváth were regarded with suspicion because they expressed a certain amount of mild criticism in their contributions to *Kultúrny Život*, the Slovak Writers' Union weekly, which even at that early stage managed occasionally to evade strict Party control. Jiří Hen-

---

[5] Only a very few like Milan Lajčiak and Miloš Krno actually applauded the execution of Clementis.

drych, who at that time was head of the cultural department of the Central Committee in Prague, threatened this 'Clementis gang' with serious consequences. He demanded that they put an end to their anti-Party activities. This and similar outbursts did not prevent Hendrych himself from getting into trouble because he was a member of the Slánský apparatus. For a short time he had to work in a minor Party position in southern Bohemia. He later considered himself a victim of Stalinism and claimed rehabilitation, which was granted a short time before the Twentieth Congress of the CPSU when Antonin Novotný, the First Secretary of the Party, suddenly attempted to present himself as a kind of liberal and surrounded himself with men of Hendrych's calibre and political background. Even Novotný himself claimed after the Twentieth Congress that he had been a victim of Stalinist methods and told his friends that he had been on the list of those who were to be arrested under Slánský and Gottwald. He never bothered to produce that list, knowing that nobody would believe its authenticity. It would not have been difficult for Novotný to manufacture counterfeit historical documents.

At the time of Slánský's arrest in November 1951, Novotný was First Party Secretary of the Prague region. He played a very active role in denouncing Slánský and the 'treacherous activities of his Zionist gang'. He kept stressing their Jewish background. On one very rare occasion at a meeting of a Party branch at which Novotný happened to be present, an ordinary Communist Party member of Jewish origin asked some questions which cast doubt on the official version of the Slánský trial. He was told by the 'Marxist and atheist' Novotný that the questioner has obviously mistaken the Party meeting for a synagogue congregation, where his place and behaviour would be more appropriate.

After the death of Gottwald in March 1953, Novotný became organizational secretary, and a few months later, in November, First Secretary of the Party. His obedient servant Bacílek, the Minister of National Security, paid tribute to him publicly for exposing Slánský and his gang. Novotný beamed with pleasure at Bacílek's praise. When in 1967 historians dug out Bacílek's tribute to Novotný, the latter was not pleased. He stated that Bacílek had done him a disservice and denied his own initiative in the Slánský purges.

II THE IMPACT OF THE TWENTIETH CONGRESS

After the Second World War the pressure of the capitalist states encircling the Soviet Union, which seemed to have worried Stalin so much, was alleviated by the establishment of the People's Democracies fashioned on the Soviet model. Despite this important development, however, Stalin did not relinquish his theory that the class war is intensified by the success of socialism. He probably thought that he had to retain this idea for internal reasons, in order to complete industrialization, the basis of his socialism. When, after February 1948, Stalin's model was adopted in Czechoslovakia, a highly developed industrial country, the emphasis on heavy industry proved disastrous to the economy of the country both in the short and in the long term. If socialist Czechoslovakia had been allowed to follow its own road, industrialization on the Soviet model would not have been its main concern. In a country with huge industrial enterprises – the engineering works of Škoda in Plzeň and the Bat'a shoe factory in Zlín – and with a highly-developed light industry, the Communists could have concentrated on those aspects of socialism which, according to Stalin, the Soviet Union could not afford. The potential Czechoslovak experiment was stifled just as twenty years later the new experiment, which appeared to Stalin's frightened heirs as an attempt to return to pre-February Czechoslovakia, was also stifled.

In February 1948 the Czech and Slovak Communists under Gottwald carried out Stalin's orders with enthusiasm. There was no need for him to use force. The native Communists themselves seemed to be quite willing to bury their previous, more independent, policy; they blocked their own Czechoslovak road to socialism, although it was perfectly passable. It would have been a good and a modern road.

Great hopes rose in the Communist world after Stalin's death; the first signs of a thaw seemed to be appearing. When in February 1956 a real thaw came in the Soviet Union with the Twentieth Congress of the CPSU, Khrushchev's revelations, however shocking and distressing, came as a relief to many Communists. Previously many of them had refused to be taken in by 'bourgeois propaganda' which had been saying for many years what Khrushchev was now saying about Stalin in his secret speech. But now they enjoyed the fresh wind blowing from Moscow. Among other important developments, the possibilty of separate paths to socialism was again admitted. In the summer of 1955, a few months before the Congress, Khrushchev had gone to Belgrade for an act of public reconciliation with Tito. At that time the visit amounted to a Soviet admission that the Yugoslav Communists had not been wrong, and that their condemnation by the Cominform had been unjust.[1] Tito was no longer a revisionist; he was publicly recognized by Khrushchev as a true Marxist–Leninist.

The documents of the Twentieth Congress proclaimed a new policy towards the socialist countries, and peaceful coexistence with the rest of the world. Stalin's thesis that wars were a necessary corollary of imperialism was replaced by the new belief that wars were not inevitable, although the character of imperialism had not changed. The new, brighter, prospects for mankind were made possible not by the new trends in the capitalist world, but by the strength and achievements of socialism. Khrushchev thus reversed Stalin's theory of the intensification of the class war and actually dismissed his paranoiac thesis of capitalist encirclement. The socialist states, he believed, could afford to live in peace with the capitalists, who anyhow were suffering from a general and permanent crisis and were in a process of disintegration.

Most socialist countries rejoiced over this change. But not Communist leaders like Rákosi in Hungary, Novotný in Czechoslovakia and Ulbricht in East Germany, who had come to power under Stalin and must have feared that they would be found guilty of the same crimes and mistakes for which he now stood condemned. All of them feigned acceptance of the new line. Even Rákosi seemed anxious to implement the new policies, although only shortly before he had been praising Stalin's concepts. But for the time being the dead Soviet dictator still had his honourable place beside Lenin in the mausoleum. Most Communist theoreticians in and outside the Soviet Union argued that the 'cult of personality' was accidental and not essential to the Soviet system, which was basically a sound and healthy one. Its followers could be proud of its achievements in the Soviet Union and in other socialist countries. Khrushchev was still surrounded by men like Molotov, Kaganovich and Malenkov, all close friends of Stalin. And what about Khrushchev himself? If these men were not removed, why should the Novotnýs and Ulbrichts be afraid, why should they hurry to carry out the proclamations of the Twentieth Congress in their own countries? If the worst came to the worst they

---

[1] The Cominform was subsequently dissolved in April 1956.

could always change, or pretend to change, as Khrushchev had done. They knew that for decades Khruschev had not only kept silent about Stalin's crimes, but had actually helped to perpetrate them.

Unfortunately, Khrushchev was far from consistent in implementing the ideas he formulated at the Twentieth Congress. He either lacked the ability or the will to imbue the Party and government with a really new spirit. The ideas of the Twentieth Congress were intended to mark the beginning not only of a new era in Soviet life but also to give new meaning to the whole socialist commonwealth of nations. Yet Khrushchev failed to introduce a fundamental change into the structure of the Party and state apparatus. He managed to dispose of his main rivals relatively quickly and in this he succeeded perhaps even faster than Stalin had done, but in a less cruel fashion. Indeed, with the exception of Beria, who was executed soon after Stalin's death, it was an almost bloodless process. Whether the ideological and political reasons given by Khrushchev for the personnel changes in July 1957, when he accused Molotov, Kaganovich, Malenkov and others of anti-Party activities, were his real motives or not, they were welcomed by those who were eagerly waiting for the ideas of the Twentieth Congress to be realized.

The Czechoslovak Communist Party was securely in the hands of Novotný; Gottwald's successor as President of the Republic was an old trade-unionist leader, Antonin Zápotocký, who, unlike Gottwald, was more of a figurehead than a real leader of the Party. The CPCz under Novotný was very reluctant in the early months and even years after the Twentieth Congress to accept its new policy, although occasionally and with much embarrassment Novotný had to pay lip-service to them. He was particularly slow in carrying out the expected rehabilitation of the victims of the purges. He released from prison two of the three survivors of the main Slánský trial, London and Hajdu, and rehabilitated a few men like Goldstücker and other former diplomats, especially those sentenced for alleged espionage in collaboration with the left-wing British Member of Parliament, Konni Zilliacus, who, in the Tito–Stalin controversy, had firmly supported Tito. Now that Tito was accepted as a good Communist again it would have been too conspicuous to maintain the pretence that Zilliacus was an imperialist spy.

But Slánský and Clementis, one the embodiment of Zionism, the other of bourgeois nationalism, were not included in the short list of those who were rehabilitated. Zionism was still a dangerous deviation because of the recent Anglo-French-Israel war against Egypt. Nationalism became a burning issue once more after the Hungarian 'counter-revolution' and the Polish uprising of October 1956. Afterwards, Tito's support for the Hungarian reformers and their abortive attempt to change the Stalinist Rákosi régime made him the odd man out once more.[2] He was vehemently condemned by Khrushchev as an exponent of 'national comunism', as the deviation was now officially called.

Novotný and most leaders of the Czechoslovak Communist Party must have watched the tragic events in Hungary with a strange kind of satisfaction, for it seemed that Rákosi, who had been one of the most violent Stalinist witch-hunters and the first to initiate show-trials, had been too hasty in rehabilitating his victims. Novotný considered it to be carelessness on the part of Rákosi to bring back to power some of those who were still alive, and to honour the dead, such as Rajk, with pomp and ceremony at state funerals. Such occasions, in Novotný's view, only added to the hysterical atmosphere of the times and helped to precipitate counter-revolution. Even Khrushchev seemed to come to this conclusion. Novotný did not intend to repeat Rákosi's mistakes, and still refused to rehabilitate most of his own victims; he even tried to prevent the dissemination in Czechoslovakia of most of the ideas of the Twentieth Congress.

As it turned out, the post-revolutionary Hungary of Kádár and post-October Poland of Gomulka became for a short time the envy of the nations of Eastern Europe and hence a cause of concern and fear for Novotný in Prague and Ulbricht in East Berlin. However the Poles soon came to realize that perhaps the only thing that had changed after October was Gomulka himself; he was soon attacked by the intelligentsia which had suppported him with such great hope when he was swept back to power by popular will. Hungary became the only socialist country which seemed to have serious intentions of implementing the anti-Stalinist measures suggested at the Twentieth Congress. Kádár, who during the Hungarian revolution and the ensuing months was considered to be a Soviet collaborator actually became the most liberal of the satellite leaders Novotný watched the developments in Poland and Hungary closely. He felt fully justified in taking a cautious line and in many ways his policy represented a return to the situation before Khrushchev's attempts at various liberal innovations and de-Stalinization. In 1957 and the

[2] Especially after the execution of the liberal leader of the Hungarian revolutionary movement, Imre Nagy, who, with his close associates, had taken refuge in the Yugoslav Embassy in Budapest. The Yugoslavs had agreed to release them for extradition only on condition that they be granted a safe conduct out of Hungary by the Russians.

following years new purges were ordered in the Czechoslovak state apparatus and many anti-Stalinist suspects lost their jobs.

After the Twenty-second Congress of the Soviet Communist Party in October 1961, in the course of which Stalin's body was removed from the Mausoleum to be buried in a less honourable place near the Kremlin wall, it again looked as if Khrushchev was serious in his anti-Stalinism. The revolutionary events in Hungary and in Poland were over and almost forgotten. The political situation in those countries seemed to have been stabilized, at least from the Soviet point of view. The relationship with Tito improved once more. Now it was Mao Tse-tung's China that had become the main object of concern to the Soviet leaders. For a very short period China experimented with the ideas of the Twentieth Congress and in this respect seemed to go even further than Khrushchev himself. Whatever subsequently made the Chinese Communists change their minds, whatever cause the Soviet rulers had given Mao Tse-tung for concern, China soon became the principal protagonist of Stalinism. Mao Tse-tung claimed to be the heir not only of Marx and Engels and Lenin, but of Stalin too.

In the bitter ideological dispute that ensued, Khrushchev condemned the dogmatic and ultra-conservative attitude of Peking and advocated the possibility of a peaceful transition to socialism and the thesis that the imperialists could be prevented from unleashing a world war. In his polemics against the Chinese Communists Khrushchev said that war was not necessary for the further expansion of Communism, and that in some capitalist countries socialism could even be achieved by parliamentary methods. Since in the Soviet Union the class struggle had virtually ceased, a dictatorship of the proletariat was no longer necessary; the state could be transformed into a 'state of all the people'. The Soviet Communist Party's new programme adopted by the Twenty-second Congress brought more liberal features into the life of the Party, in particular by stressing the need for a faster rotation of functions. All these ideas were in sharp contrast to those now held by Mao Tse-tung. He accused the Soviet leaders of the most serious heresy – revisionism. On the other hand Khrushchev saw Chinese dogmatism as the greatest crime and he continued to stress the dangers of revisionism while vigorously refuting the Chinese accusations.

Without attempting a deeper analysis of the causes of the Sino–Soviet dispute, there is no doubt as to its far-reaching effect on the socialist countries and the world Communist movement, including

Czechoslovakia. Novotný could not ignore this development. Although he sided openly with the Soviet Union in this dispute, he was suspected of pro-Chinese attitudes. Such suspicions were confirmed by his slowness in implementing the new Soviet policy expressed in the Twenty-second Congress. There were rumours circulating in the Czechoslovak Party that Khrushchev himself had had to rebuke Novotný for this reluctance. It is likely that the rumours originated only from the wishful thinking by those Communists in Czechoslovakia who were justifiably impatient about the slowness, if not absence, of liberalization in their country. Khrushchev's prodding of Novotný, if it did occur at all, was obviously not as insistent as, for example, Stalin's pressure on Gottwald a decade earlier to remove the Czech and Slovak class enemies from the Party. Whatever Khrushchev's attitude to Novotný was, the latter hesitated and conceded very little to his impatient population and those more progressive Party officials who had been looking forward to the introduction of long overdue reforms.

Despite Novotný's Stalinist attitudes he was quite popular in Moscow at that time: he had the situation in Czechoslovakia firmly in hand and there was no sign as yet of any Hungarian or Polish type of rebellion taking place in Prague or in Bratislava. When President Zápotocký died in 1958 and the question of his successor arose, rumour had it that Khrushchev intervened directly. Novotný, who was First Secretary of the Party was already the most powerful man in the country, became President of the Republic as well as retaining his position in the Party. The Praesidium of the Czechoslovak Communist Party had originally decided that the Slovak, Viliam Široký, who was Prime Minister in Prague, should succeed Zápotocký. The state news agency ČTK had already distributed officially approved photographs and Široký's biography to the mass media, ready for publication after his formal election. However unpopular Široký was, the country was shocked to hear that the even more unpopular Novotný would from now on hold the two most important jobs in the country. There is so far no official confirmation of Khrushchev's intervention on behalf of Novotný but circumstantial evidence points in this direction. Novotný enjoyed Soviet confidence not because of any progressive views he may have been thought to hold, but because he gave the Russians little trouble; this, perhaps, was Khrushchev's way of showing his gratitude.

The Prague 'Twentieth Congress' finally took place in December 1962. It was the Twelfth Congress of the Czechoslovak Communist Party. This time some steps were taken towards de-Stalinization of the Party and general liberalization throughout the country. Most of the victims of the trials – some of them freed only under the terms of an amnesty for ordinary criminals in May 1960 on the fifteenth anniversary of the existence of Socialist Czechoslovakia – were now promised full rehabilitation.[3] What Novotný actually meant with his promise of full rehabilitation soon became clear. Those who were still alive got back their Party cards and better jobs. The next of kin of the executed received financial indemnities, with the privilege of jumping the long queue for a car, which they could buy with the money. None of those who survived the trials and who were released in 1960 under the amnesty and who were now 'rehabilitated', like Švermová in Prague, and Husák and Löbl in Bratislava, were given back the jobs in the Party or in the state administration which they had held before their arrest. The reason was self-evident. Novotný was afraid of his victims' regaining positions of power. He guessed what the rehabilitated might do to their 'rehabilitator'.

The problem of rehabilitation became very important after the death of Stalin, and especially after the liquidation of Beria. In Czechoslovakia it was a burning issue which Novotný had tried to extinguish. From the early Sixties onwards, and especially after the Twenty-second Congress in Moscow, the problem was constantly raised by the most progressive elements in the Party and in the country. The need for a solution was urgent, not only for the sake of those directly affected; the reformers saw it as a means of achieving the moral rehabilitation of the Party, indeed of socialism itself, and it is no coincidence that some of the most prominent leaders of the 'Czechoslovak spring' were former victims of Gottwald and Novotný.

[3] Until now they had only been allowed to hold very minor posts as clerks in small enterprises. Husák was a clerk in the building industry, Löbl worked as a storeman in a clothing shop, and so on. None of those released had been readmitted into the Party.

I2 THE REVOLT OF THE SLOVAK INTELLECTUALS

The events of 1968 in Czechoslovakia were the result of a gradual accumulation of factors over a long period of time. The main precipitating factor was the Twelfth Congress of the CPCz of December 1962, which triggered off turbulent events in Slovakia. These events may serve to justify the statement that the Czechoslovak spring of 1968 was preceded by the Slovak spring of 1963.

Novotný's downfall in January 1968 did not come as a surprise. It was the culmination of pressure which had been growing for a long time from the ranks of progressive Party members and which had been resisted by the conservatives, above all by Novotný himself. The events of the first eight months of 1968 and even after the Warsaw Pact invasion in August of that year can be seen as part of a pattern; the revolt of a section of the Communist Party against the ineffectual way Novotný was running the country; important political and cultural events like the Czechoslovak Writers' Congress in June 1967; the student demonstrations in November 1967; and most important of all the individual actions which helped to set in motion the avalanche which was to sweep Novotný away – particularly Dubček's speech at the October 1967 session of the Central Committee in Prague, which provoked Novotný into remarking that all the Slovaks in the Central Committee were nationalists. The anti-Stalinist attitude of the politically conscious intelligentsia, as opposed to the apparently apathetic working class for whom the Novotný system apparently held some appeal, was an important factor in the period before 1968. But the significance of the growing tension in relations between Czechs and Slovaks, which under Novotný had reached breaking point, must not be underestimated. Even Dubček's Czech colleagues had to wait for the right psychological moment to act, and that moment appeared to have come when Dubček openly denounced Novotný, in particular over his attitude to Slovakia.

When in December 1962, the Twelfth Congress of the Czechoslovak Communist Party revealed more fully the crimes committed under Gottwald and then under Novotný and exposed the political trials and purges which had continued into the late Fifties and early Sixties, the position of the Party rulers in Slovakia was deeply shaken.

In 1954 Karol Bacílek, former Minister of Security, had been sent to Bratislava as First Secretary of the Slovak Communist Party. He had become a liability in Prague because he had been known to be Beria's man in Czechoslovakia. Bacílek, who had never been very popular with the Slovaks, returned to Bratislava completely discredited. In Prague his removal from office was greeted with great relief. Novotný could and actually did present his removal as a clever way of dealing with whatever was admitted of the activities of Beria's 'gorillas' in Czechoslovakia.

However, Bacílek's arrival in Bratislava as Novotný's viceroy was taken by the Slovaks as an insult. For the next nine years he ruled Slovakia, apparently with the sole aim of liquidating all remnants of Slovak self-government. Under the constitution as it was revised in 1960, on the occasion of the fifteenth anniversary of the liberation, the Slovak national organs lost all power. The new regional structure, with three regions in Slovakia, put local administration under the direct control of the central government in Prague; the regional councils in Slovakia were not directly responsible to the Slovak National Council. As in the new regions in the Czech lands, their activities were directed by the Ministry of the Interior in Prague. This caused great disappointment in Slovakia. Further, in 1964 the new arrangements, which were supposed to meet Slovak demands, were modified in such a way that the Slovak Board of Commissioners disappeared altogether. Its separate executive departments were reduced to mere committees of the Slovak National Council with almost no competence of their own.

Novotný had no illusions as to his popularity in Slovakia. Only a few months after Bacílek was finally relieved of his post as First Secretary of the Slovak Party and replaced by Alexander Dubček, did Novotný venture into Slovakia. He did not dare to visit Bratislava, but went to Košice, the capital of eastern Slovakia, where he felt he would be safer. The purpose of this visit was to suppress the dangerous ideas voiced at recent congresses of Slovak writers and especially of Slovak journalists. Novotný spoke of the spirit of unity and he described the role of the Slovak National Council thus:

> The Council used to act as the legislative body in Slovakia, while the Board of Commissioners exercised the executive power. After the victory of socialist production relations in our country we adopted a new constitution which already assumed that it would be valid at a future time when we enter communism. In the Constitution we formulated the role of the Slovak National Council and at the same time we have abolished the Board of

Commissioners. Why, comrades? I am not asserting here the right to consider the shape of social organs in a future communist society. But we must, even at this stage, create certain forms of social organization of which we presuppose that they will in principle correspond to the needs of our communist society. I say openly, comrades, that in the past we in the Politburo [the Praesidium of the CPCz] often criticized the activities of the Slovak National Council as well as of the Slovak Politburo. Comrade Dubček is here, he can confirm that the Council is making inadequate use of the jurisdiction it has in Slovakia. We recommended that it should work actively but it did not do so sufficiently.[1]

Novotný's clumsy attempt at forecasting the structure of a future Communist society was merely a pretext for what was in effect the end of what was left of Slovak home rule. Slovakia was to have the privilege of being the first region in which, according to Marxist teachings, legislative and executive power would be fully merged. The Slovaks would experience the dream of a Communist society in which there would be no room for petty nationalist aspirations, to say nothing of national institutions. Slovakia was to be the guinea-pig in Novotný's practical implementation of this Marxist philosophy. To add insult to injury, Novotný had the temerity to blame the Slovaks for not having made sufficient use of their national organs. No wonder the Slovaks took Novotný's speech as a bad joke; they could not fully appreciate it, however, as it was made by a man who was not particularly renowned for his sense of humour.

The main aim of Novotný's trip to Košice had been to calm down the mood of irritation in Slovakia. Its immediate cause was the dissatisfaction of Slovak intellectuals with the findings of the new commission headed by a member of the Czechoslovak Praesidium, Drahomír Kolder, which had been set up to investigate 'violations of Leninist norms of Party life and principles'. This commission, after spending months studying tons of material, completed its final report at the end of 1962, although most of its members had known all along exactly what had happened at the trials and who was directly implicated in them. Although the commission's report signified a new and major step towards rehabilitating the main victims of the purges, it still left much to be desired. It still contained half-truths and proposed only half-measures. The 'bourgeois nationalists' were rehabilitated in the sense that they were absolved of the crime of Titoist

[1] Quoted from the BBC Monitoring Service, 12 June 1963.

revisionism and treason. Even bourgeois nationalism was not branded as a criminal offence but only as a deviation from the proper Party line, alien to proletarian internationalism. The dead Vladimír Clementis was rehabilitated with this reservation, which was particularly stressed. So were Dr Husák, the poet Novomeský, the Spanish Civil War veteran Holdoš, amongst others. Now they were given back their Party membership cards. Novomeský could return from his forced exile in Prague and the press was told it could publish his poems and literary essays. Husák and some of his colleagues were given jobs in the history department of the Slovak Academy of Sciences. He turned down an invitation from Novotný to come to Prague as Deputy Minister of Justice – a junior position which it was hoped would corrupt him into obedience and silence. Husák saw what lay behind this offer of promotion; Novotný wanted him to be far away from Bratislava where he might exercise a dangerous influence.

Frequent visits by Novotný's emissaries to the former monastery of the Barnabites where the rehabilitation commission was working had ensured that there was no suggestion of Novotný or other members of the current leadership having been personally implicated; Gottwald was made responsible for the distortions of justice. But he had died in 1953. They found another culprit, Kopecký, the former Minister of Culture who had died more recently. These could safely be denounced as the guilty men of the Fifties. On the other hand, the report made no mention of Široký, now Prime Minister, who had been the main crusader against Slovak bourgeois nationalism and had helped to bring many men to jail, although in those days he had only been Foreign Minister. There was no mention even of Bacílek, Minister of Security during the purges and First Secretary in Slovakia until 1963. And, of course, there was not the slightest hint that Novotný himself might have had any responsibilty; he was to remain above all suspicion. Attempts were even being made to depict him as the man who did his best to bring out a just solution to the long overdue problem of rehabilitation. He was described as having been hindered in his noble task by men like Barák, Bacílek's successor in the Ministry of the Interior. Barák had been accused of embezzlement and sent to prison, although it was whispered that in fact the real cause of his imprisonment was his desire to speed up the rehabilitations. This was later officially acknowledged to have been the case.[2] The truth was that Novotný was afraid that Barák in his new function might use the evidence collected against him, and he suspected him of coveting

[2] In 1968 Barák was retried and freed.

his job as First Secretary of the Party. He decided to remove this potentially dangerous rival.

Most of the 'Zionist' culprits were rehabilitated too. But Slánský, Šváb, Šling and a few others were not absolved from the indictment of anti-Party activities and violations of Leninst principles. They were rehabilitated legally, but not politically. These dead men were still to be deprived of the honour of a posthumous return to the Party. Novotný and his associates thought it wise to leave some stain on Slánský. With his primitive kind of shrewdness Novotný expected that by discriminating in this case against the Zionists in favour of the bourgeois nationalists, he might even gain some sympathy in Slovakia, and perhaps with Husák himself. The latter had never forgiven Slánský, who was General Secretary of the Party when he and other 'bourgeois nationalists' were arrested, although Slánský himself was soon chosen as the main culprit in the 1952 trial. Husák made frequent remarks in his later writings to the effect that he still regarded Slánský as one of the originators of the drive against bourgeois nationalists. Husák failed to grasp the full tragedy inflicted by Stalinism on dedicated Communists such as himself and Slánský. In addition to this Husák seemed to forget that he was sentenced to life imprisonment two years after Slánský had been executed.

Unlike Husák, the Slovak journalist Mieroslav Hysko showed deeper understanding of the tragedy of both the 'bourgeois nationalists' and the 'Zionist cosmopolitans'. At the Congress of Slovak Journalists in May 1963, Hysko transformed this gathering, which was expected to be as dreary one as most congresses of the kind in Novotný's Czechoslovakia, into a very exciting event with far-reaching consequences. He gave an analysis of the relations between Czechs and Slovaks since 1948 and made brilliant use of the case of bourgeois nationalism in support of his conclusions. He rejected the findings of the 'Barnabite commission' on rehabilitations as insufficient. He claimed that the term 'bourgeois nationalism' should be dropped altogether from the political vocabulary because it was only a Stalinist pretext for suppressing the just aspirations of the Slovak people. He regarded the initial persecution of the bourgeois nationalists as merely paving the way for the liquidation of all those in the Party including the so-called cosmopolitans, who might possibly have challenged the Stalinist leadership and its sterile dogmatism. Stalinism was hostile not only to the Slovak intellectuals but to all intelligent men who wished to think for themselves and who were not prepared to obey Party discipline blindly. He directly accused the Prime Minister, Široký, of having been one of those most responsible for the bourgeois nationalist witch-hunt in Slovakia and for the more general witch-hunt throughout Czechoslovakia. He asked why a man like that should still remain in office. Hysko's speech hinted that other men were not without guilt, although he was astute enough not to mention Novotný himself. Anyway, everybody knew whom Hysko considered to be the man most responsible for withholding the truth from the Party and the nation. It was the first time in the history of a socialist country that a Prime Minister still in office had been the target of such serious criticism and charges at an official Party-sponsored gathering.

Hysko's speech created a great stir and encouraged other delegates to express similar views. Most of the speakers at the Congress of Slovak Journalists discarded their prepared written speeches and spoke openly on matters which had been taboo up till then. Besides Hysko, the most prominent of them was Roman Kaliský, a talented writer and journalist on the staff of the weekly *Kultúrny Život*.[3] What he had to say at this congress confirmed Novotný's misgivings about him. His main thesis was that Slovakia should have a greater say in its own affairs. He not only advocated political decentralization but also demanded economic autonomy. He was not demanding Slovak economic separatism, as Novotný alleged.

The contents of the speeches, especially Hysko's and Kaliský's, reached the ears of the public. The trade union daily *Práca* covered the proceedings of the congress in some detail. The editor of the Party daily *Pravda* hesitated for a few days but in the end decided to publish the unabridged version of Hysko's speech, thus compensating for the fact that his paper's coverage of the two days of this turbulent congress had at first been scanty.[4] In May 1963, it took some courage to publish Hysko's speech. The editor of *Pravda*, Andrej Klokoč, was not a man known for great courage, but in the heady atmosphere of those days he decided to take the risk and defy the expressed wish of the censor. Klokoč argued that, as a member of the Central Committee of the Slovak Communist Party, and as editor-in-chief, he took full responsibility for his action.

---

[3] He was formerly a deputy of the National Assembly for the small Slovak Party of Reconstruction and editor-in-chief of the daily L'ud but had lost his job because of his frequent clashes with official Communist policy.

[4] It had not reported, for example, that a motion had been passed by the congress in memory of their fellow journalists, the Slovak Vladimír Clementis and the Czech André Simone, who had both been sentenced to death and executed in the Slánský trial. This motion was passed unanimously with great applause. It was in fact the first occasion on which two victims of that Kafkaesque trial had been publicly honoured.

On the second day of the Slovak Journalists' Congress a further resolution was moved. A group of about thirty well-known journalists petitioned the congress to invite their fellow-journalists, Husák, Novomeský and Friš to state their case in public for the first time. However, the delegation from the Central Committee of the Slovak Communist Party, strengthened by Vasil Biľak, who was in charge of its ideological work prevented it from being carried. Biľak threatened strict disciplinary measures and very serious consequences if the motion were not withdrawn.

The two delegates from the Union of Czechoslovak Journalists in Prague, the General Secretary Adolf Hradecký and the editor of *Kulturní Tvorba*, Miroslav Galuška, seemed most impressed by the courage of their Slovak colleagues. Galuška,[5] addressed the congress, praising it as the first one of its kind 'when a congress was really a congress and a debate really a debate'. He had clearly been encouraged by the moral strength of the Slovak journalists who had dared to challenge the leadership of the Party, although at that stage they had chosen to attack directly only Široký and discredited men like Bacílek, who, had recently been replaced in his job as First Secretary of the Slovak Communist Party by Alexander Dubček, though he still remained a member of the Central Committee of the CPCz.

Dubček had risen quickly in Communist Czechoslovakia. He was a partisan during the Slovak uprising, and had been twice wounded. In 1949, still in his twenties, he became a district party official in Trenčín. From then on he progressed quickly in his Party career. In 1952 he was made a departmental head in the Central Committee in Bratislava and one year later became Deputy Chairman of the Central Committee of the Slovak National Front. In 1953 he was First Secretary of the Party in the Banská Bystrica region. From there he went to Moscow, where he graduated with honours in the Party College. He returned to Bratislava as First Party Secretary of the West Slovak region. From 1962 to 1963 he was one of the secretaries of the Central Committee of the Czechoslovak Party in Prague. In fact he seemed to be the most trusted young Slovak in Prague – Novotný's Prague. And then he finally replaced the old Stalinist, Karol Bacílek, as First Secretary of the Party for the whole of Slovakia. How a man who rose so quickly under Novotný became a symbol of Czechoslovak reform and anti-Stalinism remains to be answered.

[5] Galuška was known for his intelligent and courageous approach to journalism even under Stalinist conditions and later became one of the leading figures in the Prague spring and Minister of Culture under Dubček.

Certainly Dubček was not known at that time as a man cherishing new ideas. The fact that he appeared to enjoy Novotný's confidence did not then endear him to the Slovak progessives. Nevertheless, when Dubček became First Secretary of the Party in Slovakia the atmosphere changed although at the time this could not be ascribed directly to his influence. It resulted not so much from the presence of this new man in the highest office in Slovakia, as from the absence of Bacílek, whose removal from his post had been greeted with great relief as a good omen for the future.

So far, little is known about what went on in the inner circles of the Party in Bratislava under Dubček's new leadership. Only his closest colleagues may have realized that Dubček was in fact a totally different kind of Communist from Bacílek, as later events were to prove. In the spring and the summer of 1963, a short time after Dubček's promotion, the political atmosphere in the country seemed to improve; Slovak journalists felt that they could come into the open with their views and their grievances. If this had not been the case, the rather timid editor of *Pravda* would not have dared to publish Hysko's speech in defiance of the censor. While Bacílek was First Secretary a similar act of defiance would have been unthinkable. The disobedient editor would have been dealt with ruthlessly. Now, Klokoč got away with a serious breach of Party discipline with no more than a mild reprimand from Dubček and when Dubček referred to Hysko's case a few weeks later, he merely remarked that 'there can be no agreement with everything said by comrade Hysko'.[6] There were suggestions that disciplinary action might be taken against him, meetings were held in Party organizations in the mass media at which Party officials denounced Hysko's views. But by 1963 it was too late to initiate strict actions against him; the functionaries had to content themselves with making sarcastic remarks about his personal character, questioning even his sanity and making pointed references to his alcoholism. However, this psychological pressure drove him to give up his job as director of the Slovak Research Institute for Journalism. He became a Reader at the Department of Journalism in the Philosophical Faculty of the Comenius University in Bratislava, a change which would have been unthinkable under Bacílek. In those days it was not even suspected that the absence of strict disciplinary measures could have been due to Dubček's desire for reform, at least in Slovakia. In retrospect it can be assumed that, were it not for Dubček's influence, whether direct or indirect, nothing could have

---

[6] Deryck Viney, 'Alexander Dubček', *Studies of Comparative Communism*, July–October 1968, p. 23.

saved Hysko from expulsion from the Party, despite the fact that at the Party meetings organized against him by the Central Committee most of his colleagues openly sympathized with him and defended his views. It is even possible that, at that time, Dubček tacitly agreed with Hysko's and Kaliský's views and that he had become affected by the general mood of his country, especially in Bratislava.

As I have already mentioned, in 1963 Novotný refused to visit Bratislava and chose the relative safety of the Party platform in the iron and steel works at Košice. Only with his carefully selected audience, far away from the intellectual ferment in Bratislava, did he dare to denounce bourgeois nationalism once again, although its exponents had already been cleared of the criminal charges against them. In the same speech in which he forecast the development of state organs in Slovakia, he said:

> A problem which has been talked about a lot lately is that of bourgeois nationalism in Slovakia. Several comrades who had important functions in the past have been the bearers of this. I read the article by comrade Hysko in *Pravda*. I have also read a number of other articles in *Kultúrny Život* and, comrades, I say openly that both the authors of the articles and the editorial offices themselves have set out on a dangerous road. I openly say that these articles treat the question of personality cult as the fundamental and only problem with which we should deal in Slovakia and in the whole of the Republic.[7]

Then he went on to emphasize how Western propaganda was using every means at its disposal to inflame the issue of nationalism in Slovakia and to spread a mood of opposition. Little did he realize that speeches such as his did more to inflame nationalism than any amount of 'enemy propaganda'.

Of course, the ruler of Czechoslovakia did not consider nationalism in Slovakia to be the only danger facing the socialist Republic. Talking in Košice about the 'sinister aims of Western imperialists', he accused them of seeking 'under the pretext of the fight against the personality cult to unleash a battle in the sphere of culture and renew the call for freedom of self-expression'.[8] Novotný identified it as 'the freedom to attack the interest of the Party and the interest of socialism'.[9] Ironically enough, the two 'dangers' which Novotný dreaded most eventually caused his downfall: Slovak liberal nationalism and Czech national liberalism.

[7] BBC Monitoring Service, 12 June 1963.
[8] *Ibid.*   [9] *Ibid.*

In 1963 Alexander Dubček himself was very far from propagating progressive ideas. Despite this, during his time as First Secretary of the Party in Slovakia it was possible to express views which were practically forbidden in Prague and in the Czech lands. These were the days when the weekly of the Slovak Writers' Union, *Kultúrny Život*, was read eagerly throughout the country, not only in Slovakia. Actually it was the first Slovak periodical to arouse interest among the Czechs. Although the Party refused to increase the allocation of paper for *Kultúrny Život*, a few hundred copies did manage to reach Prague. Often they were sold for black market prices, or under the counter. The most progressive writers were frequent contributors: men like Eugen Löbl on economics, Pavol Štefček on problems of literature, Július Strinka and Miroslav Kusý on social philosophy, and Dr Husák himself on the Slovak national problem.

In the Party branches in Bratislava, especially those in intellectual organizations, the mass media, the universities, the Academy of Sciences, and government offices, Party officials were unable to suppress free discussion. Some of them gave the impression that they did not even wish to, and appeared to sympathize with the anti-Stalinist ideas which were being so openly expressed.

13 THE HISTORICAL ARGUMENT

From 1963 onwards Bratislava was teeming with political and intellectual activity. The most active were the historians, economists and philosophers. In all faculties of the universities and schools of technology there were large departments of Marxism–Leninism and scientific Communism. Most of the teachers and research workers, if they were any good, made genuine efforts to 'develop creatively' those Marxist principles in economics, philosophy and political theory which, under Stalin, had become rigid dogmas with no bearing on reality. If they did have any effect on practical life, then the consequences were purely negative and often disastrous.

The work of Slovak historians in this period deserves special attention. The immediate impulse for their new approach – especially to the last decades of Slovak history – came from Dr Husák, who was still unable to play a direct and active role in the Party or in the government, and from 1963 worked in the history department of the Slovak Academy of Sciences. Ironically enough, he caused more damage to Novotný there than he would have done if Novotný had succeeded in getting him into some more important job after his formal rehabilitation in 1963. Husák was not idle. He soon became the most influential man in Bratislava intellectual circles. In a very short time he wrote a book on the Slovak National Uprising. His account of this great event in the history of the Slovak people was somewhat different from the version given up till then by official Party historians, who had been obliged to distort historical truths to the detriment of the Slovak nation. Quite understandably, Husák's first aim was to clear himself of the charges against him concerning his activities as a prominent leader of the Uprising in August 1944. Stalinist historians had concentrated almost exclusively on Moscow's role in it and had belittled the importance of the underground movement at home. All the leaders and most of the ordinary participants in the Uprising were suspected of bourgeois nationalist attitudes. Husák proved convincingly that the Slovak anti-German, anti-fascist revolt was mainly the result of the activities of those Communists and Democrats who stayed in Slovakia during the war. An essential part of his argument was to show how the Slovak leaders had had to press their Czech comrades in London and in Moscow for pledges as to the future position of Slovakia in the new Republic. Husák helped to clear the names of some prominent non-Communist Slovak leaders of the Uprising such as Generals Golián and Viest, who after its suppression were captured by the Germans and executed. They were now presented as Slovak martyrs, though in the Fifties they had been branded as traitors together with their Communist friends and allies. History books had up till now referred to them, if at all, in derogatory terms. They were accused of having been conspirators working for Beneš in London and not for the benefit of the Slovak nation. Husák had the moral integrity and courage to exculpate these men from those monstrous charges. Having himself experienced similar accusations, he had some understanding for his non-Communist fellow-fighters who had been so unjustly accused.

Husák's book was published before the twentieth anniversary of the Uprising after some delay resulting from the hesitation of the press department of the Slovak Party's Central Committee. Eventually the officials, probably with Dubček's consent, ruled that a limited number of copies of the book could be published. In practical terms this meant that although the book was not officially banned, the general public could not buy it. It never even reached the bookshops, having been distributed and sold out before it got there. A second edition was not recommended.[1]

Husák also became a frequent contributor to *Kultúrny Život*. It was the only periodical which offered its columns to him, although unlike other contributors to that journal he was not a liberal progressive writer on matters of general policy. In his political and philosophical views, in as far as he expressed them at all, Husák gave the impression of being a man whose intellectual development had ceased in the late Forties when he got into trouble with the Party. He was never much of a theoretician anyway, being interested more in matters of everyday politics than in general principles of Marxist theory. His main concern was the Slovak national question. He frequently referred to the Soviet Union as the best friend of Czechoslovakia and the Slovak nation. Was he paying only lip-service to the Soviet Union? Some of his close associates wondered whether his positive attitude to that country did really spring from a genuine feeling of friendship. Was it not dictated, even in those

---

[1] A revised edition of the book was published in August 1969, and included some paragraphs which had been omitted in 1964 on the recommendation of the censors.

early days, by political expediency? Naturally, he repudiated Stalin and praised Khrushchev, to whom he must have felt gratitude as the father of the Twentieth Congress and who eventually (four years after that Congress!) had caused the prison doors to open for him and his colleagues.

Whatever the changes in the political climate of 1963 and 1964 in Slovakia, no journal except *Kultúrny Život* would have dared to publish articles written by Husák, although he was always careful not to contradict the official Party line. The more loudly he condemned Stalin personally the less loudly he denounced the ideology and political practices of Stalinism. Still, when he attempted to have his articles published in *Pravda* or other periodicals he put the editors in an embarrassing position. They would have liked to publish him, but they had Party instructions that his name should be kept out of the mass-circulated press. This was to prevent him from becoming a popular figure. But the editors of *Kultúrny Život* did not always respect this instruction. After all, the weekly had only a limited circulation and it was generally known that it did not express the orthodox Party line. If Husák were to be published in *Pravda* or the trade union daily, *Práca*, the public would be given the erroneous impression that Husák was quite acceptable to the highest authorities in the Party, and that he was not only formally but practically rehabilitated. As to Husák's relationship or contact with Dubček, at that time the latter and the Party apparatus kept a respectful distance from him. Nevertheless, or perhaps because of that, Husák became the spiritual leader of the people and came to represent the great hope of the Slovak intelligentsia. Although the official representative of the Party, Dubček was still an unknown quantity. It was inevitably felt that if Novotný had not trusted him, he would not have appointed him as First Secretary of the Party in that troublesome part of the country, and that he would not have kept him in that important post if he had lost confidence in him. On the rare occasions when Novotný came to Slovakia he always appeared in Dubček's presence, thus indicating that what he had to say was binding for Dubček and the Slovaks. Dubček neither did nor could dissociate himself from Novotný's speeches.

In August 1964, on the twentieth anniversary of the Slovak uprising, there were great celebrations in Banská Bystrica, attended by Khrushchev. Husák, although invited as one of the leaders of the Uprising, was not an official delegate; his jailer Bacílek, still a member of the Central Committee, was. Husák was seated in the back row among the less important guests; Bacílek was in the front row, where he had the honour of shaking hands with the most celebrated official delegate and guest, Khrushchev. Husák was carefully prevented from meeting Khrushchev, who was obviously not interested in meeting him and perhaps was even unaware of his presence there.

At the time another affair in Slovakia must have disturbed Novotný's peace of mind. Professor Miloš Gosiorovský, who changed from a dogmatic official Party historian into a genuine seeker of truth and facts, compiled a study in which he outlined a proposal for federation as the only solution to the strained relations between the Slovaks and Czechs. Husák, being a practical politician and knowing the disastrous effect such a suggestion would have on Novotný, carefully omitted this heretical idea from his writings. Gosiorovský ungratefully forgot that Bacílek and Široký had made him a Professor at the Comenius University, despite his lack of higher education (a deficiency in qualification which had to be compensated for by an honorary doctorate and titles). He now openly proposed the federal solution which had originally been promised to the Slovaks. He did not, and indeed could not, publish his study. All he did was circulate a few typewritten copies among the experts and his closest friends and, as a dutiful Party member, he sent one copy to the Central Committee. Gosiorovský's conversion caused a major political row. Disciplinary measures were initiated against him. Although he was neither expelled from the Party nor officially removed from his chair at the University, he was prevented from lecturing and from having anything published, not even articles less harmful in content than the propagation of federalism. Novotný must have been furious with Gosiorovský but did not dare to order his expulsion from the Party or to use other strict measures such as had been used in similar cases during the Fifties. In this case he was shrewd enough to realize that this would only add fuel to the fire and make the situation in Slovakia even worse. At this time the idea that Dubček might have exercised a restraining influence upon Novotný in his attitude to the Slovak rebels would have come as a total surprise to all but his closest colleagues.

In 1964 the rights of the Slovak National Council were further reduced although the Party propagandists did their best to present the new measures as a further step towards the dream solution of self-government which Novotný had outlined a year before in Košice. True enough, the number of Slovak commissioners was increased, but they were only figureheads – they had no executive power. This was exclusively in the hands of the cenral government in Prague. They became mere transmitters, translating Novotný's Czech instructions into Slovak. After this reorganization and the abolition of the Board of Commissioners, the Slovak National Council was only an empty symbol, a parody of Slovak nationhood.

Although there was still no open expression of disagreement between Novotný and Dubček on these fundamental matters, it later became known that Novotný was dissatisfied with the course of events in Slovakia and partially blamed Dubček for the state of affairs there. In 1965 it was rumoured that Novotný intended to replace Dubček with a more trusted man, the Chairman of the Slovak National Council, Michal Chudík. But such rumours were so frequent that they were not taken seriously, especially when nothing happened and Dubček remained First Secretary of the Slovak Party. The suggestion that Novotný had originally opposed Dubček as Bacílek's successor in that post is not borne out by the evidence. On the contrary, it seems inconceivable that in April 1963 anybody on the Central Committee in Prague could have pushed through any candidate other than the one Novotný had chosen. There is no doubt that Dubček had been his choice for Slovakia. That Novotný made a wrong decision and that Dubček – a man with an excellent Party record, even from Novotný's point of view – eventually let him down and turned against him, is another matter.

Slovak historians and political scientists were intimidated by the case of their colleague Professor Gosiorovský. For a while it looked as if they had been frightened into passivity. But they soon recovered their nerve and slowly but surely continued their research into Slovak history and society. As a result, they began to reassess the political situation in Slovakia. They were dedicated scholars with a strong sense of social duty and exercised great influence on Slovakia's changing political climate. Despite strict censorship they managed to publish hitherto unknown materials. At this time they were concerned above all with attacking Stalinist dogma and very gradually they managed to remove the distortions and lies which had been concocted about their history. The main target of attack was the concept of bourgeois nationalism which was still in use. They rejected it as a malevolent invention exploited by those in Prague whose real aim was to suppress Slovak national rights. *Kultúrny Život* willingly published their writings, though often only after bitter wrangling with the censors. These were mostly semi-educated men with only an instinctive sense of what constituted matters of dangerous content. Sometimes their instinct failed. When a case was referred to the Central Committe of the Slovak Communist Party, it was not unusual for some progressive-minded worker in the ideological department to actually help get material published. This sometimes happened even with some dailies and, of course, with scientific journals published by the Slovak Academy of Sciences.

The Slovak capital thus became the only place in the socialist world where it was possible for a weekly like *Kultúrny Život* to be published. Occasionally, its counterpart in Prague, the weekly of the Czechoslovak Writers' Union, *Literární Listy*, printed articles of a similar nature, sometimes reprints from *Kultúrny Život*, in which case there was nothing much the Prague censors could do about it. They could hardly ban articles which had been passed by their Slovak colleagues. It was a unique situation, brought about by the courage of young Slovak political scientists, and by writers and journalists, including those of the older generation who had been converted to the new, progressive cause.

In 1967 and 1968, men like Vasil Bil'ak, who in earlier years had bitterly fought all attempts to modernize Marxist theory claimed credit for the 'Slovak spring' of 1963 and 1964. Being frightened by the new developments in Prague, Bil'ak tried to inhibit similar trends in Slovakia by arguing that the Czech writers had let the Slovaks down in 1963. He now suggested that the Slovak writers should behave in the same way to the Czechs, who anyway had little understanding for the Slovak national cause. This, of course, was not true, at least in the way suggested by such doubtful converts to the progressive cause as Bil'ak and his associates in the Slovak Communist Party. What is now regarded as the Slovak spring was not Bil'ak's doing, nor probably even Dubček's. The developments in Slovakia happened despite Bil'ak's efforts. His claims that the Czech intellectuals had let the Slovaks down in 1963 had little substance, because the Czech intellectuals, as has been shown already, were under stricter control than the Slovaks. This was partly because Bil'ak's counterpart in Prague, Hendrych, who was in charge of Party ideology, had years of practical experience in this job and therefore handled the situation more efficiently. On the other hand, the Czechs had less motivation than the Slovaks, who were driven by their national frustration. Nevertheless, whenever they had the opportunity, Czech historians and other political research workers and writers in the Czechoslovak Academy of Sciences did a great deal of good and useful work in this period. On the question of Slovak national rights some Czech historians, as, for example, Dr Prečan of the History Department and Dr Hübl of the High Party School in Prague, came to conclusions similar to those of their more nationally-minded Slovak colleagues.

Literární Listy in Prague, although at times not as outspoken as *Kultúrny Život* in Bratislava, was very progressive compared with most similar periodicals in the Soviet Union, and – with a short exceptional spell in 1956 and 1957 in Poland and Hungary – in most socialist countries. Most Czech writers were no less progressive in those years than most of their Slovak colleagues. Some managed to publish works which had escaped the watchful eyes of the Prague censors. Czech film writers and directors produced films which won renown in the outside world. Czech political philosophers like Dr Kosík had no counterpart in Bratislava, where the Philosophical Institute of the Slovak Academy of Sciences was headed by dogmatists like Ladislav Szántó, who survived all the régimes, and who took part in the most vicious attacks against his progressive subordinates. One of them, Dr Miroslav Kusý, later rejected the 'idea that the Slovak political leadership was clearly more progressive than the Czechoslovak leadership in Prague'. He pionted out that 'this illusion was caused by the assumption that the liberal process began in Slovakia ... in 1963, and that its impetus came from the removal of Bacílek and finally of Široký from the Slovak leadership'. He continued:

> This illusion is fundamentally wrong. It has been created in order to suggest that there was no need for more fundamental changes in Slovakia, and why the Slovak leadership could after January 1968 stay in power in its original composition, which re-mained intact until August 1968. During the Czechoslovak spring in 1968 practically no new men entered into Slovak politi-cal life.[2]

Miro Kusý, in his effort to fight Bil'ak's crude tactics, seemed to underestimate the significance of the situation in 1963 in Slovakia. He justly questioned the motives of those who, in 1968, tried to spread dissension between the Slovaks and the Czechs when most Slovak intellectuals followed Kusý's example, supporting their Czech colleagues, just as the Slovak people joined the Czech people in their effort to create a new Czechoslovakia.

[2] Miroslav Kusý, 'A nyní demokratisace' (And Now Democratization), *Politika* (weekly), Prague, no. 4, 20 March 1969.

In addition to the activities of the historians, both Slovak and Czech economists were now beginning to examine and criticize long-standing economic dogmas. The progressives, led by Professor Ota Šik, Director of the Economic Institute of the Czechoslovak Academy of Sciences in Prague, were primarily concerned with changing the rigid system of central administrative planning, which had been introduced in the Stalin era and copied in all the socialist countries. They objected to the official Stalinist economic theory and practice which disregarded the regulating mechanism of the market. They claimed that the laws of supply and demand were also valid in a socialist system and compatible with a more flexible system of planning which could make use of scientific methods and even benefit from the experiences of modern capitalism.

The reformers advocated a greater degree of independence for individual firms and enterprises, a greater scope for economic decision-making, not only by the government but on the lower managerial level, the workers should participate in management through their workers' councils. The reformers also demanded the abolition of the economic ministries. These central government departments prevented managers of individual plants from using their own initiative. Instead of ministries, which were in fact just huge state monopolies for each important branch of industry, group managements should be created with freedom of economic action within the limits of an all-state plan. This plan would be drawn up only in broad outline, and not in detail as had been the invariable practice in previous years. The function of state planning authorities should be essentially one of coordination conducted, through modern methods of financial and fiscal policy. Within the reform scheme the banks, and especially the Central Bank, would revert to the role they so usefully play in the modern economic world, from which Czechoslovakia could not and should not be isolated. The economy would not lose its socialist character, because the basic means of production would still remain in public ownership. Some reformers, including Professor Šik, went further and proposed the introduction of a private sector, especially in the sphere of the services, and also proposed licensing various groups of craftsmen and artisans.

The reformers were convinced that the main cause of economic stagnation was excessive capital investment which in the beginning had been justified and had produced positive results. But now emphasis should be shifted to the consumer industries and capital accumulated from higher consumption could be used for the modernization of industry. The increased quantity of consumer goods could be sold more profitably on world markets earning valuable hard-currency which together with foreign credits would help to provide industry with new technology. The reformers advocated higher wages and argued that increased production should be achieved with the help of more modern machines, and not as a result of an increase in the labour force. In earlier years the government had been proud of its increase in the labour force, but this had not been accompanied by the kind of increase in production for which the reformers now hoped.

The debate on economic reforms continued in Prague and in Bratislava from the moment when, in the early Sixties, Professor Liberman introduced his proposals for reforms in the Soviet Union. His suggestions, compared with those put forward by the Czechs, were rather timid, but the spell had been broken. Liberman stressed the importance of the profit motive – not so much as an incentive for socialist enterprise, which would still have to be guided by a central planning department – but more as an indicator of economic results. Hitherto they had been judged only by the value of the gross product. As the Soviet government was contemplating putting Liberman's ideas into practice – if only experimentally in some regions – economists in Czechoslovakia saw no reason why they should not emulate the Soviet example.

At times it seemed as if at least some progressive ideas had been officially accepted by the highest authorities. Even before 1968, Šik, as a member of the Central Committee, was alleged to have been in Novotný's confidence. In fact most of the reforms, even the more modest ones, were shelved, although few dogmatists in Czechoslovakia, in contrast to the Soviet Union, dared to oppose them openly. The head of the State's Planning Commission, Oldřich Černík, who was one of the Deputy Premiers of the government in Prague, was considered to belong to those who did not agree with the reformers. After all, they were opposed to the central planning authority which was exercised by Černik's powerful department. In contrast the new premier, Jozef Lenárt, the Slovak Communist who had replaced Široký in 1963, was known to favour economic reform. Lenárt was a younger man who, during the war, had studied in a business school sponsored by the famous Czech shoe-magnate Baťa and had actually worked for this firm. Not without nostalgia Lenárt used to remark publicly on the brilliant methods of his former employer, who had made Czechoslovakia world-famous as a major industrial power. That was one of the reasons why he did not see eye to eye with Novotný on the question of economic reform.

To Novotný it seemed a good idea to placate the discontented Slovaks by replacing the quasi-Slovak Široký with this man who had been too young at the time of the Stalinist purges in Czechoslovakia to play a prominent role in them. Lenárt, as Prime Minister, had to manage the economy from a Czechoslovak, not a purely Slovak point of view. It was not known whether he favoured any degree of Slovak autonomy. In fact, none of the Czech reformers were particularly interested in the Slovak aspect of the problem and this was bitterly resented by Slovak economists. One of the latter was Professor Victor Pavlenda, who became a candidate member of the Central Committee of the Slovak Communist Party soon after he returned from Moscow where he had taken a postgraduate degree in economics.[1] Originally he was considered to be quite a safe man from the Soviet, and therefore from Novotný's point of view. But when the first blossoms of 'the Slovak spring of 1963' appeared, he began to devote himself to the study of Slovak economic problems. He and his colleagues made full use of the opportunity to discuss economic matters in comparative freedom. Pavlenda advocated the case for a Slovak national economy so outspokenly that he got into trouble with old-fashioned economists in the Slovak Communist Party like Michal Sabolčik, who continued to be Novotný's obedient servant. But it was too late to denounce Pavlenda as a bourgeois nationalist, for, by this time, the Slovak Novotnýites were on the defensive.

In October and November 1966 Pavlenda wrote a series of articles for the official Party daily, *Pravda*, in which he argued that as far as Slovakia was concerned the new Fourth Five-Year Plan, which was to be introduced following the total failure of the third one, contained only half-measures and did not take the region's economic

---

[1] In August 1968 Viktor Pavlenda became one of the Secretaries of the new Central Committee of the Slovak Communist Party, responsible for economic affairs. After April 1969, when Husák replaced Dubček, Pavlenda lost his job and all his Party functions and was sent to Stockholm as Czechoslovak Ambassador. In 1970 he was recalled and offered a minor job in a state enterprise like his colleague H. Kočtúch.

potential into account. He openly suggested that the economic development of Slovakia could only be undertaken by the Slovaks under conditions of political autonomy. He came to the conclusion that, if this was to be realized in Slovakia, the country must first of all be recognized as a national political region within the system of a single socialist economy. Only political autonomy would guarantee Slovakia a satisfactory economic life, because national equality always stimulates economic progress and national initiative grows with improving economic and social conditions.

In fact, economic and social conditions had improved in Slovakia despite Stalinism. This may indeed have been one of the reasons why Slovak national consciousness had increased. Economic dissatisfaction is not always the main source of nationalism; very often nationalism becomes overt with the improvement of economic conditions. Slovak nationalism would have existed and grown even if the country had had no reason to complain of unjust economic treatment from Prague.

Pavlenda was partially aware that national fulfilment cannot be achieved by purely economic progress. In this he was much nearer to to the crux of the matter than when he exaggerated the extent to which Slovakia's economic disadvantage resulted from its subordination to Prague which had not made enough provision for the industrialization of Slovakia. This was, at that time, the Slovak economists' main argument, although on the other hand they stressed that Slovakia must learn to live on her own resources.[2]

Whether or not the thesis is valid, it is true that Slovakia has greatly improved its economic position since 1945. L'ubomír Lipták, one of the most independent-minded Slovak historians in the late Sixties, accepted the fact, and admitted that industry and culture in Slovakia showed amazing leaps forward. He wrote: 'One need only look out of the window of the train to see, in a few hours, more new buildings than were constructed in all the twenty years of the pre-Munich Republic.[3] To illustrate this point he quotes: '231,000 people were employed in Slovak industry in 1948; by 1960 the number has increased to 400,000. In the building industry the increase has been from 93,000 to 142,000. Industrial production has increased by 587 per cent. Agricultural output has grown by 40 per cent, in

---

[2] After the removal of Dubček from power in April 1969 the debate was soon stopped by Dr Husák who was obviously worried that Moscow might regard it as a symptom of bourgeois nationalism.

[3] L'. Lipták, *Slovensko v 20. storočí* (Slovakia in the Twentieth Century), Bratislava, 1968, p. 314.

comparison with the situation before the war.'[4] He accepts as an indisputable fact that the change in the social structure of the Slovak population was even more impressive. There was considerable movement from small enterprises and overpopulated agriculture into industry. Although Lipták criticizes the position of Slovakia within the political framework of Czechoslovakia, he admits:

> The number of people employed in the school system, in cultural institutions, rose so fast that it represents a quantitative jump which only the greatest optimist would have forecast. By 1960 the number of pupils in specialized secondary schools had risen from 15,422 to 68,894, and the number of students in the universities from 9,000 to almost 30,000. By then there were more university teachers in Slovakia than there were students before the war.[5]

No Slovak nationalist would refute these facts. Some merely argue that the position would have been even better were it not for Prague's deliberate policy of giving priority to Czech interests. The special correspondent of the *Financial Times*, reporting on the Slovak scene in 1967, wrote:

> Since the Communists came to power in 1948 the Slovaks have not fared badly. Before then Slovakia was overwhelmingly agricultural. Since then hydro-electric schemes, the Slovnaft oil refineries at Bratislava (at the end of the pipeline from Russia), the giant steelworks at Košice in East Slovakia, railway electrification and a large number of smaller industrial projects have raised Slovakia's industrial output to a level higher than that of the whole of Czechoslovakia in 1949. Slovakia has in fact benefited from investment funds raised in the Czech lands.[6]

The correspondent noted, however, that industrial development had been going ahead in Bohemia and Moravia at the same time, so that the Slovak share in Czechoslovakia's industrial output was still only about 21 per cent. The Slovak population of 4.4 million was just over 30 per cent of the country's total, hence production per head was less than in the Czech lands.

The correspondent of the *Financial Times* was making a rather bold assumption when he stated that 'the situation will now be complicated by the new economic system, brought into full effect at the New Year, 1967'.[7] The fact is that economic reform was not

[4] *Ibid.*, p. 314.   [5] *Ibid.*, p. 314.
[6] *Financial Times*, 'Can the commuters catch up?', 7 February 1967.
[7] *Ibid.*

introduced, except that some industrial ministries were reorganized. They were reduced in number and their powers delegated to the general managers of the 124 industrial groups, representing various branches of the economy. The main aim of the reformers was to achieve economic discipline by accepting market conditions in a planned economy. But this part of the reform was sabotaged, with Novotný's blessing, by the state planners in the office of Oldřich Černík.

Slovak economists welcomed this partial reform, although they deplored the fact that the majority of the general managements were situated in Prague. Still, profits made by efficient factories would be used to cover losses made by inefficient ones. According to the *Financial Times*, in many cases the inefficient factories which benefited in this way were in Slovakia where the 'new factories have splendid buildings, but too little and insufficiently good machinery'.[8] This was, of course, the Slovak economists' primary bone of contention. Prague might have been responsible for those splendid buildings, but then it was also responsible for the poor machinery, which was mostly bought or produced in the Czech lands under the management of central government departments. The Slovak national organs had no say in the matter. Hence the Slovak economists felt some resentment against those Czech reformers who still tended to think Slovakia's main economic asset was her relatively cheap supply of labour although the really progressive Czech economists however were perhaps not so cynical as to 'hope that if market forces were to prevail in Czechoslovakia, Czech industry would again be in a better and stronger position and would continue to attract Slovak workers',[9] as the correspondent of the *Financial Times* suggested.

The Slovak economists were certainly bitter about the migration of Slovak labour to the Czech lands. Tens of thousands of Slovaks were forced to settle there permanently because they could not find employment at home. It was felt that these Slovaks, or at least their children, would be lost to the nation. The Czech local authorities did not bother to provide Slovak schools for them. This 'de-Slovakization' probably worried the nationalists more than the purely economic aspects of the matter. No nation, and for that matter, no region, welcomes a situation in which a large part of its population finds it necessary to emigrate, even if it is a case of inner-state migration. The Slovaks believed that if their part of the country had been founded on a sounder economic basis, it would have been able to

[8] *Ibid.*   [9] *Ibid.*

absorb most of its labour power, in which case not only Slovakia, but the whole of the Republic, would have benefited.

One of the most outspoken critics of the Czech government's economic policy towards Slovakia was Professor Kočtúch.[10] Although he admitted that Slovakia had overcome its economic backwardness, and as a result of an increased rate of economic growth, had to some extent caught up with the Czech lands, he complained that 'the higher rate of growth failed to maintain an equal speed, and the absolute differences actually increased in this period'.[11] Kočtúch came to these conclusions although he stated that official estimates of the 'national property and national wealth have not yet been statistically calculated'.[12] He hoped that these matters would be the subject of studies undertaken at the Research Institute for Investment Theory in Bratislava. Despite the serious lack of reliable statistics on the development of the Czechoslovak economy since 1945, he defended his general conclusion that there had been an increase of absolute differences to the disadvantage of Slovakia. He argued that there were objective as well as subjective reasons for such development. 'The objective reasons are provided by the fact that an economically less advanced country cannot skip necessary phases of its progress. However subjective factors, such as the drive against Slovak bourgeois nationalism, which hindered Slovakia's economic development, could have been avoided.'[13] Kočtúch also included in the category of subjective factors wrong directives sent from the central authorities which had proved a serious obstacle to the rational use of Slovakia's resources.

Kočtúch repudiated the charge that the Slovak economists were advocating economic separatism 'in this age of international economic cooperation and integration'.[14] However, he considered the present eastern orientation of the Republic's economic policy to be advantageous for Slovakia, because 'this eastern part of the country is close to the Soviet Union, Czechoslovakia's most important business partner'.[15] Considering the development of the Czechoslovak economy as a whole, he questioned the sense of 'transporting substantial, continuously increasing amounts of raw materials, semi-finished products and primary agricultural products from the Soviet Union

[10] In August 1968 he became a member of the Central Committee of the Slovak Communist Party, in addition to his existing membership of the Slovak National Council. In 1969 he lost both positions and in 1970 was expelled from the Party.

[11] Hvezdoň Kočtúch, *The Economic and Social Development of Slovakia*, Bratislava, 1968, pp. 121–2. [12] *Ibid.*, pp. 110–11.

[13] *Ibid.*, p. 121. [14] *Ibid.*, p. 128. [15] *Ibid.*, p. 129.

to the Czech lands, resulting in a migration of the Slovak labour force to the western parts of the country'. It would be more effective to concentrate on building up a modern processing industry in Slovakia in which these raw materials could be used. Analysing the main features of development in the Czechoslovak economy, he pointed out that while 'the Czech lands suffer from an acute shortage of labour, in Slovakia there is an abundant population of working age, mainly women, approximately 200,000 persons'.[16] The economy was characterized for example by the fact that while per capita production of coal in Czechoslovakia exceeded production in other countries, there was a shortage of coal, and while, in per capita production of iron, steel, rolled steel, and concrete, Czechoslovakia was one of the leading countries of the world, there was a general shortage of metals in the processing industries. Per capita sums of capital investment exceeded not only those in other socialist countries, but also those in Great Britain, France and West Germany. Nevertheless, Czechoslovakia suffered from a production shortage as a consequence of errors in capital contruction plans, unfinished constructions, and the excessive number of small-scale and uneconomic factories. Czechoslovakia was economically very dependent on capitalist countries because of 'insufficient consideration of the possibilities of the east-oriented policy within Comecon'.[17]

To summarize the position of the most prominent Slovak economists in this debate: their main line of argument was that the raising of Slovakia's economy to the level of the more developed Czech lands – since 1945 the official policy of the Communist Party – had not really been accomplished. Slovakia's industrialization had been too slow. Party directives had not been carried out, either because they were unrealistic or because their initiators had only used them as propaganda slogans, without any real intention of putting them into practice. Slovak economists maintained that, under the prevailing form of administrative direction from Prague, economic integration of the two national regions, which they welcomed as unavoidable and desirable for both Czechs and Slovaks, was subjected to political expediency. The centre underestimated the interests of Slovakia. Prague stressed that its policy of 'equalization' was 'an act of conscious and generous support of the whole state economy to the Slovak region'.[18] But instead of taking into account such essen-

---

[16] *Ibid.*, p. 129.   [17] *Ibid.*, p. 132.
[18] Jan Marček and others, 'Nedozreté ovocie ekonomickej reformy' (The Unripe Fruit of Economic Reform), *Nové Slovo*, no. 28, Bratislava, 10 July 1969.

tial factors as productivity of labour in dynamic economic growth 'equalization' was measured solely in terms of indices of employment, consumption and, of course, the share of capital investment. Slovak economists argued that existing measures could never enable the Slovak economy to 'reach the stage where it could stand on its own feet'.[19] They complained that although in all economic plans there was a section on the industrialization of Slovakia, it was in fact only an insignificant appendix to the plan. During the whole period since 1945 a long-term and all-embracing plan for the industrialization of Slovakia had never been drawn up.

There is some truth in these charges. However, all the evidence shows that Slovakia has been developed economically and its potentialities substantially increased, although not always in the most desirable direction. Previously emphasis had been laid on the extensive economic development, not only of Slovakia, but of the whole country. Now, together with their Slovak colleagues, the Czech reformers advocated an intensive system of development which, instead of demanding further investments and expansion, would use existing plants and resources in a more scientific and technically efficient manner.

Whatever the force of Slovakia's complaints, it is now generally accepted that, while during the first Republic the region was about 40–50 years behind the Czech lands in industrial development, by 1968 the gap had been reduced to about 10–15 years. In 1968 Slovakia's *per capita* national income had reached that of the Czech lands in 1958. Most Slovak economists were accustomed to Slovakia's economic difficulties in relation to those of the whole country. But in fact Czechoslovakia as a whole had fared badly, especially in the Novotný era. This became quite evident in the Sixties. The Third Five Year Plan, started in 1961, was designed to be a further step in the industrial equalization of Slovakia with the Czech lands. This final aim was expected to be reached by 1975. By 1970 the weekly working hours were to have been reduced to 36 and by 1975 to 30 hours. National income in Czechoslovakia was to be increased by 40 per cent, but by the end of 1961, the first year of the new Five Year Plan, it had actually decreased. Czechoslovakia was the only industrially advanced country in which this had happened. In the following years Czechoslovakia's entire economy stagnated, so that instead of the expected 40 per cent increase in the national income, there was an increase of only a little over one per cent. Czechs and

[19] *Ibid.*

Slovaks were most affected by the fact that individual consumption, planned to increase by 30 per cent, had in reality fallen.

Thus, after more than twenty years of socialist reconstruction and expansion, it was finally admitted that Czechoslovakia's economy had failed to progress. The principles on which it was built had become completely outdated. After the failure of the Third Five Year Plan, long-term planning was temporarily suspended and replaced by ad hoc short-term plans, improvised from year to year. But even this did not bring about the expected results. Novotný was reluctant to introduce thoroughgoing economic reforms. Much was being said and written on this subject but almost nothing was done.

15 THE DEBATE CONTINUES

As we have seen in the previous chapters, Novotný remained a hard-line Stalinist in his attitude to the Slovaks. He would have liked to take harsher measures against those who he still considered bourgeois nationalists but it was already too late. Although the virus of the Twentieth Congress of the Soviet Communist Party took a long time to reach Czechoslovakia, it had in the end a deeper and more widespread effect there than in the other socialist countries. Not that Novotný and his trusted men in Slovakia looked on helplessly at the slow process of ideological disintegration. But it was somehow out of date to use the crudest methods of suppression. One of the Slovak Novotnýites, a fairly young but conservative Communist official, Michal Pecho, head of the ideological department of the Slovak Party, wrote that 'federation of the two nations would be a step backwards', although he quoted Lenin that 'in certain situations, under conditions of strong nationalist feelings, federation could be a step forward'. He admitted that 'it is no secret that from time to time views have been expressed to the effect that the constitutional framework and its legal model have not been proved satisfactory, and that the Košice Government Programme has not been systematically realized'.[1] This was an extraordinary case of understatement. The truth was that such views had not been expressed merely 'from time to time' as Pecho put it. This might have been the case in the Party press and the mass media directly under Pecho's control, but the conviction that the Slovaks had not got what they had been promised, above all a federal solution had for a long time been deeply felt and had frequently been publicly expressed.

Pecho's chief in the Party, Vasil Bil'ak, who was Secretary of the Central Committee of the Slovak Communist Party responsible for ideology, was more emphatic in his condemnation of nationalistic views in Slovakia. He stated most definitely that federation would be a step backwards. Together with Novotný he claimed that the Party resolutions of December 1963 and May 1964 had urged the Slovak National Council to make greater use of its powers. In fact the

[1] Michas Pecho, O *národnostnej otázke* (On the nationality question) Nová Mysl (monthly), Prague, 22 February 1966.

original intention of these resolutions had been to perpetuate the system in which Slovakia no longer existed as a political entity. These resolutions were intended to offer an ideal solution for which the Slovaks should be grateful. Bil'ak spoke more bluntly than Pecho, who saw in the Party resolutions only a 'positive measure for the development of the constitutional concept'.[2]

These attempts by Party officials in Slovakia to argue against nationalist views were not very successful. It is significant that Pecho wrote his treatise in the Czechoslovak Party monthly, *Nová Mysl*, while Bil'ak was expounding his less scientific but more hard-line essay on Slovak nationalism in the Prague Communist daily *Rudé Právo*.[3] (A limited number of about 30,000 copies was published in Slovakia. Few people read it.) It is not known whether Bila'k offered his article to Klokoč, the editor of the Slovak Party daily *Pravda*, who would probably have published it but with little enthusiasm. Obviously, Bil'ak preferred to express his unpopular views to a Czech public where there was less interest in federation.

Meanwhile *Kultúrny Život* continued to advocate progressive and liberal policies. Although an intellectual journal, it was widely read and very popular. It did not confine itself to literature and art, as the Party would have liked it to do, but offered its columns to economists who were often more progressive than Pavlenda and Kočtúch, such as Eugen Löbl.[4] Some of the latter's views, which he began to express in *Kultúrny Život* in 1963, amounted to a complete reappraisal of the principles of Marxism–Leninism, including its fundamental thesis that productive labour is the source of all wealth. He stressed the importance of science and the human intellect as the main driving forces in the revolution of our time, regardless of the ownership of the means of production. These were not original ideas judged by Western standards but in a socialist country they sounded extraordinarily new.

Long before the outbreak of the big crisis in the second half of 1967, which led to the January 1968 session of the Central Committee in Prague and the replacement of Novotný by Alexander Dubček, the situation in the Party and in the country had become very confused, although there were no outward signs of a serious rift in the Party Central Committee, nor in the Praesidium itself. The economic

---

[2] *Ibid.*   [3] Vasil Bil'ak, *Rudé Právo*, 2 March 1966.

[4] He was Deputy Minister of Foreign Trade until November 1949, when he was arrested and later sentenced to life imprisonment in the Slánský trial. He was one of the most outspoken critics of Stalinism, not only as an economist, but as a political thinker. He left after the Soviet invasion and now lives in the United States.

difficulties of the country were in the foreground of the discussion and despite censorship, many views on this subject were expressed. Creative artists too, both in Prague and in Bratislava, managed from time to time to achieve some measure of freedom of expression. By 1966 most of those works which had been banned in the Fifties and early Sixties had been passed for publication. There was practically no limitation on what could and should be translated from Western literature. The question of whether to publish controversial books written in the socialist East was, however, a more delicate one. The speedy publication in Czechoslovakia of the works of Erenburg, Dudintsev and Solzhenitsyn, for example, might have been taken by the Russians as a deliberate insult.

Novotný was slowly losing the battle on the cultural front. This was the period when Czechoslovak films became renowned for their avant-garde nature and gained world recognition, including Hollywood Oscars. Czech and Slovak playwrights were free to write practically anything; after some wrangling with the censors their plays were produced, often without any alterations. Creative artists ignored frequent admonitions and threats from the authorities that measures would have to be taken against them if they did not conform. They did not. This was partly because of their moral courage and integrity, and partly because, at that time, they knew that Novotný was too weak to carry out his threats. In fact Novotný's only real victims were some of his subordinates, Party officials working on the ideological front who were blamed for having handled the situation incompetently. There were frequent changes in the ideological department of the Central Committee, especially in the ranks of those who were in charge of the press and censorship. The only 'administrative measures' taken were the dismissals of these fairly unimportant men. Novotný expected personnel changes in the Party apparatus to exercise a warning influence on creative artists.

It is hard to explain the mentality of some of these Party officials. Perhaps they wanted to prove to the intellectuals, whom instead of detesting they actually respected, that they were quite open-minded men, capable of appreciating the specific problems of artistic expression. The most revealing case was that of Pavel Auersperg, Novotný's former personal secretary. Novotný trusted him to the extent of putting him in charge of the ideological department. He was expected to create order amongst the undisciplined ranks of writers, artists and scientists. But in a short time Auersperg had shown himself to be as helpless in fighting 'liberal and revisionist' tendencies as his predecessors had been. Novotný was angry, and Auersperg was dismissed for his relatively liberal treatment of the intellectuals. He had in fact been unable to suppress them by the old Stalinist methods and perhaps also, being a careerist, he had come to doubt the future of Stalinism in Czechoslovakia. He was possibly quite innocent of any genuine liberalism and was simply used as a scapegoat when Novotný and his chief ideological adviser, Hendrych, realized that they were powerless to take effective measures against the intellectuals. Nevertheless Auersperg remained a member of the Central Committee. He opposed Novotný in 1967 and 1968; on the other hand, he became one of the Russians' most reliable collaborators in the decisive days before the Russian invasion and afterwards, and eventually became head of the International Department of the Party in Prague. He was one of thirty-three men who actually signed the mysterious letter asking the socialist allies to save Czechoslovakia from counter-revolution.

Another was Bohuš Chňoupek',[5] a former Deputy Minister of Culture, and for many years the Moscow correspondent of the Slovak daily, *Pravda*. He was known to be Moscow's man, and played a questionable role in journalistic circles after his return to Bratislava in 1966. While a correspondent in Moscow, he was alleged to have denounced Slovak liberal writers and journalists to the Russians. He excelled in these activities during the 'Slovak spring' in 1963. His chief line was discovering Zionist plots amongst the Czech and Slovak intellectuals. He was known to have compiled a list of Slovak journalists and writers with a Jewish background. Those who happened to have Jewish wives were branded as Zionists, potential conspirators and enemies of the state. In 1966 he became chief of the Slovak Party weekly, *Predvoj*, with the aim of combatting the progressive influence of *Kultúrny Život*. He managed to attract a few second-rate journalists, mainly by offering them large salaries – as was the usage in the Party press. This weekly was distasteful to most Slovak intellectuals including Dr Husák who in 1969, after *Predvoj* changed its name to *Nové Slovo*,[6] used it too against *Kul-*

---

[5] After the 1968 invasion he was made General Director of Czechoslovak Radio in Prague. In 1970 he became Czechoslovak Ambassador in Moscow and in 1971, obviously for his services rendered to the Soviets, he got the job of Minister of Foreign Affairs.

[6] The original *Nové Slovo* (The New World) had been published during the Slovak Uprising and after the war when it became the most distinguished mouthpiece for Slovak journalists until it was suppressed in the early Fifties, following Husák's arrest. Husák regarded *Nové Slovo* as his personal journal and was chairman of its editorial board until 1950, and again from 1968 onwards.

túrny Život although for years it had been the only periodical which dared to publish his articles and had been instrumental in re-establishing him as a respected political figure in Slovakia.

Bohuš Chňoupek made the Party weekly a ruthless antiliberal platform, with the full support of Bil'ak and Pecho who preferred men like Chňoupek to have leading jobs in the mass media in Slovakia. When Chňoupek moved to Prague as Deputy Minister of Culture, his successor in *Predvoj* was the notorious Stalinist poet Milan Lajčiak who in the Fifties had hailed the execution of Clementis as a great victory for the Slovak people and deplored the fact that not all those accused in the Slánský trial had met with the same fate. Another Stalinist of this calibre, Dr Miloš Marko, the former ČTK correspondent in Moscow, became director of the Slovak radio. That was one of the reasons why few people, if any, considered Dubček, who, as First Secretary of the Slovak Communist Party, was in a superior position to Bil'ak and Pecho, to be a man of progressive views.

By now the so-called Slovak spring was virtually over. Although Dubček himself could not be blamed directly for this retrogressive development, those who might have given him some credit for the liberal atmosphere in Slovakia of 1963 were inclined now to criticize him for not sufficiently protecting his country from the frosty winds blowing from Novotný's Prague.

In the Party and State apparatus it was another Slovak, the Prime Minister in Prague, Jozef Lenárt, who at that time managed to convey the impression of favouring liberal changes, particularly the economic reforms proposed by Professor Ota Šik. It was known that Lenárt was mockingly denounced by Novotný as an ally of the intellectuals. This was a fairly serious accusation. Yet it was not the Bat'a-trained Jozef Lenárt who turned against his old Party leader in the decisive days of December 1967 and January 1968, but the Moscow-trained Alexander Dubček who in 1968 became recognized and genuinely loved as the respected leader not only of his own Slovak people, but of all Czechs and Slovaks, who saw in him the embodiment of the Czechoslovak spring.

It is not surprising that Czechoslovakia caused concern, and sometimes even alarm, in Moscow and most of the socialist capitals long before the anti-Novotný storm broke. At a closed Party meeting in 1965, Ulbricht's secretary for ideology went so far as to criticize the revisionist tendencies in Czechoslovakia, hinting that the leadership of the CPCz was to blame for not handling things more firmly. This unusual step caused misgivings in Prague, not only among the intellectuals. Novotný himself was said to be deeply hurt because he suspected that the rebuke from Berlin had been inspired by Moscow. He ordered Koucký, the ideological secretary in Prague, to tell his East German colleague to mind his own business. At the same time Ulbricht's comments provided an excellent pretext for Novotný to point out to Czech and Slovak intellectuals that they should appreciate his difficulties with his allies. They were therefore asked to respect the Party line.

About the same time it became known in well-informed circles in Czechoslovakia that Party organizations in the Soviet Union were examining a confidential letter from their Central Committee which expressed grave concern over the cultural situation in Czechoslovakia. The ever-watchful Soviet guardians of the Party line in all socialist countries stated in that letter that Prague had become 'the seat of modern revisionism'. This was an additional reason why to the Russians Novotný did not appear to be an ideal Party leader, although they must have been aware that under the circumstances he was probably the best one they could get in Czechoslovakia. The Russians had not forgotten that in October 1964, when Brezhnev and Kosygin replaced Khrushchev, Novotný had done what was perhaps the most decent thing in his political career. He had written a letter to his Moscow superiors on behalf of the Central Committee of his Party expressing surprise and concern over the manner in which the change had taken place. The letter could have been interpreted to mean that the Praesidium was not particularly enthusiastic about the change itself and this unusual gesture cannot have endeared Novotný to Brezhnev and Kosygin.

At that time Novotný was allowing, if not directly inspiring rumours that it was he who stood between the nation and the Russians who were pressing him for stricter measures against cultural workers. Novotný was trying to present himself as a man resisting friendly Soviet offers to send troops to Czechoslovakia 'to defend the Western frontier'. Whether this was true or not, nobody in Czechoslovakia really believed that their highly unpopular leader had the courage to resist clearly formulated Soviet demands. The Czechs' and Slovaks' reaction to these rumours was to suspect Novotný of trying to win popularity at home. No matter how hard Novotný tried he could not succeed in changing his image with his own people, even though the Russians may have suspected Novotný of 'Rumanian tendencies'.

The year 1967 did not start too inauspiciously for Novotný in Slovakia. The Slovak Writers' Congress which took place in the spring was uneventful. A general mood of apathy pervaded the Congress. Very few writers took part in the debates. They concentrated their attention on organizational, cultural and personal matters and avoided political issues. The only commotion was caused by a third-rate woman writer who complained of being unfairly treated by the Slovak Writers' Publishing House which, she alleged, refused to print her books. This Congress was in a way a victory for Bil'ak, who made a fairly moderate speech in which he conveyed the impression that he was going halfway to meet the nationalist and liberal demands of the Slovak writers. It was a move calculated to pacify the more progressive writers, and lull them into a less oppositional attitude. Bil'ak's change of heart had occurred very late and very suddenly and most participants at the Congress suspected him of using only more sophisticated methods of manipulation.[1] There was no reason to doubt that they resented Novotnýism and its representatives in Bratislava.

Bil'ak tried to present Slovakia to Novotný as a united and consolidated region with little trouble on the cultural front. According to Bil'ak, the Slovak intellectuals were less dangerous than the Czech

[1] Vasil Bil'ak is a former tailor's journeyman from the easternmost part of Slovakia and speaks with a heavy Ukrainian accent. He had not, up till now, been known for his Slovak patriotism and he was certainly not regarded as a liberal who believed in cultural freedom. But it occurred to him that it might be profitable to feign interest in Slovak national affairs in a country where men like Husák and Novomeský, although still kept out of office, were the undisputed spiritual leaders. If he had to compete with them for popularity he must act as a Slovak patriot and defend Slovak national rights. This was the only way to gain sympathy with the Slovak people and with the restless intelligentsia.

writers and artists who by now had begun their offensive against the dogmatists and neo-Stalinists.

In Prague the first challenge came at the Czechoslovak Writers' Congress held on 27–9 June 1967. Unlike the Slovak Congress this turned out to be an occasion of historic importance. Most of the speakers demonstrated that long years of forced silence could not break the spirit of a nation and its most distinguished writers. The most powerful attack came from Milan Kundera and from Ludvík Vaculík, one of the editors of *Literární Listy*. Kundera set the tone of the whole Congress. He was one of the first to speak, as a member of the Writers' Union Commission, which together with the ideological department of the Party prepared a preliminary draft for discussion at Plenary Sessions of the Congress. It was Kundera who foiled the Party's carefully laid plans. The Party was represented on this occasion by Jiří Hendrych, the Secretary of the Central Committee, at that time believed to be approved by Brezhnev as Novotný's heir-apparent. Stressing freedom as a necessary condition for the development of the arts, Kundera said:

> I know that when freedom is mentioned some people get hay fever and reply that every freedom must have its limits. Of course every freedom has its limits, given by the state of contemporary knowledge, education, prejudice, etc. Yet no progressive period has ever tried to fix its own limitations... Only in our case is the guarding of frontiers still regarded as a greater virtue than crossing them.[2]

He said that he did not like fascism and Stalinism being equated. He thought that fascism had created a morally simple situation because it left the humanist principles and virtues intact by being opposed to them. Stalinism on the other hand, the heir of a great humanist movement, retained many of its original attitudes, ideas and slogans. To watch such a humanist movement being totally perverted into something which destroyed every human virtue, which transformed love for humanity into cruelty to people, gave tremendous insights into the very foundations of human values and virtues.[3]

Instead of concentrating on purely literary topics, Ludvík Vaculík spoke on the problem of power and its abuse. It was an open challenge, an outspoken critique of the Novotný régime. It was the most courageous speech at this Congress and probably at any public gathering of its kind in a socialist country. He did not distinguish between

---

[2] Quoted from Z. A. B. Zeman, *Prague Spring*, Penguin Special, 1969, pp. 58–9.
[3] *Ibid.*, p. 59.

power exercised by governments in socialist and capitalist countries. Although Vaculík did not say so, he implied that monopoly of production, one of the basic characters of the Stalinist type of socialism, can lead to the abuse of power. In one of the most remarkable passages of his 45-minute speech he stated:

> Where the government stands for a long time, the citizen falls. Where does he fall? I will not try to please the enemy and say that he falls on the gallows. Only a few tens or hundreds of citizens do that. Our friends know that it is sufficient because it is followed by the fall of, perhaps, the whole nation, into fear, into political indifference and resignation, into petty daily cares and little desires, into dependence on gradually tinier and tinier overlords, into a serfdom of a new and unusual type, impossible to explain to a visitor from abroad. I think that there are no citizens in our country any longer. I have got proofs for that, collected over many years' work on newspapers and in broadcasting. I don't have to go far for a fresh reason. This Congress did not take place when members of our organization decided, but when our master, after having considered the problems before him, gives us his kind permission. In return he expects, as has been the custom in the past thousands of years, that we shall pay tribute to his dynasty.[4]

The master, a very prominent representative of the Novotný dynasty, Hendrych, was listening to these heretical words. He was fuming with rage. Especially when Vaculík continued:

> I speak here as a citizen of a state I should never like to give up, but in which I cannot be content. I have in mind the affairs of the citizens, but here I am in a sensitive position. I am a member of the Communist Party as well, and therefore should not and must not talk about Party affairs. But it so happens that there is almost nothing that, at a certain point of discussion, does not become a Party affair. What can I do when both of them, my party and my government, have done their best to merge their agenda? It has also created a difficult situation for us citizens assembled here. Party members are bound not to talk about important aspects of most key questions in front of non-members, who, in turn, have not got access to meetings when one can discuss those questions significantly, so that both sides are limited in the personal freedom to talk to each other as equals.[5]

[4] *Ibid.*, p. 62.   [5] *Ibid.*, pp. 62–3.

Others spoke against censorship. Some went as far as to maintain that even during the most oppressive period of the Austrian monarchy censorship had not been as widely exercised as in this socialist country.

Some of the writers questioned the principles of Czechoslovak foreign policy. It was a few weeks after the Six Day War and Israel's victory evoked, if not the admiration of the Czech and Slovak people, at least the satisfaction that Soviet weapons had proved so inefficient. Pavel Kohout associated himself completely with the Israeli cause. He drew an analogy between that small country and Czechoslovakia during the Munich crisis, threatened by Hitler and other hostile neighbours, such as Hungary and Poland. But Israel had decided to fight, against so many odds, and had won. He suggested that the countries which had helped the Arabs, such as the Soviet Union, were not only militarily but also morally defeated. It was a direct criticism of the Czechoslovak government for so blindly following Soviet foreign policy. Pavel Kohout then read the letter on censorship which Solzhenitsyn had recently sent to the Union of Soviet Writers, and which Novotný's censors, following the Soviet example, had prevented from being published. He said that he had to read a translation of the version published in the French paper, *Le Monde*.

This part of Kohout's protest was supported by Novomeský, who wrote a letter to the Congress in which he attacked the illegal practice of censorship. The Slovak poet could not attend the Congress because of ill-health, but his was the only manifestly anti-Novotnýite contribution made by Slovak writers to the progressive atmosphere of this gathering. It was the Slovak poet Lajčiak, a diehard Stalinist – and proud of it – who in defiance of the general mood of the Congress and most of the speeches, defended dogmatism in politics and socialist realism in the arts. Not all the speakers had the courage of Kundera, Vaculík, Kohout or Liehm. Liehm analysed the more subtle problems posed by various cultural policies of the government and examined the unfavourable situation created for the arts by imposed uniformity. The most conservative Czech writers, such as Ivan Skála, Jan Drda and Jarmila Glazarová, and some Slovak writers did not take part in the discussion, but wrote a letter to the Congress which was read out by the Chairman. They resented much of what had been said at the Congress, and claimed that an atmosphere of nervousness and tension had been created. They dissociated themselves from the political context of some of the speeches.

Professor Eduard Goldstücker, a well-known literary critic and essayist, delivered a speech in which he attempted to avoid a clash with the Party and the diehards in the Writers' Union. He spoke on the conflict between politics and art, expressing himself in a way which would be acceptable to most of the progressives and to those whom he feared would use the occasion to clamp down once again on the intellectuals. Goldstücker spoke not only as a man of progressive views, for which he was known and respected, but as an experienced tactician with considerable knowledge of the man with whom he was dealing. His effort to find a compromise solution did influence the final resolution of the Congress. Goldstücker was subsequently elected President of the Czechoslovak Writers' Union. He was not merely being modest: was quite sincere when he made it plain that he did not consider himself the most suitable person for this position and accepted it only as a temporary arrangement.

The Czechoslovak Writers' Congress undermined the already weakened foundations of Novotný's régime. After what happened there Novotný seemed to lose self-confidence. He ordered the expulsion from the Party of those writers who had, in his view, committed the worst offences against Party discipline. But this was only a half-measure for a Stalinist leader and even this decision was only taken after two months' hesitation, at the September session of the Central Committee of the Party. The writers' weekly, *Literární Listy*, was put under the control of the Ministry of Culture, an action which did not achieve much. Most of the readers stopped subscribing to the journal, cancelled orders and claimed the return of subscriptions. No writer of any significance, not even conservative, was prepared to contribute to it. The chairman of its editorial board was Jan Zelenka[6] a journalist of dubious character. A few third-rate journalists, believing that they ought to comply with Party discipline, worked as sub-editors. Not a single member of the former staff of *Literární Listy* agreed to work for this new propaganda sheet of the Ministry of Culture.

In Bratislava, Vasil Bil'ak, who supervised the Slovak writers, was very pleased that his own wards had not participated in the Czech writers rebellion. He was openly proud of this and used it as further proof of the consolidated cultural front in Slovakia. He pointed out how peacefully the Slovak Writers' Congress had ended and altogether how disciplined the Slovak writers were, compared with Czechs. In Bil'ak's eyes the Slovak poet Lajčiak was the hero of the day for what he had said at the Congress in Prague.

However, the situation was in fact quite different from the one

[6] In August 1968 he was made General Director of Czechoslovak Television.

portrayed by Biľak. Only a few Slovak writers had taken part in the Congress in Prague, which they had expected to be as dreary an affair, as their own. When they heard what had happened there, some of them blamed Juraj Špitzer, the Slovak literary critic and editor of *Kultúrny Život*. As the Slovak secretary of the Writers' Union, he had helped to prepare the Congress in Prague. They blamed him for not informing them or warning them of what might happen at the Congress. Špitzer had probably suspected what the atmosphere at the Congress was going to be like, although he could not have known what Vaculík, Kundera and others were going to say. On one occasion he sought to defend himself by admitting that he had anticipated, though he had not known for certain what was going to happen, and by pointing out that if he had mentioned this to anybody he would have risked the Party authorities' getting to hear of it. If they had, they would have taken measures to prevent its taking place. The Slovak progressives were not totally convinced by Špitzer's explanation and thought that he could have done more to secure their presence at the Congress.

Meanwhile the Party in Bratislava was more concerned with another problem. In August 1967, while on a trip to Vienna, the writer Ladislav Mňačko issued a statement that he would not return to Czechoslovakia as long as its government refused to renew diplomatic relations with Israel. He condemned Czechoslovakia's subservience to the Soviet Union in matters of foreign policy. Mňačko was a Moravian Czech who lived and worked in Slovakia. Although he was not a Jew, he used the Israeli issue, which he viewed as a moral rather than a political matter, to denounce Novotný's régime. His interview on Austrian television was watched by thousands of Czechs and Slovaks who at that time regarded Austrian television as their main source of information and contact with the outside world. Mňačko declared that he did not consider himself a refugee. Among other things he accused Novotný of Stalinism and anti-semitism in refusing to allow the full rehabilitation of Slánský and most of his colleagues of Jewish origin. In various articles and statements he predicted the imminent downfall of Novotný and his régime. He then went to Israel, where he settled for a time in a kibbutz and wrote his book, *The Aggressors*.

In Slovakia Mňačko's action was regarded with mixed feelings. It embarrassed some of his friends, who knew his histrionic inclinations and thought that, under the new circumstances, he could have done more for the progressive cause if he had stayed at home. His Czech colleague Kohout, who was known to have pro-Israeli sympathies and was certainly not a man who had any wish to please Novotný, criticized Mňačko's behaviour and blamed him for not having spoken at the Writers' Congress which was where he should have expressed his views. Later it became known that Mňačko, who was present at the Congress for a short time had, instead of siding with the progessives, actually signed a petition together with the Czech Stalinist Ivan Skála, in which he denounced the risky course the debate was taking. This was a bitter pill for those to swallow who, in the later controversy over the Mňačko case, wanted to defend his action.

This affair had many reverberations in Slovak intellectual circles and deeply divided the cultural front. It was the immediate, though not the primary, cause of a crisis that erupted in the Praesidium of the Slovak Writers' Union and on the editorial board of *Kultúrny Zivot*. This journal defended the right of the individual to express his views anywhere as a matter of principle, especially when he was not given the opportunity to do so at home. *Kultúrny Život* argued that Mňačko should not be condemned just because he said what he had to say abroad. The Czechoslovak Writers' Union refused to condemn Mňačko's defection, arguing that this was a case to be dealt with by the Slovak Writers' Union. The latter actually expelled him from its ranks, in accordance with the decision of the Praesidium of the Central Committee of the Czechoslovak Party to strip him of his Party membership and of all honours and titles. The Ministry of the Interior deprived him of his Czechoslovak citizenship.

These were harsh measures and they only added to the indignation of those who defended Mňačko. A few months later, after January 1968 and Novotný's downfall, the issue was revived once more when Mňačko expressed his wish to return home without waiting for the government to re-establish diplomatic relations with Israel. One night, quietly and without fuss, he came back to Bratislava. His views were widely known in the country, although opinions about him differed. People remembered his prophetic forecast of Novotný's imminent downfall and most of them realized that it was not so much Israel that was in Mňačko's heart, but the fate of his own country. The Israeli–Arab problem important as it was in the context of the world situation, was only a side issue in Czechoslovakia. It served to clarify many other matters of more immediate concern. It became a criterion for progressive views. Most people regarded it as a matter in which the Czechoslovak government could have shown a more independent line – as for example Rumania had done – if it had wished to reflect the real wishes of the people.

At the end of August 1967 Novotný came to Turčiansky Svätý

Martin (now Martin) to take part in the celebrations marking the centenary of the first Slovak high school, founded in 1867 under the auspices of the deeply cherished old Slovak cultural institute, Matica Slovenská. Matica had been established in that northern Slovak town in 1863, a gesture of goodwill by the Austro-Hungarian monarchy towards the Slovaks, who had nevertheless continued to be deprived of all political rights as a nation. Matica Slovenská published books and periodicals (including the best known one, the literary monthly, *Slovenské Pohl'ady*) and organized lectures on Slovak culture. The institute was soon closed down by the Hungarians, but was re-established some decades later in 1919, after the foundation of the first Czechoslovak Republic. Matica's functions were then extended to provide cultural contacts with Slovaks living abroad. This became one of its principal activities. Obviously, in the days of the Slovak State, Matica was instrumental in fostering Slovak patriotism. However, as it was run mostly by Protestants in a predominantly Protestant region, its policies never fully coincided with the aims of the clerico-fascist Slovak State. The activities of Matica Slovenská were badly affected after February 1948 when the Czech Stalinists virtually dictated not only its political, economic and social ideas, but its cultural policy in Slovakia as well. Matica seemed to them too much of an embodiment of Slovak traditions. They limited its functions to those of a kind of National Library and stopped all its contacts with Slovaks living abroad. In the early Fifties Matica's *Slovenské Pohl'ady*, the oldest Slovak literary monthly, was transferred to the safer hands of the Publishing House of the Slovak Writers' Union in Bratislava, where it would be nearer the Central Committee of the Slovak Communist Party.

Novotný came to Martin with the intention of redressing all the wrongs which Matica had suffered, but his behaviour there was so tactless that he achieved just the opposite. After his public speech, which ignored the current political atmosphere in Slovakia, he had a private argument with a number of Slovak cultural workers and political officials, including Bil'ak. They challenged Novotný, pointing out to him that he did not understand the mentality of the Slovak people. The quarrel mainly concerned Matica's cultural contacts with Slovaks abroad. Novotný said that in Prague there was an approved society for cultural relations with Czechoslovaks living abroad. He argued that this society was sufficient to deal with such delicate matters, which should be directed from one centre. He implied that in this matter other than merely cultural questions were involved. After all, many thousands of Slovaks and Czechs, for example those living in the United States and Canada, were foreign citizens with other loyalties than to the Socialist Republic. Although the Slovaks who were present could see what he meant, they did not agree with his reasoning. The most outspoken of them was the director of Matica Slovenská, Pavol Paška. Paška assured Novotný that the officials of Matica were also aware of the problem but were quite competent to deal with it, perhaps better than the Central Government office in Prague. The Prague society, in any case, was more concerned with propagating Czech culture and rather neglected the Slovak part of its function, even though rather more Slovaks than Czechs lived abroad. Surprisingly, Bil'ak who accompanied Novotný, agreed with his opponents.

The episode in Martin ended with resounding defeat for Novotný. He left the place in a fury. With his usual lack of grace he omitted to take with him the official present, a few volumes of rare Slovak books published by Matica. This incident gave rise to the caustic remark that he was probably afraid that the packet contained a time-bomb.

I7 THE OPEN CLASH

The September 1967 session of the CPCz Central Committee in Prague was held after the rebellious Writers' Congress. The party cell of the Writers' Union had refused, despite Novotný's wishes, to take any disciplinary measures against its members. Novotný and Hendrych were determined to have their revenge on the writers, although the Central Committee was not convened solely for the purpose of dealing with them and with the situation on the ideological front. As usual there were other points on the agenda; at this particular meeting the reorganization of the Party apparatus was to be discussed.

Novotný had no difficulty in getting his way as far as the writers were concerned. He still had absolute power over the Central Committee, and, of course, over his inner cabinet, the Praesidium, which at that time consisted of ten members. (Formally, the Praesidium is responsible to the Central Committee, but it is in fact the highest decision-making body in the Party and in the country.) Ludvík Vaculík, A. J. Liehm and Ivan Klima were expelled from the Party. Pavel Kohout received only a minor punishment; Jan Procházka, whose new liberal stand must have particularly annoyed Novotný, lost his alternate membership of the Central Committee. Not long before he had been regarded as the poet laureate of Novotný's court at Hradčany.

Nevertheless, something extraordinary happened at this September Plenum. Dr František Kriegel, the Chairman of the Foreign Relations Committee of the National Assembly, voted against the expulsion of the writers and all other disciplinary measures.[1] Two other members of the Central Committee, encouraged by Kriegel's example, abstained from voting. It was the first time during the whole of Novotný's rule that somebody had dared to spoil the idyllic atmosphere of complete unanimity and harmony prevailing in the Central Committee and had challenged the Praesidium's recommendation. This was tantamount to challenging the First Secretary himself.

[1] By profession a doctor, Kriegel had been a Communist before the war, and had fought with the International Brigade in Spain. Being of Jewish origin, he was persecuted during the Fifties, and rose gradually to important posts in the Party and in the National Assembly only after the Twentieth Congress of the Soviet Communist Party.

A month later, at the October session of the Central Committee, less courageous men than Kriegel began to speak more freely, criticizing fundamental aspects of Party policy. In September they had dutifully voted for Novotný's revenge against the rebellious writers. Now they came out with proposals which would have meant a great improvement in and acceleration of the reforms. The agenda included a report on the methods of Party work. One of the first speakers in this discussion was the Slovak First Secretary, Alexander Dubček. When he began speaking nobody suspected what was going to happen. In a subdued rather than emphatic manner, Dubček claimed that the Party should lead not by methods of forceful pressure but by relying on the voluntary support of the working masses. He stated that there was insufficient contact between the Party and large sections of the population. As a result, the population was critical of Party policy. A new policy should be adopted and presented as a programme of action which everybody could understand and support. As to the Slovak question, he said that the sharpening of the conflict was the result of an artificially created situation and of clumsy handling. Finally, he stressed the need for more socialist democracy in the Party.

Dubček must have been motivated by political ideals rather than any personal antagonism to Novotný as he had presumably known for a long time what kind of a man Novotný was. A well-known Slovak political writer, Ján Uher, who worked under Dubček in the ideological department of the Slovak Communist Party, attempted to explain what had gone on between Dubček and Novotný in all their years of close collaboration, especially after Dubček became First Secretary in Slovakia. Between 1963 and 1968 Dubček had had to swallow many bitter pills. According to Uher, he often argued with Novotný but had to give in to him because he did not want – as he used to say to his closest friends – 'to complicate matters and deepen the rupture'.[2] These issues were not of a personal nature but were 'very important matters of principle, involving the interests of the Party and of socialism not only in Slovakia, but in the whole of the Republic'.[3] This explanation sounds plausible enough. One is inclined to be impressed rather than surprised by Dubček's patience during those long years when he managed to hide his real feelings towards Novotný and his policies.

At the October 1967 Plenum Dubček no longer stood alone. He

---

[2] Ján Uher, 'Osobitosti slovenského vývoja' (The Special Features of Slovak Development), Výber (fortnightly), Special Edition, Bratislava, March 1969, p. 35.   [3] Ibid., p. 35.

had chosen the right moment to express his dissent. He was supported not only by most Slovak, but by many Czech, members of the Central Committee, men such as Kriegel and Voleník. On the other hand he was opposed by Martin Vaculík, the Party Secretary of the Prague region, and Chudík, the Chairman of the Slovak National Council, who accused Dubček of using the platform in order to settle personal accounts with Novotný. Dubček's reaction to this was restrained and dignified. He presented a verbatim report of his speech at the previous Praesidium meeting during which he had spoken on the same subjects. Events took a more dramatic turn when Novotný accused Dubček of laying too great an emphasis on the national question, and of expressing views which were basically nationalistic. Without giving any direct evidence, he actually accused the Slovaks of not keeping to the argreement reached at the common session of the Praesidia of the Czechoslovak and Slovak Central Committees of 1965, which had laid down the principles of a common policy with the aim of bridging the differences between Slovakia and the Czech lands, differences which were a result of historical developments.

Vasil Bil'ak followed Novotný onto the rostrum. He expressed dissatisfaction with Novotný's line of argument. Even more emphatically than Dubček, he repudiated Novotný's description of Dubček's views on the Slovak question as nationalistic. Bil'ak argued that a situation had arisen in which conflict between the two nations was growing. There was much anti-Slovak feeling in the Czech lands and in Slovakia there were anti-Czech feelings. Novotný, Dubček and Bil'ak were careful not to use the phrase 'bourgeois nationalism', but they certainly had this bogy in mind. Novotný had revived it whenever he thought it opportune. Now, however, the Slovaks had become so sensitive to the slightest hint of this threat, that this time they were provoked into open defiance on the sacred soil of the Party Central Committee in which nobody had ever before dared to challenge the leader.

After the October 1967 Plenum the situation in the Praesidium had become so strained that Novotný was afraid to re-convene it. It did not in fact meet for six weeks. Novotný knew by now that the Praesidium had ceased to be the instrument of his will, just as the Central Committee had ceased to be the instrument of the Praesidium. Hendrych, the most important man on the Praesidium besides Novotný, was exhausted from the strain of his nerve-wracking dealings with the rebellious writers and intellectuals, and went to Italy for a holiday. It was rumoured that he would not return to his post. The official outcome of the October Plenum was that Novotný promised to prepare a detailed analysis of the situation in the central bodies of the Party and the State with suggestions about how to coordinate their work and define their competence. He was expected to submit an analysis of the work of the Praesidium, the Secretariat and the individual departments of the Central Committee. This was to be completed by the end of November.

In the meantime another event exposed the weakness of Novotný's régime and his personal position. On 31 October 1967 the students in the largest university hostel in Prague, at Strahov, demonstrated against their unsatisfactory living conditions. They invited journalists to come and see how they lived. The students seemed to be particularly annoyed by the frequent power cuts. One of these power cuts occurred just as the journalists arrived at the hostel. The students marched from Strahow towards the city centre, but were stopped by the police, who suggested that they choose representatives to voice their complaints. The students refused, and the police began to disperse them with tear gas and truncheons. Three students were arrested, and many were taken to hospital.

The Strahov incident provoked repercussions in student hostels and university faculties throughout the country. The students of the Philosophy Faculty of Charles University in Prague sent a petition to the Minister of Education demanding the punishment of the policemen responsible for the events of 31 October, the banning of the use of tear gas against peaceful demonstrations, and requesting that individual policemen should not remain anonymous but should wear discs with identification number.

The Minister of Education seems to have taken up the students' cause for he managed to persuade his colleague, the Minister of the Interior, to dissociate himself from his own subordinates and punish them. The situation became so confused that nobody knew who was on whose side. This confusion was reflected in the mass media. Some of the daily papers refused to condemn the students, although their editors were being briefed by the Party secretariat to do so.

This was the atmosphere at the time when Novotný, with an official Party and government delegation, went to take part in the celebrations in Moscow to mark the fiftieth anniversary of the Bolshevik revolution. This annual visit was a routine affair, but this time, there was one difference; the First Secretary of the Slovak Communist Party was not included in the delegation. Instead of Alexander Dubček, Michal Chudík, the Chairman of the Slovak National Council the most obedient of all Novotný's Slovak servants, accompanied his master.

Novotný came to the November 1967 Plenum of the Central Committee empty-handed, without the analysis he had promised in October. He could not give a satisfactory explanation for his failure to produce it, and this did not improve his position; he was already on the defensive. This was a new experience for him; he had always been the strong autocrat, attacking and aggressive, but the October Plenum had somehow broken his spirit.

At the December Plenum of the Central Committee he actually apologized to Dubček, and tried to appear critical of his previous attitude to the Slovak comrades. He also tried to explain away his invitation to Brezhnev to come to Prague to help him handle the worsening situation in the Praesidium and in the Central Committee, but he could not explain why he had acted on his own, without consulting the Praesidium. Although the main topic on the agenda was the reorganization of the central state organs, most members of the Central Committee were more interested in discussing the more urgent question of the concentration of state and Party functions in the hands of one man, and in particular the combination of the office of First Secretary of the Party with that of the President of the Republic. Both offices were held by Novotný. Similarly, members of the Party Praesidium held important jobs in the government, such as the offices of the Prime Minister, the Chairman of the National Assembly, and the Chairman of the Slovak National Council. The majority of the members of the Central Committee criticized this lack of division of roles. Some of them pointed out that there was a crisis in the Praesidium which was rendering it incapable of action; it was, they maintained, unable to solve important problems facing the country and the Party. The main point at issue, as everybody knew, was that Novotný's two functions should be divided. The progressive members of the Central Committee stressed another crucial point: the sovereignty of the Central Committee to which the Praesidium was responsible. The Committee's function should not be merely that of rubber-stamping decisions made by the Praesidium. They resented the fact that up till then the Praesidium itself had been an instrument of Novotný's autocratic rule.

Although in his October speech Dubček did not deal primarily with the Slovak question, but discussed the role of the Party and the meaning of socialism, few people doubted that in the first place he was acting as a Slovak leader. Novotný was wrong in accusing all the Slovaks in the Central Committee of nationalism, and of plotting against him. Actually, the two other Slovaks on the Praesidium, the Czechoslovak Premier, Jozef Lenárt, and the Chairman of the Slovak

National Council, Michal Chudík, supported Novotný against those who wanted him to give up his job as First Secretary of the Party. Neither Dubček, nor Lenárt had designs on Novotný's job; if anyone did, it was one of the Czech members, such as Kolder, Černík or Hendrych. Hendrych had for long been regarded as Novotný's heir apparent. It had been rumoured that he was Brezhnev's choice, long before the Soviet leader was called in by Novotný in December to save his position. But Hendrych's incompetent handling of the Writers' Congress a few months before had not strengthened his position in Soviet eyes, although the strict measures which he afterwards ordered against the writers might have improved his standing. Hendrych now became the most vehement anti-Novotnýite in the Praesidium. He accused him of being responsible for the confusion in the Party and the country.

When Brezhnev visited Prague in December 1967, he spoke with every member of the Praesidium separately. The content of his discussions is not known but the longest talk he had was with Dubček. When they parted after four hours conversation, Dubček did not look like a schoolboy who had been severly reprimanded by the Soviet headmaster for being rude to his form-master Novotný. Dubček assured his closest associates that his talk with Brezhnev had been a comradely, friendly affair. However, one thing may be safely asssumed; when Dubček left Brezhnev, his composure was not due to any suggestion made by Brezhnev that he should be Novotný's successor. He must have been an ambitious man, otherwise he would not have risen so quickly in the Party hierarchy and got top job in Slovakia, but his ambition was not so great that he wanted the top job in Czechoslovakia: if for no other reason than that it must have seemed out of his reach as a Slovak. As the premier Lenárt was also a Slovak, that would have been too much for the Czechs to accept.

Yet this was exactly what did happen. When the Central Committee met again on 3 January 1968, it decided that the functions of First Secretary and President of the Republic should not be held by the same man. Most of the members of the Committee suggested that Novotný should give up the more influential job and keep the post of President of the Republic. This was confirmed, but the Praesidium got into difficulties over the question of who should succeed him as First Secretary. It was Novotný himself who proposed Dubček. The Praesidium accepted this proposal with relief. Thus Dubček, the least likely candidate, regarded by members of the Praesidium as the least controversial and least ambitious amongst them, was put forward to the Plenum of the Central Committee as the only candidate on whom the Praesidium could agree. There was a unanimous vote in favour of Dubček as First Secretary of the Czechoslovak Communist Party.

The Central Committee, which since October had been divided on most issues into three groups – the progressives, the centre and the conservatives – accepted this solution as the most expedient one, and with the feeling that this was only a temporary arrangement. Dubček himself accepted it on that assumption, as he told a group of editors two weeks later when they came to him to congratulate him and to be briefed on the course that the mass media should take in the new situation. He seemed unsure of himself, not convinced that he was up to the job. At the briefing, he stressed the principle of continuity in Party policy. He did not suggest any major changes. On the contrary, he advocated restraint and moderation. His main request was that the mass media should not create difficulties for him in his new job.

At this stage, Novotný had little reason to be particularly worried about his future. The January Plenum of the Central Committee kept him in the Party Praesidium as President of the Republic. This body remained basically unchanged. There were three new members, who were meant to strengthen the anti-Novotný side, but actually of these three only Špaček proved to be a real progressive. The resolution adopted by the January Plenum made it clear that Novotný had been relieved of his function at his own request; it then went on to praise him in a way which was highly unusual in socialist countries when such important personnel changes are made. The Central Committee claimed that

> thanks to comrade Novotný the Party has, during the past years, achieved significant successes in the country and in the world Communist movement. The Central Committee therefore values highly and appreciates the dedicated work which, in this complicated and difficult period, comrade Novotný has carried out with so much self-sacrifice for the benefit of the Party and the Republic.[4]

Announcing that the Central Committee had elected Alexander Dubček as First Secretary, the communiqué stressed that in his person 'the continuity of the Party leadership was being preserved, bearing in mind his long years of work in the Party'.[5]

The population was pleased that Novotný was no longer the First Secretary, but Party members in particular were taken aback by the arrival of Dubček as Party leader. The warm words of praise for the

[4] *Rudé Právo*, 6 January 1968.　　　　[5] *Ibid.*

fallen leader filled them with misgivings. The emphasis on continuity of Party policy did not sound very promising. Continuity was the last thing the country wanted. What the people of Czechoslovakia, inside and outside the Party, wanted above all was to put aside the discredited policies of the Novotný era. They hoped that this would be the aim of the new leadership, and that this was the meaning of the change. If the policies which had proved disastrous for the country were to be continued, what was all the fuss about? Why did Novotný have to go, if he was such a great man, full of merits, and worthy of such high praise and gratitude? Therefore, mingled with a feeling of relief that Novotný had suffered at least a partial set-back, was a feeling of frustration, particularly among the more progressive elements in the Party. They were disappointed, but instead of being paralysed into passivity, they went on to the offensive. The conservatives were steadily losing political ground.

In Slovakia, although people were worried by the style of the communiqué which had announced Novotný's departure, a state of near-jubilation prevailed over the fact that a Slovak had had the courage to tell his Czech boss his mind and had replaced him in his Party job. When Dubček returned to Bratislava late in the evening of 5 January hundreds of people came to greet him at the airport. Many of them were Party and government officials and newspaper editors who came to remind the new leader of their existence and of their loyalty to him. The really progressive Slovaks, although pleased by Novotný's partial fall, were perhaps not nationalistic enough to see a Slovak victory in Dubček's appointment. They foresaw the psychological difficulties and political implications of this change.

At this stage, the Russians were not too worried by the turn of events in this important satellite country. Whatever Brezhnev learned from his individual discussions with members of the Czechoslovak Praesidium in December, he seemed to have no desire to interfere with the immediate course of events. He could not have argued convincingly against the principle which he himself had applied when he got rid of Khrushchev; his method had been far less democratic than that used by the Czech and Slovak Communists in dealing with their First Secretary. The new Soviet leaders had also accused Khrushchev of concentrating too much power in his hands. The principle of collective leadership had been to a greater or lesser extent re-established in the socialist countries, the most striking exception being Rumania, where in this matter as in some others they went in a different direction to that of the Russians. At a time when in Czechoslovakia the progressives were attempting to divide power, the First Secretary of the Rumanian Party, Ceauşescu, became President of the Republic. This step was justified by the need to cut down on unnecessary bureaucracy and to rationalize overlapping government and Party functions.

At first the Soviet press published only short news items on the Czechoslovak leadership. Party members were allegedly sent a confidential circular which explained what was going on in Czechoslovakia. The gist of this circular was that Novotný had been removed from his Party post because he could not handle the complicated situation in the country. Novotný was obviously too weak to take a firm stand against the revisionists. It was now Dubček's task to put things in order. On 29 January 1968 Dubček went to Moscow for a short visit. He returned apparently unworried. The Soviet leaders still had little reason for concern over events, or rather the absence of events, in Czechoslovakia. In the first few months after Dubček took office things moved very slowly indeed. The conservatives felt confident that they would manage to keep Novotný's system without Novotný. It was the progressives who were becoming restless and impatient, wondering what Dubček was up to. Except for Dubček's election, and his visit to Moscow, nothing of importance happened in January.

February began with the Seventh Congress of the agricultural co-operatives, at which the new First Secretary of the CPCz indicated rather timidly the reforms he intended to introduce. On the whole he spoke in the spirit as at the October session of the Central Committee. On 4 February Dubček met his Hungarian colleague Kádár at the frontier, and had a friendly exchange of views. On 7 February he had a meeting with the Polish leader Gomułka, which as became known later in Party circles, was less friendly. On the same day the Praesidium of the Czechoslovak Communist Party discussed in very general terms the preparation of the Action Programme.

On the eve of the twentieth anniversary of the February events of 1948, when the Communists took over complete control of the country, the Praesidium of the Soviet Communist Party sent the usual cordial greetings to their Czechoslovak comrades. On 22 February there was a joint session of the Central Committee of the Communist Party, the Central Committee of the National Front, and the Government, at Prague Castle. The main speaker was Alexander Dubček; he spoke of the political legacy of February and stressed the duty of Communists to uphold that legacy. He claimed that the deformations which had occurred in the country had not been caused by the ideas of February but by their abuse. He stressed the urgent need for a solution to the economic problems of the country by introducing essential economic reforms, but he also stressed the need for 'strengthening the planned economy as an instrument of economic policy'.[6] The new First Secretary spoke of the national problem and particularly of the relationship between the Czechs and Slovaks. He reminded his audience that the proceedings of the last Central Committee had rightly emphasized the importance of the national problem in Czechoslovak political life. He said: 'It has to be made quite clear that those who regard any manifestations of national activity with suspicion do disservice to our movement and to our state'.[7] This was an unusual reference to a problem which was supposed to have been solved in all the People's Democracies and, of course, in the Soviet Union. Now Dubček was suggesting that in Czechoslovakia the national question had not been solved, but only shelved. Still, the leaders of the socialist countries who were present at this occasion, Brezhnev, Gomułka, Ulbricht, Kádár, Ceauşescu, Zhivkov and the Yugoslav, Vlahović, did not express any concern in their fraternal addresses over the recent development in Czechoslovakia (later referred to as the 'post-January' one). Nearly two months after the January session of the Central Committee, little had happened to justify the claim that it marked an historic turn of events in the country.

Novotný was still President of the Republic. On 25 February, at a mass meeting in Prague Old Square to celebrate the Communist victory of 1948, with the People's Militia surrounding the platform, he stood beside Dubček, looking very self-confident. The new First Secretary of the Party gave the main speech, in which he hinted at better things to come; but his tone was very much in the spirit of the occasion, and gave no indication of the possibility of any return to the type of democracy which Communists had abolished twenty years ago. Novotný, too, delivered a ceremonial speech, which differed little from Dubček's except that Dubček's was clearly prepared by more competent and perhaps even more progressive speech-writers than Novotný's.

Slovakia, too, was modest in its expectations, but the fact that on 28 February the Czechoslovak National Assembly in Prague had endorsed a law affording Bratislava the status of capital of Slovakia, was hailed as a great achievement, a major national victory.

[6] *Rudé Právo*, Prague, and *Pravda*, Bratislava, 23 February 1968.
[7] *Ibid.*

On 5 March 1968 the Praesidium of the Czechoslovak Communist Party discussed the information services in the Party and the mass media generally. It laid down the principle of freedom of speech and proposed a change in the existing press law and the abolition of censorship. This was the first concrete measure of really great importance following the January change in the leadership. For the workers in the mass media this was a clear sign that the days of censorship were numbered, although it was not formally abolished by the National Assembly for several months. At the same meeting, the well-known liberal, Špaček, was put in charge of the mass media; he was appointed as the new head of the ideological department of the Central Committee.

The Party Praesidium was still more powerful than the National Assembly, officially the highest legislative body in the land. Journalists therefore felt that there was no point in waiting for the new press law to receive legislative approval. Although the censors still sat in their offices at the printing presses and at the radio and television studios, after 5 March nobody took any notice of their existence, even though some censors still thought that their advice might be useful. They sat there with nothing to do but look back with nostalgia to the time when their decisions had been sacrosanct. These decisions had in the past been made on the spot, sometimes after consultation with higher officials in the Central Office of Publications. In theory the censor's decision could have been over-ruled by the editor, who was ultimately responsible to the Party for all that appeared in his paper, including the advertisements. Still, when the censor stood firm, the editor usually obeyed. It was wiser to avoid trouble. It was an old-established maxim among Communist editors that there would be more trouble if they printed controversial material than if they did not print it at all. For journalists the crime of commission was always graver than the crime of omission. Only in the last stages of the Novotný régime did some editors manage to get their way, in spite of the censors. But even then only the periodicals of the Writers' Unions in Bratislava and in Prague (partly because of their limited circulation, but also because of the courage of their editors and the strength and influence of their organizations) published articles which would clearly anger the Party officials and Novotný himself.

The abolition of censorship from 5 March 1968 marked the real beginning of the Czechoslovak spring. It signified a radical change in a political practice common to all socialist countries, where in one way or another, under various names and disguises, strict control of the mass media is an essential condition of government. The significance of the step taken by the Czechoslovak Party Praesidium under Dubček cannot therefore be over-estimated.

The first test case for the Czechoslovak mass media, now liberated from censorship, was provided by the defection of Major-General Jan Šejna to the United States. This event did great damage to Novotný. Šejna represented a perfect success-story of the Novotný régime. An uneducated man and an unscrupulous careerist, Šejna was made a general in his early thirties, and became one of Novotný's closest advisers on military matters. As Chairman of the Party branch of the General Staff he was more powerful than the Minister of Defence himself. He must, therefore, have been implicated in the alleged attempt by conservative officers to solve the political crisis in favour of Novotný, if necessary, by a military *Putsch*. The story of this affair has never been fully told. It was officially dismissed as a 'fabrication of the right-wing opportunists', as Dubček's supporters, and, of course, Dubček himself, were soon to be called.

General Šejna, the most faithful of Novotný's supporters, assumed by all to be an arch-enemy of the imperialists, was willing to betray his country and his Party to the United States. This dramatic story was a godsend for the progressives, who made no secret of their delight. Czech and Slovak journalists, although not trained for scoops of this kind, took it up with relish, despite the official version that Šejna's defection was simply a result of his black-market activities in the seed business. Although Dubček himself instructed the mass media to present the official version of the affair, they disobeyed him, even though he implied it was the wish of their Soviet allies because top secrets of the Warsaw Pact were involved.

Šejna defected on 25 February 1968, before the decision of the Party Praesidium to abolish censorship. The censors had received instructions to enforce the official version of Šejna's flight to the West in the mass media. But the journalists did not wait for the formal introduction of the new press law; they saw no reason why, in a case like this, they should not use their professional skills. The Šejna affair gave them a unique chance to come out openly against Novotný and his supporters, for Šejna had been one of them. They ridiculed the suggestions of black-marketeering and concentrated more on the political and moral aspects of the affair. Anyway, they could hardly have given any more secret information than Šejna himself had already given to the intelligence services of the United States.

Šejna's defection was a real blow to Novotný. The mass media openly attacked the conservatives who were in a state of helpless fury. Whatever the American government and the CIA had intended when they granted Šejna asylum, they had the effect, indirectly, of strengthening the progressive movement in Czechoslovakia. Now, things began to move fairly fast. Novotnýites in the trade unions, such as Oldřich Pastýřik, the Chairman of the Trade Union Council, and his two secretaries Kozelka and Pašek, who defended Novotný at the crucial sessions of the Central Committee, were forced to resign under pressure coming from their more liberal colleagues. The Praesidium of the National Assembly passed a vote of no-confidence in the Prosecutor General, Bartušek and the Minister of the Interior, Kudrna. On 14 March the Praesidium of the Party took measures to implement the immediate and complete rehabilitation of the victims of the Stalinist purges. The same day, the progressive Communist Čestmír Císař, who had been sent into exile by Novotný as Ambassador to Rumania, was appointed head of the Central Committee's Deparment of Education and Culture. Also on the same day, the Deputy Minister of Defence, General Janko, committed suicide, probably because he was implicated in the Šejna affair – not in his illegal seed-business, but in more serious matters such as the alleged attempted *Putsch* by Novotný's generals.

In Slovakia on 15 March the Plenum of the Slovak National Council removed its Chairman, Michal Chudík, from office. He was replaced by Ondrej Klokoč, the editor of *Pravda*, who in 1963 had published Hysko's article attacking Viliam Široký, the Prime Minister then in office. More significantly, the Plenum voted unanimously for a speedy solution of relations between the Czech and Slovak nations on a federal basis. Now the Slovaks, as well as the Czechs, began to enjoy the fresh air of the Czechoslovak spring. The Dubček era had begun in earnest.

Preparations were under way for the Fourteenth Congress of the Czechoslovak Communist Party. District conferences were held, and delegates were elected to regional conferences at which delegates were elected to attend the Congress. The district conferences gave ordinary Party members a genuine opportunity to express their views. They openly criticized the work of higher Party organs and of the Party apparatus. The delegates to the regional conferences and the new members of the Party district committees were elected by secret ballot. This was another major innovation. The old Party Statutes of Gottwald and Novotný were still formally valid. They could be altered officially only by the Party Congress. (The Central Committee published its draft-proposal for new statutes on 10 August 1968, but because of the Soviet invasion this was not implemented.) The Central Committee of which Dubček was now First Secretary had, without waiting for the official acceptance of the new statutes, voted on important issues by secret ballot. Oddly enough, although all the members of that Central Committee had been elected under Novotný at the Thirteenth Party Congress in 1966, with a hard core of conservatives, all the progressive measures put forward by Dubček and his colleagues were now carried by safe majorities, and in some cases even unanimously. Dubček was taking a considerable risk when he introduced the secret ballot, for the Central Committee had faithfully supported Novotný up till then. It was further proof that, after all, he was the right man in the right place. The result of his initiative was to strengthen his hand considerably. He could justly point out that all major decisions had been reached by truly democratic means.

The mood of most delegates at the district conferences was one of hostility towards Novotný, and dissatisfaction with his policies. They resented the fact that he was still President, and had been praised in the official communiqué of the January Plenum. After all, he was responsible for the political and economic situation and the crisis in the Party. Many resolutions demanded his resignation as President of the Republic. Responding to the revolutionary call sounded by the Central Committee and the Praesidium, the district conferences now carried the movement to the grass-roots level; the radical mood spread through the whole country. Meetings were held and were attended by the general public, not only by Party members. The biggest gathering of this kind was held in Prague on 20 March, at which Marie Švermová, Professor Goldstücker, and Dr Husák from Slovakia were present. These had all been victims of the Stalinist purges and none of them had been allowed back into political life, despite their formal rehabilitation. These well-known leaders of the reform movement were joined by Smrkovský, one of the very few rehabilitated Communists who had been restored to his membership of the Central Committee and was Minister of Forestry at that time; by Professor Ota Šik, the father of the economic reform, who was high in the Party hierarchy; by the writer Kohout, who had taken such a bold stand at the Writers' Congress; and other popular national figures.

The main theme of these meetings was a demand for consistent democratization and rehabilitation, and for the resignation of Novotný.

On 22 March 1968 Novotný resigned from office as President of
the Republic. The National Assembly accepted his decision with
great relief, because after the Šejna affair his position had become
indefensible. He was replaced by Ludvík Svoboda, an army general
held in high esteem both in the Czech and the Slovak parts of the
country.[1] Smrkovský was made a member of the Praesidium of the
Party, and Čestmír Císař was elected one of the secretaries of the
Central Committee.

In Slovakia too, there was a great increase in political activities.
Husák, Novomeský and other former 'bourgeois nationalists' were
not yet in high office either in the Party or in the government. Their
political future was by no means certain or settled yet, but as
delegates to the district and regional conferences they could take an
active part in the progressive movement sweeping the country. By
now Slovakia was proud of the fact that the Slovak Dubček had become the embodiment of new ideas and had full understanding of the
Slovak national cause. At that time Husák fully supported Dubček
and was regarded as a progressive Communist. But in March, at the
district conference in Bratislava, he spoke about two problems of
democracy and freedom. He stressed the need for more democracy
but referred to the necessity of 'defending freedom and democracy
in our socialist sense'.[2] Not that Dubček or the Czech progressives
had given the slightest grounds for the suspicion that they had in
mind any other sense of freedom and democracy, but Husák laid so
much emphasis on this point that he gave the impression that it was
of the utmost importance to be on guard against those forces 'whose
activities do not correspond to our aims and plans'.[3] When he spoke
about democracy he reminded his audience of responsibility, of
the dangers which could threaten the Party and actually harm it.
'Some people would welcome that development', he warned.[4]

On 8 April 1968 Husák became Deputy Premier in the new

---

[1] He had been the commanding officer of the Czechoslovak brigade which
fought alongside the Soviet Army; he was dismissed in the Fifties, although
he had been an active supporter of the Communists in February 1948. After
his dismissal he had worked as a clerk in an agricultural cooperative until
1957 when Khrushchev visited Czechoslovakia and asked what had happened to his old friend Svoboda. He was immediately given back his general's
uniform, and presented to Khrushchev, but still was not taken back into
the army.

[2] *Výber*, Bratislava, March 1969, Special Edition, p. 39.

[3] *Ibid.*   [4] *Ibid.*

Czechoslovak Government formed by Oldrich Černík, who succeeded Jozef Lenárt. A few weeks later Husák wrote:

> There is a broad spectrum of views on our problems, ranging from old and conservative to ultra-radical. There are people amongst us who are vying with each other to invent ideal systems incorporating freedom, institutions, guarantees, which...propagated on a mass scale would lead to anarchy in our social life, making united action impossible, weakening the Party and the Government. The freedom to criticize is being overstressed; far more urgent is the need to unite people in a positive programme, to solve immediate daily problems. People are advocating opposition for the sake of opposition, criticism for the sake of criticism. Some people are over-zealously competing in radicalization like small boys competing to see who can spit furthest. Some of them are fishing in troubled waters. The situation is being exploited by forces which believe neither in socialism nor in democracy; under the slogan of democratization they create an atmosphere of terror; under the disguise of high-sounding slogans they are pursuing their own personal aims and are playing the power game.[5]

Once back in power, Husák became a different man to the one he had been when, forced out in the cold, he had worked in moral and political opposition to the Novotný régime. In those days he had even used liberal arguments and had talked about democracy and human rights – subjects which, as Deputy Premier in Prague, he now seemed to resent. Now his speeches were devoted to warning the people against the abuse of freedom. As he was one of the most important men in Slovakia he therefore helped to create the impression that Slovakia was less progressive, less revolutionary, than the Czech lands. This was a false picture and did not correspond to the facts. What was true was that the Slovaks were united on the issue of the federal solution to the national problem – a solution which was fully endorsed by the Action Programme of the Czechoslovak Communist Party on 5 April 1968.

[5] Gustav Husák, 'Dejinná príležitosť' (The Historical Chance), *Pravda*, Bratislava, 9 May 1968.

19 THE NEW COMMUNIST MANIFESTO

The Action Programme of the CPCz incorporated all the fundamental changes which were designed to give socialism a human face.
It was the Communist Manifesto of Czechoslovakia's bloodless revolution.[1] The document did not represent the views of the most radical
elements in the Party and in the country. Rather it was the result
of a compromise.

The Action Programme had not abandoned any of the basic
principles of Marxist theory. Its main aim was to create conditions in
Czechoslovakia which would enable those theories to be put into
practice. It was not intended as a blue-print for all socialist countries,
but merely as a modern, up-to-date plan of action for socialism in
Czechoslovakia. Some of the theories it expressed were hardly more
radical than the documents of the Twentieth and Twenty-second
Congresses of the Soviet Communist Party. The Czechoslovak
Action Programme emphasized principles similar to those proclaimed
by Khrushchev, but with a greater sense of urgency. For example it
stated:

> Antagonistic classes no longer exist in our country; all social
> groups are becoming closer together...Measures must be taken
> to ensure the participation of the country in the technological
> and scientific revolution that is taking place in the world...closer
> cooperation between industrial and agricultural workers and the
> intelligentsia is essential.
>
> Opportunities for social initiative, open exchange of views and
> democratization of the whole social and political system are
> vitally necessary if a socialist society is to remain dynamic. Our
> success in world competition, and our ability to fulfil our ob-
> ligations to the international workers' movement...depend on
> this.[2]

However, there were passages in the Action Programme which
must have alarmed the more conservative leadership of Brezhev and

[1] This study cannot give a detailed treatment of the Action Programme but
only a brief indication of its main features.
[2] These quotations have been translated from the Slovak original, published
as a supplement to the daily *Pravda*, Bratislava, 6 April 1968.

Kosygin. It must be remembered that since the Khrushchev era developments had taken place in the Soviet Union which were quite different from those advocated at the Twentieth Congress. But even Khrushchev would have regarded the passages on the leading role of the Party as outright heresy. For example:

> In the past, the Party believed it should concentrate all power in its own hands since it regarded itself, falsely, as the instrument of the dictatorship of the proletariat. This harmful attitude weakened the initiative and responsibility of state, economic and social institutions, damaged the Party's authority, and prevented it from carrying out its real functions. The role of the Party should not be that of a guardian, whose directives are binding for all organizations and without whose permission no step can be taken.

More alarming to neo-Stalinist ears was the passage concerning the mass media:

> The working people...can no longer be dictated to by an arbitrary power, as to what information they may or may not be given, what opinions they may or may not express publicly... Public opinion polls must be taken into account when important decisions are being taken, and their results published. The Central Committee of the CPCz considers it urgently necessary to define...in a press law in what circumstances a state body can forbid the propagation of certain information (in the press, radio, television, etc.)....There must be no more distortion of the facts either in political or economic matters. Enterprises should publish their balance sheets; more foreign newspapers should be imported. Leading representatives of state, social and cultural organizations should give regular press conferences, and state their views on topical issues.

The section on the implemetation of constitutional freedoms of assembly and association is no less radical.

> These must be ensured this year so that the right to form voluntary associations is guaranteed by law in accordance with the interests of our citizens, without bureaucratic interference and without creating a monopoly for any individual organization.

The Action Programme stipulated that

> freedom of speech must be guaranteed by law. . .so must the right to travel abroad. . .a citizen should have the legal right to

stay abroad if he so wishes and should not be forced unnecessarily into the position of an emigré.

The Action Programme was not strikingly original in its attitude to the national question. The principle of federation had after all been recognized from the very beginning by the Soviet Union as a fundamental theorem. But in Czechoslovakia where, only a few months before, the very word had been anathema, it reflected a basic change of attitude. The Action Programme presented a genuine plan for federalization. It condemned the hitherto unequal, 'asymmetric' arrangement under which the Czech national bodies were identical with the central ones. This meant that they had greater powers than the Slovak national bodies.

> This prevented the Slovak nation...from taking an equal share in the creation and realization of a state-wide policy...The Slovak national bodies found that they had little influence on the state machinery...The result was that the Slovaks believed they were governed by Prague.

Summing up the problems, the Action Programme proposed:

> It is essential to recognize the advantages of a socialist federation which allows two equal nations to live together in a common socialist state...It is therefore necessary to draw up and pass a constitutional law to this effect...thereby solving the status of Slovak national bodies in our constitutional system in the nearest future – before the elections to the National Assembly and the Slovak National Council take place. It will have to:
>
> ❋ constitute the Slovak National Council as a legislative body and the Slovak Council of Ministers as a collective executive body, and ministries as individual executive organs of the Slovak National Council, extending the real powers of all these organs so that the division of legislative and executive powers between the state-wide and the Slovak bodies may basically comply with the principles of the Košice Government Programme;
>
> ❋ entrust the directing of national committees in Slovakia to Slovak national bodies and...set up a Slovak ministerial office for internal affairs and public security;
>
> ❋ allow Slovak national bodies to draw up and approve an economic plan and budget for Slovakia...Establish ministerial economic executive bodies within the Slovak National Council which would reorganize Slovakia's manufacturing industries;
>
> ❋ appoint State Secretaries to central departments, especially

in the Ministries of Foreign Affairs, Foreign Trade and National Defence, and make the Secretaries members of the government;

✱make it impossible, politically and constitutionally, for the Slovaks to be out-voted in matters concerning relations between Czechs and Slovaks, and the constitutional status of Slovakia;

✱also to ensure the principle of equal rights for both nations concerning appointments to central bodies, the diplomatic service, etc.

In the interests of strengthening the unity, cohesion and national individuality of all nationalities in Czechoslovakia – of Hungarians, Poles, Ukrainians, and Germans...we deem it necessary to stress that the principles of our Programme in respect of our two nations also extend to other nationalities. To that end it is necessary to stipulate constitutional and legal guarantees of complete political, economic and cultural equality. It is necessary to see that the nationalities are represented, in proportion to their numbers, in our political, economic, cultural and public life, and in elected and executive bodies.

In the section dealing with the rationalization of Slovakia's resources, the Programme stressed that 'the economy of the Czechoslovak Socialist Republic represents an integration of two national economies which makes it possible to increase the economic potential of our entire society'. The programme acknowledged that

the past development of Slovakia within the unified Czechoslovak economy was marked by major changes in economic and living standards. Slovakia has become an industrially advanced. agriculturally developed part of the Republic...However, these undeniable achievements were accompanied by serious problems. Although Slovakia's contribution to the national income increased from 14·2 per cent in 1948 to 24·4 per cent in 1965, this does not seem adequate when compared with the possibilities of growth which exist in Slovakia: its favourable geographical position, and more highly skilled workforce...new developments in the chemical industry, metallurgy, fuel and power, agriculture, and in the exploitation of natural resources...The potential for growth was not utilized, either in industry or in agriculture. The tertiary sphere, particularly in the development of scientific research, has lagged greatly behind. Slovakia's development was not sufficiently coordinated...It is of decisive importance for Slovakia's long-term economic development to raise substantially Slovakia's participation in the creation and the utilization of the national income and to solve the task of creating a balanced economy by 1980. This necessitates faster economic development in Slovakia than nationally. The prerequisite of this is to give strong support to progressive structural changes, to intensify agricultural production and the processing industries, to develop the tertiary sector in all spheres.

With a critical reference to the new system of management proposed by the Prague reformists, the Programme states that 'this system in its present form has not created sufficient scope for separate national developments. Past adjustments of the plan are inadequate'.

Although all the principles of the Action Programme were unanimously approved by the Central Committee, the Slovaks were anxious to have them implemented as soon as possible. It was an understandable and natural attitude. Unfortunately it was abused by some Slovak Party officials, mainly by Vasil Bil'ak, who after Dubček's elevation to Prague, was made First Secretary of the Party in Slovakia. He was obviously worried that the more radical parts of the Action Programme would be given priority and therefore thought that it might be safer to exploit the national feelings of the Slovaks and their traditional mistrust of anything coming from Prague.

Bil'ak was worried by developments in the Czech lands, where the liberalization process was moving too fast for his liking. Like his Czech conservative colleagues, he was concerned, partly by the pace of the movement but mainly by its direction. Bil'ak feared that the removal of discredited politicians which had begun in Prague with the dismissal of some officials who had been close to Novotný might serve as a dangerous precedent for Slovakia. Therefore, at this decisive hour, Bil'ak started emphasizing the unity of the Slovak nation, arguing that the situation in Slovakia was different from that in the Czech lands, that Slovakia had in fact undergone a process of de-Stalinization in 1963 and that there was a little left to be done in this field. He maintained that the most urgent task was the federalization of the Republic, thereby hoping to isolate Slovakia from the liberalism of Prague.

Most Slovaks knew that federalization could not be considered separately from democratization, that one was the prerequisite of the other. If this democratization did not take place things might develop as they had done in the Soviet Union, where the principle of federation was laid down in the Constitution and formally implemented in the structure of the state, where the Ukrainians and the Byelo-Russians even had their own Ministers of Foreign Affairs, but with no independent policy – foreign or domestic. Federation without political freedom would be a mere sham. So when Bil'ak coined the slogan, 'Federalization before democratization', it caught on only with a few Party officials who thought that their position in Slovakia would be safer if they joined Bil'ak.

Husák, by now Deputy Premier in Prague, followed a similar line. He too helped to convey the impression that the immediate national interests of Slovakia should take priority over everything else. This had its effect in the Slovak mass media, which tended to give greater opportunity of expression to those who were inclined to stress the national principle, the federalization of the Republic. That was certainly the intention of those who directed the Slovak mass media – in particular, the conservative head of the Ideological Department of the Slovak Central Committee, Michal Pecho. Although there was no direct censorship he realized that he had to try and control the mass media in order to safeguard his position, since many of his comrades in Prague had already been removed and their places taken by progressives like Špaček and Císař. The directors of Slovak radio and television were still the men who for years had faithfully obeyed all the Party directives. So were most of the editors of the daily news-papers, with the exception of the editor of the youth paper, *Smena*, who, only shortly before, had been dismissed from his post because he had published a letter which Clementis had written to his wife on the eve of his execution. In July 1968 the man who had replaced him as editor had the decency to resign, requesting that the former editor be given back his post. This was the only case of its kind in the Slovak mass media. That was one of the reasons why the editors who, since the abolition of censorship, were now expected to reflect Party policy, were not always obeyed. They could no longer command respect, for they had lost their moral authority in the eyes of their subordinates. Slovak journalists and writers also wanted to enjoy to the full the newly won freedom of the press. The fact that the editors themselves did not know whom to obey nor what the Party policy actually was, or was going to be tomorrow, sometimes infected them with a kind of mental paralysis in which they let their subordinates do as they liked. Occasionally when individual writers had not bothered to present copy for the editor's approval the latter made critical suggestions after the article had already been published. If possible, writers tried to avoid seeking the opinion of the editor, who often welcomed this, because if there was trouble later, he could claim that his advice had not been sought and that therefore he was not responsible.

With, therefore, the absence of strict control, the workers in the Slovak mass media managed to express progressive views, in addition to relaying most of the best programmes from Prague television and radio. On the other hand, Bil'ak's men prevented similar materials from Bratislava from being included in the Prague programmes. This happened, for example, with the television talks given by well-known Slovak progressives such as Roman Kaliský, Pavol Števček, Zora Jesenská, Miroslav Kusý, Eugen Löbl and others. Their occasional appearances were seen only by Slovak audiences, so that the Czechs would not gain the impression of a similarly liberal and radical mood in Slovakia. Bil'ak wanted to preserve the image of a Slovakia that was concerned less with democracy than with federalization. He was partly successful in this. Most Czechs thought that federation was really all that the Slovaks cared about, which, of course, was not the case. It was only one of their demands, made more urgent by the fact that in the past they had so often been cheated of their rights.

Kultúrny Život consistently upheld its progressive line. On the particular issue of 'federalization versus democratization' its policy was sensible. It stressed the danger of putting the question in such a form at all. Despite the chauvinistic mood which Bil'ak was trying to provoke, the editors of *Kultúrny Život*, fully supported all the progressive demands made by Czech liberals. even though they continued in their genuinely patriotic Slovak policy. They stood for the implementation of all parts of the Action Programme, not only for that section dealing with the national question.

20 THE SLOVAK RESPONSE

Despite the Soviet leaders' antipathy towards nationalism they seem to have thought that there would be no harm in Slovakia having a federal status similar to that of the fifteen national republics of the Soviet Union if the Slovaks could be used to restrain those Czechs who were concentrating on the even more dangerous heresies proposed in the Action Programme. Soviet fears were based on the emphasis which the Czech reformers were now laying on the idea of a Czechoslovak road to socialism. Their fears grew when they began to suspect that the Czechs and Slovaks meant to export their heresy to other socialist countries, by claiming that their kind of Marxism would be the first real socialism. This infuriated the Russian leaders, although it was not a conscious attitude on the part of the Czech and Slovak reformers.

That the Czechoslovak experiment might end in a fiasco did not seem to worry the Russians and their satellites. Had they believed this to be the danger they would probably have let things take their course, allowing the Czech and Slovak reformers to reveal their foolishness to the world. Dubček himself would have been completely discredited in his own and other socialist countries: this would have been a real triumph for the Russian type of socialism. However, this was not the case. The Russians seem to have been convinced that the Czechoslovak experiment was both attractive and potentially viable, and that this new socialist laboratory was being managed by very intelligent and dedicated men, Communists and non-Communists alike. When it occurred to them that in Slovakia a situation might develop which would make it more difficult for the experiment to be brought to a successful conclusion, they toyed with the idea that now was the time to encourage the Slovaks into a more nationalistic attitude. They found their man in Bil'ak, and were even counting on Husák who for this particular purpose seemed to be acceptable to them.

In the first months of 1968, the Party under the new leadership did not adopt federalization as its policy. The old Gosiorovský project was still officially condemned and almost forgotten. But gradually

Bil'ak, now First Secretary of the Party in Slovakia—came to realize that this idea would meet with great approval in Slovakia where even the most progressive were imbued with patriotic sentiments. Bil'ak expected the Slovaks to give priority to federalization at the expense of a speedy introduction of other measures on which he was not too keen.

Whatever the longstanding and immediate causes of Novotný's downfall, in Slovakia his inept treatment of the national problem enhanced nationalistic feelings. Bil'ak and his friends in the Slovak Praesidium and the Central Committee of the Party which had remained unchanged until the Extraordinary Congress after the invasion, thought that by exploiting Slovak nationalism, they could rally opinion in Slovakia for themselves and their cause by whomever it was inspired. Except for his approval of the federal solution, not one instance can be quoted of Bil'ak having taken a progressive course, be it in economic reform, in granting freedom to the mass media or above all, in democratization of the Party and the state.

He was not surprised to be branded as a conservative as he told his trusted friend in the Slovak Praesidium Miloš Hruškovič in the spring of 1968 at the Bratislava Party conference.[1] In an interview in the Slovak Party paper Hruškovič gave first-hand evidence of the true attitude of Bil'ak and the Slovak Praesidium to the events in Czechoslovakia. He said: 'In the course of the first half of 1968 federation became a very practical and mainly political question. The Praesidium therefore had to pay full attention to it.'[2]

Hruškovič confessed:

> If the process of democratization in Slovakia was retarded, I admit that we in the Praesidium dissociated ourselves from the forms and subsequently from the consequences of democratization which was taking place in those days in the Czech lands. For example, in our instructions to the regional and district councils, we deliberately did not give the green light for the establishment of workers' councils. When it was said in those days that the Praesidium had not supported this kind of democratization, I did not consider it then and do not consider it now, as something accidental. Many things we had done deliberately.[3]

The very words of the interview prove beyond doubt which measures the Slovak Praesidium under Bil'ak was deliberately block-

[1] *Pravda* (daily), Bratislava, 22 January 1970, p. 5.
[2] *Ibid.*   [3] *Ibid.*

ing. Hruškovič fulminates against the mass media which, according to him, abused its freedom. He gives ample evidence of how Bil'ak and his Praesidium tried to hamper the introduction of democratic measures in Slovakia. Hruškovič admitted this policy at a time when Husák, after the removal of Dubček from office, managed to 'normalize' the situation in Czechoslovakia to the delight of Brezhnev.

Long before Bil'ak's secret meeting with Shelest of the Praesidium of the Soviet Communist Party, in the Tatra Mountains in June 1968, the men in the Kremlin knew well who in Bratislava, or for that matter in Prague, were their friends and whom they could trust. To the best of their knowledge, Bil'ak and Hruškovič were no great democrats, not only in the matter of workers' councils. As to the position of the Party, Bil'ak consistently adhered to the Soviet model. As Hruškovič put it in the same interview: 'All the time we were convinced that if January had to bring some good to our society, it must not happen by weakening the Party, by undermining its foundations.'[4] In the latter instance, the role of the Party, Dubček's programme presented something new. Although in the view of most Slovak and Czech Communists and non-Communists it would have only strengthened the position of the Party, it was the most dangerous part of the Czechoslovak experiment – for Brezhnev and his men in Czechoslovakia.

Jozef Lenárt, the man who remained faithful to Novotný in the critical days of January 1968, and who became First Secretary of the Party in Slovakia in 1970, replacing the less reliable Štefan Sádovský, boasted in his address to the Slovak Communist Party Congress on 13 May 1971: 'In 1968 it was of the greatest importance that a group of comrades headed by comrade Vasil Bil'ak...gave preference to the solution of the juridical structure of the state on a federal basis... thus pushing into the background questions which the right-wing opportunists were pressing, particularly the so-called process of democratization.'[5] Lenárt could not have been more open. He only omitted to add, by whom they were encouraged.

The introduction of a federal system, provided it were implemented on their model, seemed to the Soviets far less dangerous. They now thought it worthwhile to woo the Slovaks and make them insist on federalization even. Moreover, under the circumstances, it would have seemed indefensible to prevent Czechoslovakia from adopting a federal system (in the state structure, not in the structure of the Party) when the Russians themselves considered this to be the best arrangement for nations living in one state.

[4] *Ibid.*   [5] *Výber* (fortnightly), Bratislava, 1971, no. 11, p. 7.

Despite Bil'ak's efforts most Slovaks were not impressed by these tactics which more than smacked of demagogy. Unfortunately for him and for the Russians, few people fell into this trap.

There were occasions when they might have done. Although the Czech liberals accepted federalization in principle and were inclined to understand the national aspirations of the Slovaks better than Novotný and his predecessors had done, even they did not always find the right psychological approach to the Slovaks. For example, in the famous progressive manifesto, the 'Two Thousand Words', written by Ludvík Vaculík and signed by many prominent Czechs, they made the mistake of not including amongst the signatories Slovaks, who would willingly have put their names to the document. It was also a blunder to publish it initially only in Czech papers. If its authors had contacted prominent Slovak progressives, its impact in Slovakia would have been much greater. To make things worse, the relatively few words out of the two thousand which related directly to Slovakia seemed to show a lack of understanding of the Slovak mentality.

Thus on the subject of federalization, the manifesto stated:

> Let us consider federalization as a matter of solving the question of nationalities, and otherwise merely as one of several important measures designed to democratize the system. In itself this particular measure may not necessarily give even the Slovaks a better life. The problem of government is not solved by having separate governments in the Czech lands and in Slovakia. Rule by a state and Party bureaucracy could still go on; in Slovakia indeed such rule might be strengthened by the claim that it had 'won more freedom'.[6]

To say the least, this was not appreciated by the Slovaks, although most of them agreed with the other ideas in this radically progressive manifesto. And, of course it was not appreciated by the Slovak General, Kodaj, who denounced it in the National Assembly as a counter-revolutionary document and achieved its formal condemnation by the Praesidium of the CPCz. In Slovakia it was not recommended for reprinting. It was, however, published by the youth daily *Smena* two days later despite the disapproval of Bil'ak, who by now had no legal powers to enforce censorship.[7]

[6] '2000 slov' (Two thousand Words), *Literární Listy* (weekly), *Mladá Fronta, Práce, Zemědělské Noviny* (dailies), Prague, 27 June 1968, *Smena* (daily, Bratilava, 29 June 1968; translation by *Times Literary Supplement*, 18 July 1968.

[7] Censorship had been officially abolished by the National Assembly on 26 June 1968, a day before the publication of the 'Two Thousand Words'.

On the one hand the Slovaks knew it was not Vaculík and the Czech progressives who were endangering the promised federation. On the other, Vaculík's words, however true and well-meant, could not fully convince the Slovaks of the good will of the Czechs – although only very few Slovaks accepted Bil'ak's warnings that the Czech liberals would again betray their cause. On one private occasion, Bil'ak (off the record, in the presence of editors) implied that if he had to choose between democratization and federalization, he would decide for the latter even if it meant the separation of Slovakia from the Republic. He hinted that the Soviet leaders would not reject such a possibility.

Despite his earlier attitude during the Slovak uprising, Husák did not suggest any such separatist solution to the Slovak problem. But he did little to counteract Bil'ak's activities. Instead in *Nové Slovo* and in public speeches, he tried to weaken the position of the Slovak progressives. He even inspired a rift in the Praesidium of the Slovak Writers' Union and in the editorial board of *Kultúrny Život*, when he persuaded his closest friend, Novomeský, and two other writers, Válek and Mihálik, to resign from it and to join his *Nové Slovo*. Nevertheless, Husák's weekly remained an uninspiring platform for those who, faced by the artificially created dilemma – democratization or federation – decided in favour of the latter.

At the height of the nation's concern and uncertainty about what was going to happen in Čierna Nad Tisou, where the Czechoslovak Party Praesidium, after long hesitation, had given in to Soviet pressure and agreed to discuss the fate of Czechoslovakia with the Soviet leaders, Husák chose to publish his own manifesto in *Nové Slovo*. It was intended as a counter-appeal to the Czech 'Two Thousand Words' and also to counteract a magnificently written petition to the Czechoslovak Party Praesidium published on the eve of the meeting at Čierna. The latter's authors were the well-known Czech progressive writers, Kohout and Hanzelka. It was published simultaneously by the Czech *Literární Listy* and the Slovak *Kultúrny Život* and read by both authors on television. It appealed to the nation's leaders not to abandon the progressive course and pledged the full support of the people. It claimed to stand for socialism, sovereignty, freedom and alliance.[8] Within a few hours it had been signed by millions of people in the Czech and Slovak parts of the country.

Husák nationalist manifesto was signed by a group of quite well-known Slovak personalities. It solemnly declared 'to the Slovaks and

[8] Known in Czech as the Four S's – standing for Socialismus, Suverenita, Svoboda, Spojenectvi.

those Czechs who are willing to listen' that 'Slovakia's unequal position is intolerable. It is high time to put the plan for federalization on an equal basis into practice, thus our relations with the Czechs would become truly fraternal.'[9]

The Slovaks were in no particular mood for this kind of warning. Their eyes and ears were turned to Čierna, as they awaited the result of their leaders' meeting with the men from Moscow. When, after four tense days, the President of the Republic, Ludvík Svoboda, spoke on television, his reassurances that the post-January course would be continued were not convincing. The old man could hardly conceal his own sorrow. The nation wondered what had happened. Svoboda was aware of the true nature of the situation since he had attended the meeting with the Soviet leaders, although he could not have known what had passed between Brezhnev and Dubček when they met for a private talk after the official session was over. It was at this secret meeting that Brezhnev probably tried to force Dubček to promise to do things which he could not and would not do. Dubček was convinced that Brezhnev was wrong and that his own cause was right.

The tension in Czechoslovakia relaxed somewhat after Brezhnev together with the leaders of the 'satellite states' – Germany, Poland, Bulgaria and Hungary – came to the Slovak capital and on 3 August signed the 'Bratislava Peace'. This was supposed to be an act of reconciliation. The people of Bratislava received it as such and welcomed even Ulbricht, although the latter is on record as expressing surprise that the festive crowd did not cheer him as much as it did the representatives of other fraternal Parties. This was hypersensitivity on his part. The biggest applause was given to Dubček when he appeared with Brezhnev. Both men embraced and kissed. Most Slovaks saw Dubček as the saviour of the Slovak people. In remote villages devout old women were burning candles for their beloved leader. For the first time, they did not seem to mind that he was a Communist.

Being an ambitious politician Husák must have envied Dubček, who this time had unwittingly pushed him out of the limelight. Although at times a respected political leader, Husák had never been the idol of the Slovak people: he was not the kind of man whom people take to their hearts. Only in the days of his unjust persecution by the Czech Stalinists did they feel compassion for the man who, after all, had suffered for the same reason that they suffered – simply because they were Slovaks.

[9] *Nové Slovo*, Bratislava, 3 August 1968.

Husák, who still held no party function, had little liking for Bil'ak and made no attempt to conceal his attitude towards him and his associates in the Party apparatus. For example, while agreeing that the progressive trend in 1963 was more pronounced in Slovakia, Husák said at the special Party conference held in Bratislava on 4 and 5 July 1968: 'The question was who was responsible for it; by whom was it done, where and against whom.'[10] He argued with Bil'ak, maintaining that the idea that the whole Slovak leadership had been progressive was not justified. He said that the political renaissance in Slovakia had been extinguished by Slovak hands (meaning Bil'ak). Husák questioned the assumption that those who had turned against Novotný in the autumn of 1967 and the spring of 1968 could now be considered as always having been progressive. He pointed out that in 1951 the same men had held posts in the Party apparatus. In 1960 they still held them, so also in 1963 – and they were still there in 1968. 'So we have such miraculous people', he continued, 'that they are capable of going through all kinds of metamorphoses; they have been most faithful to Gottwald, Novotný, Široký, Bacílek, Dubček, and they will be most faithful to God knows whom else.'[11]

It is possible that in this speech Husák was hinting at Dubček himself, who had held important Party jobs in the previous periods and had suddenly turned against Novotný. Maybe, as early as July 1968 Husák was already trying to suggest that he was a better man than Dubček. For while Dubček was making a brilliant Party career, Husák had either been in prison or forbidden to take part in politics. But Dubček was already a national hero, and had proved himself a genuine convert. By now most people were convinced that he must have been against Novotný all the time and had only been waiting for the right moment to challenge him openly. So Husák's subtle allusions to Dubček's role in the past seemed to most people unjust. But Husák wanted to draw attention to his own liberal and progressive views in addition to his firm and uncompromising stand on the national question. Referring to democratization, he stated:

> It would be very dangerous if the situation developed in such a way that in the Czech part of this state new men, not discredited by their behaviour in the past, were coming to the fore with a clear, progressive programme, while in Slovakia we remained in a kind of semi-finished state, with a democratic phraseology but with less democratic intentions or sometimes even practice.[12]

[10] *Výber*, Bratislava, Special Edition, March 1969, p. 34.
[11] *Ibid.*   [12] *Ibid.*

He said that it would be a tragedy if Slovakia were to become a conservative bastion in the state-wide struggle, a pillar of support to the conservative elements throughout the Republic, and if the Slovaks and the Czechs were to clash over this issue. But bearing in mind the national question, he emphasized that 'in a federation, Slovakia would be able to administer its own political, economic, national and other affairs. Slovakia must choose a national and Party leadership that would enable it to realize a really progressive national policy.'[13] How insincere these words were, was shown only too sadly by his subsequent attitudes.

Another issue, and the attitude of various leaders to it, particularly in Slovakia, illustrates the political mood of the country at that time. After January 1968 the convocation of the Fourteenth Congress of the CPCz became an urgent matter. This Congress would elect a new Central Committee, a new leadership, and legalize all the revolutionary measures which had been taken, but which would only be strictly valid once they had been officially endorsed by the Congress, the highest decision-making body of the Party. The progressives were pressing for an early date. Their main concern was to remove from the Central Committee the conservatives who, under the pressure of public opinion and to save their own immediate political careers, had apparently joined Dubček and voted for most of the reforms he introduced. These conservatives tried to postpone the Congress for as long as possible. Finally on 1 June the Praesidium of the CPCz decided to hold it on 9 September 1968.

In Slovakia this was a particularly burning issue. While most Czech organizations passed resolutions demanding that the Congress should take place at the earliest possible date, Bil'ak, the First Secretary of the Slovak Party, declared at the regional conference in Banská Bystrica that even should the Czechs hold such a Congress, the Slovak Communists would not regard it as their own. They would dissociate themselves from it and not attend it.[14] He was speaking only for himself and for those few men in the Party apparatus who were afraid that the Congress might put an end to their careers. The majority of Slovak Party organizations called for the convening of the Congress and in the end Bil'ak had to give in, but only after Dubček had intervened. The Slovak demand in fact went even further. Instead of the Slovak Party Congress being held after the Czechoslovak one (its main function being to apply the latter's decisions to Slovakia), as was usual, most Slovak Party organizations

13 Ibid.   14 Quoted in *Pravda*, Bratislava, 2 July 1968.

agreed to the suggestion of the Bratislava regional conference that the Slovak Congress should take place before the CPCz Congress in Prague. This was the wish not only of those who wanted to push forward the federal solution but also of the progressives, eager to prove that the Slovak Communists were not lagging behind the Czechs in their desire for democratization.

21 THE AFTERMATH OF THE INVASION

On 21 August 1968, following the invasion of the country the previous night, Dubček, Černik, Smrkovský and Kriegel were arrested and later taken forcibly to Moscow. On 23 August they were joined by President Svoboda, allegedly at his own request. On the way Svoboda had to stop in Bratislava and was asked by the Russians to take Husák on to Moscow with him. Svoboda must have welcomed this, for he knew Husák to be a courageous man who had not succumbed to long years of mental and physical torture in prison during the Fifties. He probably thought that it would be a good thing to have Husák in Moscow to counter-balance Bil'ak, Piller and Švestka who had also been invited to the 'negotiations' by Brezhnev. Officially their presence was required to complete the full strength of the Czechoslovak Praesidium; in fact it was known that these three had refused to vote for the condemnation of the invasion passed by the Praesidium of the Party. It was reported that in Moscow Svoboda was the most outspoken opponent of Brezhnev and his associates, and that he threatened to commit suicide. But in the end he too returned to his country as one of the Czechoslovak representatives who had signed the 'Moscow protocol', described as an agreement but recognized by the Czech and Slovak people as nothing other than an outright *Diktat*.

Whatever Husák said in Moscow, whatever his stand had been there, when he returned from Moscow and went straight to the Slovak Communist Party Congress (convened on 26 August despite the occupation) it was obvious that he had accepted the task of convincing the angry delegates of the expediency of the new policy which Brezhnev and his armed forces had imposed.[1] Husák's behaviour almost immediately after his return suggests that Brezhnev must have had his reasons for insisting on Husák's presence at the

---

[1] Ing. M. Hruškovič, the Slovak Deputy Premier in Prague, revealed in an interview given to the Slovak Communist Party daily *Pravda* (22.1.1970) that Husák and Bil'ak telephoned from Moscow that the Slovak Congress should not be held; the delegates should wait until the return of their leaders. This demand was agreed to by the Bratislava Party Committee on 25 August but in defiance of that decision the Slovak Party extraordinary Congress took place the following day.

post-invasion discussions. Unquestionably the military action taken by the Warsaw Pact allies against Czechoslovakia had fundamentally changed the situation in the invaded country. But the nation expected Husák to act with greater moral integrity. The invasion was indeed a far-reaching reality, frightening at that time even for Husák, but he seemed to be too ready to accept it as a necessity. The delegates of the Fourteenth Congress of the Slovak Communist Party were most shocked by that part of Husák's speech in which he condemned the Congress of the Czechoslovak Communist Party which had taken place secretly in a factory hall in the Prague working-class suburb of Vysočany. The CPCz Congress had been hastily convened immediately after the occupation because of the danger that the invaders would prevent the Congress being held on the date originally fixed, i.e. on 9 September. It was held on 22 August while Dubček and most of the members of the Praesidium of the Party were in Moscow. The Vysočany Congress elected a truly democratic new Praesidium headed by Dubček and the progressive members of the former Praesidium, men like Černik, Smrkovský, Svoboda. They excluded Bil'ak, Kolder, Piller, Rigo, who since January had shown a hesitant if not altogether negative attitude towards the implementation of the Action Programme. It was also rumoured that these men had signed the letter asking the Soviet and other Warsaw Pact armies to come and 'liberate Czechoslovakia from the counter-revolution endangering the achievements of socialism'.[2] In their place, Šik, Goldstücker and the Slovak Husák were elected on to the new Czechoslovak Party Praesidium. Although it was the first high Party function to which Husák had been appointed since his days of imprisonment, he did not recognize its validity. He challenged the legality of the Vysočany Congress and resigned from the Praesidium and from the new Central Committee. Husák's act was precisely what the occupying powers needed. According to one version, before going to Moscow Husák had dissuaded the Slovak delegates from going to Prague for the Fourteenth Party Congress by pointing out the possibly unfavourable consequences of their presence there to the

---

[2] As was later stated by the Praesidium, this was not true. Such a letter was actually sent, but it was signed by men like Auersperg, Novotný's former Private Secretary, Hoffman, the former Minister of Culture, and his deputy Chňoupek, and others of a lower calibre than the originally suspected members of the Praesidium. In April 1969 the latter were given an official public apology for this insult. This rehabilitation was of rather doubtful value to them because it tacitly suggested that collaboration with the Soviet and other socialist allies was dishonest, rather than a matter for praise and an act of true proletarian internationalism.

immediate political interests of Slovakia. However, fourteen Slovak delegates managed somehow to overcome alleged transportation difficulties said to have been caused by the Russians at the Slovak–Moravian border town of Břeclav, and which have been suggested as the main cause of the Slovak absence.

The new Czechoslovak Central Committee which Brezhnev and Husák did not recognize, condemned the invasion even more sharply than had the previous Praesidium. This new Committee was a body which the aggressors would have had difficulty in handling when compared with the old Central Committee and the old Praesidium, some of whose members had come back from 'negotiations' in Moscow as broken men.[3]

By successfully helping the Russians to achieve the annulment of the Vysočany Congress, Husák seemed to have gained their favour and confidence. They were ready to repay him in concrete terms by not insisting on the annulment of the Slovak Congress at which Husák had been elected First Srecretary; and by allowing Biľak, who was not even elected onto the new Central Committee of the Slovak Communist Party to be replaced temporarily. However the Russians thought it necessary to keep Biľak in the Czechoslovak Praesidium at all costs. He remained a member of the old Central Committee of the Czechoslovak Party when, immediately after their return from Moscow, the old Praesidium declared the new one elected at Vysočany, and the new Central Committee illegal.

An extraordinary situation arose. In Bratislava the delegates to the Slovak Congress had removed all Stalinists from the Central Committee. In their place they elected progressive men and women; writers like Pavol Števček, Miroslav Kusý, Zora Jesenská and Svetozár Štúr, the chairman of the Slovak Journalists' Union and a leading commentator on Bratislava Radio, who had helped to organize the clandestine broadcasts during the days of the invasion; in addition economists like Hvezdoň Kočtúch and Viktor Pavlenda.

The new Slovak Central Committee put its trust in Husák. He was after all the only leading politician now in Slovakia, Dubček being in Prague, who had played an important role in the overthrow of Novotný. Objectionable as some parts of his speech to the Congress immediately after his return from Moscow had been, it did contain

---

[3] Dubček recovered from the shock fairly quickly but continued to come under heavy criticism from the Russians. They accused him of not keeping to the terms of the Moscow 'agreement' just as they had tried to justify the invasion by accusing him of not keeping to the terms of the Čierna and Tisou and Bratislava agreements.

positive elements with which the progressives could agree, especially in the new situation arising from the presence of foreign troops. Speaking of the invasion itself, Husák used cautious and not wholly unacceptable words. He said,

> Through no fault of our own we got into a situation in which the territory of the Czechoslovak state was occupied by the armies of the five friendly nations. I do not have to go into detail about how our people reacted to this. Whatever its situation, a nation needs political leaders who will think in a very sober way and take into account all the facts when considering how to deal with such a crisis. We saw only two possible ways. To lead the people into resistance? From the very beginning the leadership of our Party and of our state decided that we were incapable of puting up an armed resistance and that we should not do so, and gave orders to the army and all other armed forces to act accordingly. The Party leadership looked for another way, the way of political settlement, which would lead us out of this difficult situation, and would give us back our full freedom...and enable us to realize our own ideals under progressive leadership. I know today that such solutions are regarded with a certain scepticism. I do not intend to describe the Moscow settlement as a historic victory. Today everywhere, even in the West, people say that the return of the leading representatives of the Party and the state to the positions is no small matter. We should not indulge in illusions: what else was there to do?[4]

At the same time he told delegates: 'I fully back Dubček's conception; I took part in its formulation. I am going to give him my full support; either I shall stand by him or I shall go.'

Husák was either fooling the delegates or fooling himself. As he was no political innocent the first alternative is more probable, particularly for example when he expressed his conviction that the occupation would not last for years, but merely for a relatively short period, 'while the situation was being normalized'.[5] He assured the delegates that 'assuming a sensible attitude on the part of the Communists and other honest people of our nations this problem too will be solved'.[6] He failed to mention that the situation in Czechoslovakia had only become abnormal after the invasion. The aggressors had not come to normalize it.

The reaction of the Czech and Slovak people to the sudden and uninvited presence of their allies is well-known. It is difficult to

---

[4] V*ýber*, Special Edition, March 1969, p. 27.   [5] *Ibid.*   [6] *Ibid.*

compare and analyse individual acts in various parts of the country, which in some cases overstepped the limits of passive resistance actually recommended by the Party Praesidium during the fatal night of the invasion and by the Vysočany Congress. The first general picture, corroborated by subsequent evidence, shows that the Slovaks reacted in much the same way to the invasion as did the Czechs. True, in a few towns in Slovakia martial law was imposed by the Soviet military authorities, whereas this did not happen in Bohemia and Moravia.[7] But this does not necessarily mean that resistance in Slovakia was more widespread. The people of Prague and Plzeň in the Czech lands, of Brno and Ostrava in Moravia, of Bratislava and Košice in Slovakia, indeed of virtually all the Czechoslovak cities, towns and villages through which the invaders had to pass, responded with hatred and despair, contempt and helplessness. In some places there was active expression of these sentiments.

On the whole, however, the population obeyed its leaders' requests not to put up armed resistance. Under the circumstances this would have turned a national tragedy into a catastrophe of unpredictable dimensions. The people of Czechoslovakia could not expect any help from outside. There had never been the slightest suggestion of it. Such a hope would have been desperate and altogether naïve. Thus, in this respect, there was no disappointment, no disillusionment, because there were no illusions. Thirty years earlier, during the Munich crisis, the allies of democratic Czechoslovakia considered it more expedient to give in to Hitler and sacrifice Czechoslovakia in order to save the peace. The help of the Soviet Union was conditional upon military intervention by France and upon a request from the Czechoslovak Government. But in August 1968 the Soviet armies came to Czechoslovakia uninvited to save her from what they considered to be a greater threat than that represented by Hitler in the autumn of 1938; they came to suppress heresy in their own ranks. The Czech and Slovak people had no wish to abandon socialism; they had merely decided to take it seriously. That was their unforgivable sin in the eyes of the Russian orthodox practitioners of the creed. It was a most dangerous heresy. It challenged not only the Soviet interpretation of Marxism, but above all, Soviet supremacy within the socialist camp.

The Slovaks did not react to the invasion in 'a realistic and sober manner', as Husák would have liked them to do. On the contrary,

[7] Philip Windsor and Adam Roberts, *Czechoslovakia 1968*, London, 1969, p. 124.

they now joined forces with the Czechs and put aside their quarrel over the achievement of their equal national rights. Their hatred of the invaders made the Slovaks forget their less serious grievances against the Czechs. Compared with the situation now facing them, these seemed to them insignificant. In the first days and weeks after the invasion when the fate of the whole Action Programme was at stake, with its new ideas of political freedom and economic reform, the Slovaks missed no opportunity to express their views. Dubček was still in power in Prague and the post-January Party Praesidium (with the exception of František Kriegel, whose speedy removal was Brezhnev's first condition and first triumph) was almost intact. Černík's Government was pledged to the implementation of the Action Programme. Most of the progressives had not yet been replaced by men more willing to collaborate with the Russians. Dubček refused to introduce censorship. Most periodicals, including *Rudé Právo*, the Prague Party daily, continued to publish materials very similar to those they had published before the invasion. Not surprisingly, *Literární Listy*, and *Reportér*, the weekly of the Czecho-slovak Journalists' Union, continued to demand the fulfilment of all the ideas of the Czechoslovak spring, despite the presence of foreign troops. Indeed their tone was perhaps slightly more embittered and impatient because of their presence.

Despite Husák's exhortations, the Slovak writers in their weekly, *Kultúrny Život*, refused to feign friendship for their Soviet and other fraternal allies. In one of the last issues before its suppression *Kultúrny Život* published a series of answers to the question 'What next?', which were in fact the reactions of Slovak intellectuals to the invasion.[8] The editor, the young and brilliant literary critic Jozef Bob, was one of the first to reply:

> What next? This. . .is the question that we have been asking again and again during the past few days. We seek an answer, although we know full well that the issue has already been decided. . .We do not recommend running our heads against a wall. But when we are forced to come to terms with 'reality' let us not lose the conviction that there exists a reality that is more sublime and humane, (that it exists) deep within us, in 'the Rock of Ages'. The greatest tragedies are those which, while humiliating people and nations, seem interminable, without a definite and foreseeable end.

[8] The following excerpts are quoted from *Survey* (quarterly), London, October 1968, pp. 33–8.

Pavel Števček,[9] a former editor of *Kultúrny Život* answered:

> The history of our nations – although it does not record a breach of faith of this kind – has armed us: with the force of ideas, with hope, with truth and justice. It is again our duty to use these tested weapons. For again the existence or non-existence of the Slovaks and Czechs and of their common state is at stake. Were it not for this, every individual might make his own personal attempt to survive in a suit of armour fashioned from his own grief, bitterness and passivity. I am convinced that again – oh God, how many times already! – the time has come when it is worth while making sacrifices for this nation and for this society, to make sure that we shall regain our lost freedom and that we shall be allowed to be ourselves again...The times in which we are forced to live are not the times of words, and particularly not the times of free words. Therefore let us declare, while we still may, that we shall not forget. We shall not forget that the tracks of their tanks have crushed the old tradition of sincere friendship, a friendship which had its heroic history, its moral laws and rules. We shall not forget Danka Košanová,[10] whom they murdered, nor the dozens of other victims who were criminally slain. We shall not forget that they even ordered us to wash the blood off the paving, to level the grave mounds, and to blot out signs. These are crimes and wrongs which are not subject to historical re-habilitation...breach of faith, aggression, invasion, treason, the criminal killing of innocent people, etc. I believe that we must make the greatest possible effort to preserve the continuity of the post-January policies of the Dubček leadership, of the concept of democratic socialism. At the same time we see with despair that it was precisely for this that we have now become the subject of power politics, because of an idea that frightened them more than anything in the world.

Roman Kaliský[11] wrote:

> We are an occupied country. We are alone. We have sobered up from our last illusions. We are an occupied country despite the fact that after the 'negotiations' in Moscow the leading

[9] Števček was dismissed from his post in 1965. In August 1968 he became a member of the Central Committee of the Slovak Communist Party; in April 1970 he lost his Party membership.

[10] A seventeen-year-old girl who was killed by the Russians on the steps leading to the Comenius University in Bratislava.

[11] A well-known journalist, formerly on the staff of *Kultúrny Život*. From 1967 he worked in Slovak television until his dismissal in October 1968.

representatives of the CPCz and of the Slovak CP speak of the situation which has arisen purely as a result of the arrival of the Warsaw Pact armies on our territory. When my neighbour forces my door in the middle of the night, turns my home into a shambles and kills my children, a local reporter may write about an 'unexpected visit by a neighbour', but this does not change the facts. Forcing an entry will still be forcing an entry, and murder will still be murder. There are no people who perished due to an unfortunate accident during the invasion, there are no people who were killed in action, there are only fellow citizens who were murdered. Because those who respond with deadly fire to bare hands raised against tanks and to stones thrown at armour are guilty of murder. Not only from the moral, but also from the legal aspect. Even if there were ten instead of one Slavín[12] with the graves of Soviet soldiers who died in the Second World War, this could not undo a single murder. . .

We are being asked to keep calm and to judge the situation coolly and soberly. All right, let us talk about the situation which has arisen and not about the occupation. Only this situation has not arisen. Atmospheric disturbances or earthquakes occur. The situation in which we find ourselves was created by the USSR with the aid of other 'allied countries' and their armies. And we are supposed to normalize this situation. This is really too much to ask of us. There can be only one normalization that can be real: the withdrawal to the last man of foreign troops. Any other normalization would be illusory, camouflage.

The leadership of the CPCz and the government may become reconciled with the Moscow 'Accord', particularly if forced to do so, and do all they can in the context of what they promised or of what they are permitted to do. The nation need not, must not become reconciled. This may and will produce tension between the people and those representatives for whom this people went with bare hands against tanks and machine guns. Let us hope that this tension will be at least a moral corrective of government policies; that the government will realize the limits beyond which it must not go, and beyond which it must not retreat, whatever the cost, whatever the consequences.

We have sobered up from our lost illusions: we have freed ourselves from the illusions of alliance, fraternal and internationalist ties, and from Slavophile illusions. We have come

12 A cemetery on a hill overlooking Bratislava, where there are several hundred graves of Russian soldiers killed during the liberation of Slovakia.

to know from our personal experience whom these slogans serve when they are needed for the promotion of great-power interests through brute force.

Milan Hamada[13] answered the question thus:

> I am afraid that time is not only working for us, but also against us. I am afraid that in addition to the politician who begins to forget his own human dignity and the human dignity of those whom he leads, there has already appeared the politician who literally exploits the existing situation with professional detachment...There are times when we must not ask for something which we have the right to demand at once...We are now wont to emphasize the importance of cold reason. As a writer, it is my experience that a literary work which is merely the product of cold and rational calculation is devoid of life. It seems to me that this applies to any human work, including a political action...yet let us remember that what is left to us of those things which we can regard as our own and which bear the stamp of social and human independence and sovereignty is the independence and sovereignty of spirit. We must never give up this independence and sovereignity of spirit for anything, not even to make a quick profit. For if we violated our spiritual sovereignty there would be nothing left that could confirm our human dignity and our truth.

On the other hand Štefan Drug: a Marxist literary critic who changed from being an earlier supporter of Stalinism in Slovakia to a devoted liberal in the late Sixties believed that 'reason and sober deliberation are our only effective allies this time too'. But to avoid being misunderstood as having accepted Husák's advice, Drug continued:

> This does not mean that we have to bow in despair and defeatism, nor does this mean that we have to wait in passivity and inactive silence. Let us try to preserve – with all our strength and under any circumstances – the unique and astounding unity of all sections of our two nations, of the people and of the government, demonstrated in the past few days.

At least some of the Czechoslovak political leaders, certainly Alexander Dubček and at that time President Ludvík Svoboda,

---

[13] A young literary critic known for his brilliant essays in the 1960s condemning official 'socialist realism'.

shared the feelings of the writers. The very fact that Brezhnev did not insist on Dubček's resignation and gave up the attempt to establish a workers' and peasants' government, which was one of the variants he had in mind if the present Czechoslovak leaders refused to sign the Moscow protocol, was a slight comfort in the uncertain atmosphere of those days. But Brezhnev had scored a victory in getting Dubček and Svoboda to agree to explain to their people that the presence of the fraternal troops, was, if not actually necessary or welcome, at least inevitable, in view of the situation which was said to be only temporary. When Dubček came back from Moscow, he genuinely believed he would be able to save something of the post-January policy, as incorporated in the Action Programme.

Inevitably, after the first weeks of hatred and bitterness, the mood in Czechoslovakia became calmer. Despite the presence of foreign troops things did not look as bad as they had done during and immediately after the invasion. The mass media continued to express support for the principles of the Action Programme. The personnel changes in Prague radio and television affected only the highest posts. For the time being the Soviet and the Czechoslovak leaders were satisfied by the absence of open anti-Soviet propaganda and the avoidance of the words 'invasion' and 'occupation' when alluding to the arrival and presence of the Warsaw Pact troops. There were few signs of open collaboration with the invaders. In Prague *Literární Listy* was still being published. *Reportér* and *Politika* were banned for a short time; but when they came out again, they made little attempt to be more cautious.

In Slovakia, Dr Husák, as First Secretary of the Slovak Communist Party, soon revealed his true intentions. Knowing the attitude of writers and journalists towards him he banned the publication of *Kultúrny Život* for an indefinite period. He suggested that the Slovak Writers' Union should found a new weekly with a new editor and without most of the existing members of the editorial staff. Husák maintained that these measures were necessary, although he stressed that the situation in Slovakia was different from that in the Czech lands where the rot of right-wing opportunism and revisionism was much more widespread. In fact there was little difference, except in the methods used by Husák in Bratislava and Dubček in Prague. At this stage, however, even Husák's measures were relatively mild.

Husák now concentrated on the final implementation of the federal arrangement as promised by the Action Programme. He insisted that the Czechoslovak Federal Republic be proclaimed on the fiftieth anniversary of the foundation of the first Republic on 28 October 1968. He must have known that Brezhnev would not object to this. It is probable that he had secured a promise that there would be no interference with the introduction of a federal constitution. It was a cheap price for the Soviet Union to pay – it was the price for Husák's services (the persuasion of the Slovak people that it was to their advantage to be on good terms with their Soviet ally). But when the solemn occasion took place, and the highest representatives of the Czechoslovak Communist Party and the government, Dubček, Svoboda, Černík, Smrkovský and Husák, gathered in Bratislava Castle to proclaim the Federal State which was to be effective from 1 January 1969, although the population of Bratislava and the Slovak people did not resent this move, they were far from jubilant. There were no big celebrations, no marches, and the mood was not festive. The Slovaks had misgivings about the conditions under which the recognition of their nationhood had been achieved. They suspected that it was not an achievement at all – only a present conferred on them by a foreign intruder in return for their good behaviour.

22 THE FEDERAL REPUBLIC

The constitutional law introduced on 28 October 1968 brought fundamental changes to the sections of the Constitution dealing with the status of Slovakia. The new Czechoslovak federation was to consist of two national states enjoying equal rights: the Czech Socialist Republic and the Slovak Socialist Republic. Both renounced a part of their sovereignty to the common federal state, but as the new constitutional law laid down: 'the sovereignty of the federal state does not absorb the sovereignty of the national states. Both sovereignties exist and function in parallel.'[1] This principle is spelled out with great emphasis. It permeates the whole text, as does the principle that the new arrangement 'is based on Czechoslovak conditions which are being fully respected, its specific feature being that it consists of two national members of equal status and rights'. On the economic side 'it is the task of the national organs to safeguard the optimal development of the national economies'. They are responsible for economic planning, for the administration of national budgets; they supervise the control and use of national wealth and 'are responsible for all activities in connection with the national economy as far as they are not by law (with safeguards against outvoting) transferred to the federal organs'. The main function of the latter 'is to influence the principles which determine the division of the social product and of the national income, to develop economic relations with other countries, and to safeguard the principle of equalization of both national economies by creating equal conditions and opportunities for them'. The federal organs are to support 'progressive forms of integration of enterprises of both national regions under conditions of a unified market and a unified monetary system'. A common price policy is necessary in a unified market. It is the duty of the federal organs to create a unified wage and labour policy, and a common policy on social security for the whole state.

In foreign trade it is necessary 'in the interest of a favourable participation in the international division of labour to ensure a

[1] This and the following passages of the constitutional law of 28 October 1968 are quoted from *Pravda* (daily), Bratislava, 29 October 1968, no. 267.

unified policy', although the new constitution abolished the administrative monopoly of various foreign trade enterprises.

The section on federal and national organs does not mention the
principle of the division of powers between the legislative, the executive and the judiciary. It stresses instead that 'the power of the
federal organs is complete only in connection with the competence
of the national organs'.

The highest organ of state power, and the only legislative body
in the Federation, is the Federal Assembly, which consists of two
Houses: the Chamber of the People and the Chamber of Nations.
Both are equal in status. The consent of both is required in order
to pass federal laws. Each Chamber votes separately on a simple
majority principle. But on constitutional issues a majority of three-
fifths is required in the Chamber of the People. On such issues the
Chamber of Nations has to have a majority of three-fifths of the
Czech deputies and three-fifths of the Slovak deputies, an arrangement designed to eliminate the possibility of one national group
outvoting the other. Therefore on constitutional issues in the
Chamber of Nations, in which both the Czechs and Slovaks are
represented equally (a subsequent law stipulated that each should
have 75 deputies), the national groups vote separately. Thus any
changes affecting the constitutional status of the Czechs and the
Slovaks can be made only with the agreement of a three-fifths
majority of both national groups. This measure was intended to protect the rights of the Slovaks, who in the Chamber of the People,
consisting of 300 deputies, are in a minority of about one-third.

In the federal government, jobs are to be allocated according to
the principle of democratic proportional representation of both parts
of the Federation. 'This should determine the number of Ministers
and the importance of individual government departments. Each
Minister is to have as his deputy a State Secretary who is a full
member of the government. In principle, when the Minister is a
citizen of one national state the State Secretary will be a citizen of
the other.'

The special law implementing the constitutional changes introduced two kinds of federal government bodies: Ministries and
Federal Boards. Only in the Ministries were there State Secretaries.
The federal Ministries, such as those of Foreign Affairs, of Defence,
of the Interior, of Planning, of Finance, of Foreign Trade, of Labour
and Social Affairs, were larger government departments because
their competence was of a state-wide, federal character in matters
where the integrating element was more important than the national

one. To begin with there was no agreement on the necessity of having a federal ministry of the Interior, but in the end, when problems of internal security became pressing, it was agreed that besides national ministries of the interior, there should also be a federal one.

The Federal Boards, whose main function was to coordinate the work of various national ministries, were to be the following: the Price Board, the Board for Technical Development and Construction, the Board for Industry, the Board for Agriculture, the Board for Transport, the Board for Post and Telecommunications, and the Board for Press and Information. At first it was proposed that justice and education were to be the sole responsibility of the national ministries, but this experiment in independence was considered too risky and Federal Boards of Justice and Education were set up in the same way as for other national Ministries.

In addition to Federal Ministries and Boards, various other federal bodies were to be set up, such as: the Federal Office of Statistics, the Office for the Administration of Federal Material Reserves, the Office for Patents and Inventions, the Federal State Bank, and the Supreme Federal Court and the Military Court of Justice.

The national bodies were to be: the Czech and the Slovak National Councils, the governments of the Czech and Slovak Socialist Republics, the Slovak and Czech Supreme Courts and the Office of the Prosecutor General. The federal constitution was to become valid on 1 January 1969; in the meantime all the special laws and by-laws implementing the constitutional change were to be prepared and passed.

In the final section of the constitutional law full tribute was paid to the Action Programme of April 1968. Most of its proposals for state federalization had been incorporated into the new Constitution. But the Action Programme had stated expressly that federalization would affect the Party as well as the State. After referring to 'a constitutional arrangement of relations between our two nations that will fully express and guarantee their equality and right of self-deternmination', it specified that 'the same principles shall be applied to the pattern of the Party and social organizations'. In a country in which real power is vested in the Party and not in the Government, the federalization of the Party was a matter of the utmost importance. When it became clear that in Dubček's Czechoslovakia this situation might be changed and the power of the government strengthened, the fraternal socialist armies intervened to prevent the implementation of such a dangerous idea. In addition, federalization of the Party on the same principle as that of the state would have weakened the position of the Party by shaking its very foundation, that of democratic centralism. So that no doubt should remain, Oldřich Černík, the Prime Minister, introducing the constitutional law in the National Assembly on 27 October, enumerated the 'factors which would make for the cohesion of the Federation, and the firmness of the unity of our nations'. The very first factor he stressed was 'the unified political system exercised through the leading role of the Communist Party of Czechoslovakia'.[2] In other words: federalism in government, but centralism in the Party. The Action Programme was to be accepted, in so far as it concerned the federalization of the State, but rejected in so far as it proposed the federalization of the Party.

Husák, who had previously been prominent in the battle against 'asymmetry' in state and Party structure, now seemed reluctant to press the Czech Communists to set up their own Central Committee. He was quite satisfied with having achieved 'symmetry' between the Czech and Slovak governments, and between the National Councils. He was now willing to tolerate a far more important asymmetry, i.e. that in the structure of the Party. The setting up of the so-called 'Bureau for the Administration of Party Affairs in the Czech Socialist Republic' was an unsatisfactory substitute for a Czech Party with its own Central Committee. A more important factor was that it satisfied the Soviet Union and its few reliable friends in Czechoslovakia. It met their demands; the Party was left intact. Although Dubček was deeply reluctant to give in to any of Brezhnev's demands, he had to give way on this most fundamental point – a firmly centralist Party which would tolerate no experiments in pluralism or federalism. Husák preferred the excuse that the Central Committee of the Party could not make such a change: only the Party Congress could. The officially recognized Fourteenth Party Congress, which was supposed to have been held on 9 September 1968, had been postponed until 1971.[3]

If 'legal' means could be found, as in fact they were, to create from scratch a Czech National Council where none had existed before, and a second Chamber of Nations where none had existed

[2] *Práca* (daily), Bratislava, 27 October 1968.
[3] It was opened on 25 May 1971. It decided against federalization of the Party, underlined the federal against the national principle in the State structure. It abolished the Action Programme of 1968 as a revisionist and counter-revolutionary document. Dr Husák, who was reelected First Secretary of Czechoslovak Communist Party, thanked the Soviet Union and other allies for intervening in August 1968, 'for the brotherly help which they rendered us.'

before, all without any elections, but by various nominations, man-
ipulations and personal changes, and even fundamental changes in
the constitution, surely if it were really the wish of the Praesidium
of the Party and of the First Secretary, federalization of the Party
could have been carried out even without a Party Congress.

The federal arrangement implemented on 1 January 1969 had seemed
to provide a framework in which both Czechs and Slovaks could
have lived their own national lives within a common state. The
Slovaks, being the smaller of the two nations, were more acutely
aware of the need for a change in their constitutional position.
Federation could have offered the most suitable solution to the problems of these Slav neighbours who, in the course of recent history,
had been brought even closer together than in the past. With the
exception of the interlude during the Second World War, when
Hitler gave the Slovaks formal but not actual independence, few
have questioned not only the reality but also the desirability of a
common state with the Czechs.

The Slovaks deplored the tragic circumstances under which they
had achieved their cherished goal, and they were fully aware that
federalization of the Party was at least as important as, if not more
important than, federalization of the State; that without the former
the latter was in practice likely to be something of a sham. Nevertheless, it is safe to assume that they welcomed their position in the
federation. The Czechs also learned to adapt themselves to the new
situation. The new arrangement was expected to lessen the tension
between the two nations.

In fact, a marked improvement did take place – but only as a
result of the invasion and the continued foreign occupation. Their
common resentment of the invaders united the Czechs and Slovaks
far more than the new constitution. The natural response to the
danger so acutely felt by both peoples has now changed into a
feeling of frustration and misery. This has been created by the loss
of both nations' national independence. The truth of the matter is
that Brezhnev and his men in Czechoslovakia did not succeed in
exploiting Slovak – Czech political and national differences for their
own purposes.

Although the political mood in Slovakia was little different from
that in the Czech lands, Dr Husák claimed that the Slovaks were on
the whole ready to listen to reason and agreed with his policy. Un-
doubtedly Husák's tactics went down relatively well with the Slovak
'new class' of Party and state bureaucrats, which, despite previous
attempts to curtail Slovak national rights, had emerged during the
two decades of Communist rule. It was a social group of considerable
strength and influence. Despite the unsatisfactory constitutional
position of Slovakia, most of the important posts in the Party, in the
state administration and in the growing nationalized industries, were
held by Slovaks. As in the Czech lands during the first years of
Communist rule, it was often the men without any formal university
education, and in some cases those who had not even finished
their secondary education, who were recommended by the Party
and nominated to university posts. This happened particularly in
the departments of political and social science established in each
faculty in all institutes of higher education. By the late Fifties however most of the leading posts had been taken over by educated men
and women from the various universities, schools of technology and
from the Central Party School in Bratislava which had a quasi-
university status. Almost all of them became staunch supporters
of Dubček when they realized that his programme was genuinely
anti-centralist.

However, when Dubček, as the new First Secretary of the Party
in Prague, became more concerned with a movement of general reform, the nationalist-minded section of the Slovak new class looked
for leadership to those Slovak politicians who gave priority to the
nationalist content of the post-January political developments. Husák
became their natural leader. The old Party official, Bil'ak, saw that
Husák was once more becoming a prominent figure, and so he tried
to save his own position by adhering to an even more nationalistic
programme. But, discredited by his Stalinist past, Bil'ak's sudden
conversion did not impress anybody. He had no support amongst
the people and, what is more important in a Communist country
for a man with political ambitions, he was not now supported by the

Slovak new class. After the invasion, it had become evident that Dubček had no political future since he had lost the confidence of the Soviet leaders and the new class in Slovakia had opted for Husák.

In a nation which within the lifetime of one single generation has witnessed so many changes of régime, the new class follows shifts in the personal fortunes of political leaders with particular interest. When, at the end of August 1968, Husák became First Secretary of the Slovak Communist Party, and when, in April 1969, he replaced Dubček as First Secretary of the Czechoslovak Party, he knew that he could rely on that social group in Slovakia and on their counterpart in the Czech lands. It was significant that diehard dogmatists like Kapek, Kolder, Švestka and other former Novotnýites praised Husák as early as the November 1968 plenum of the Czechoslovak Central Committee, when Dubček was still First Secretary. At this plenary session it became clear that the reform movement was going to be reversed. The Russians were at last getting their way. They were achieving much more than they had done immediately after the invasion. Then all they had obtained was Kriegel's removal from the Praesidium of the Party and that of Pelikán and Hejzlar as General Directors of Television and Radio respectively. It was obvious that they had not brought hundreds of thousands of troops to Czechoslovakia merely to get rid of these three men and it was also obvious that they had no intention of allowing Dubček's proposed reforms to go ahead.

For the time being they left Dubček, Smrkovský, Černík and, of course, President Svoboda, in office.[1] If the Soviet leaders had behaved rashly when they gave the orders for the invasion of Czechoslovakia, when the brisk military operation was marked by a total absence of political subtlety, after the invasion they had the wisdom not to push things too far or too fast. They even allowed the leaders of the Czech and Slovak 'counter-revolutionaries' to return to their posts. It was an astute move which the country accepted with relief. In the first few weeks the Soviet leaders did not press Dubček too hard to renounce his reform programme. From their point of view it did not matter whether all the sections of the Action Programme were revoked in a few months or in a few weeks. It is evident now that Dubček did his best to retreat in the slowest possible manner, but

---

[1] By 1971 all the leaders of the Czechoslovak spring except Svoboda who obviously changed his views, were expelled from the Party. It can be assumed that all of them – again with the exception of Svoboda – would have suffered the same fate even had they shown willingness to collaborate with the Russians unreservedly, which some of them attempted, e.g. Černik.

after his involuntary visit to Moscow during the invasion he knew that retreat was inevitable, and this became obvious at the November session of the Communist Party Central Committee. *The Times* correspondent wrote: 'The final resolution adopted by the CPCz Central Committee...makes dismal reading. It is humbly self-critical in tone and in places, contradictory, reflecting the deep divisions of opinion within the Committee itself.'[2] The correspondent considered as most disturbing the statement in the resolution that the press, radio and television must be regarded primarily as instruments for the implementation of state and Party policy. Those parts of the resolution which blamed right-wing forces and opportunistic tendencies in the post-January developments for everything that had gone wrong were equally ominous. The resolution complained that the Party and state apparatus and bodies of power, particularly those of the security forces and the judiciary, were unduly blamed for the mistakes of the Fifties; and it condemned attempts to discredit honest comrades because of their open internationalist relationship with the Soviet Union.

Nevertheless, despite its sombre tone, the November resolution was not a total retreat from the Action Programme; this is shown by the promise to continue the rehabilitation of citizens unjustly persecuted in the past. It praised the recently enacted federalization law, and professed willingness to continue economic reform. Šik himself was not yet openly criticized, but the November resolution spoke already of reforms which would be characterized by central planning rather than by flexible management. In addition to Dubček, most of the reformers such as Smrkovský, Černík, Císař, and Špaček kept their Party and government offices. At that stage it seemed that the Russians wanted them to stay and undo themselves the things which they had done. Thus they would discredit themselves in the eyes of the people who had identified them with the much-cherished reforms. This, if accepted as the only explanation, would present an oversimplified version of the matter, but as a single factor it seems to be the nearest to the truth.

Dubček must have been fully aware of the Russian attitude to him, but he seemed not to be too eager to make way for men whom the Russians did trust. It was an almost schizophrenic situation. Rumours circulated in Party circles that Dubček had actually expressed his intention to resign because he realized that in the end the Russians would not let him continue with his

2 Michael Hornsby, 'Prague's Dispiriting Retreat', *The Times*, 20 November 1968.

progressive policies. But he was persuaded to stay on, and it seems that the Russians were among the most insistent persuaders. Dubček had not discredited himself sufficiently; he had not renounced his programme and the Russians had not yet found a suitable successor. Therefore Brezhnev and his trusted men in the Czechoslovak Praesidium awaited an opportune moment to remove Dubček – by letting him resign. They knew that he was still the respected and loved leader of his country. This was shown by the public-opinion polls which were still conducted, despite Soviet disapproval of this subversive type of sociological research. Dubček consistently came first in popularity, always by more than 90 per cent, followed by Smrkovský, Svoboda and Černík. Husák must have been deeply hurt, for a few weeks before he became Dubček's successor in Prague he appeared at the bottom of the list in an opinion-poll held in his native Slovakia. He received only 23 per cent support. Husák's lack of popularity did not appear to worry the Russians. After all, the Soviet Party leaders' positions are based on more solid and tangible factors. Nevertheless, Husák could not feel comfortable in view of Dubček's popularity. At this stage he coveted not so much his post as First Secretary of the Party as his place in the hearts of the Czech and Slovak people.

However, the reactionaries (either on their own account, or at the promptings of Brezhnev and his representative in Czechoslovakia, the Soviet Ambassador, Chervonenko) felt that things were not moving in their direction. Husák was willing to come to their aid and to use all his rhetorical skill to put forward their point of view, however unpopular. Indeed he tried to present himself as a kind of martyr who was expected to sacrifice his own popularity for the sake of a reasonable and necessary settlement, which naïve people, misled by opportunist politicians, were unwilling to accept. Such had been the case when in August 1968 the Soviet leaders demanded to have the extraordinary Fourteenth Congress of the Czechoslovak Communist Party declared invalid. Husák accepted the task of executing the will of the occupying powers. He maintained that the Vysočany Congress could not be valid because the Slovak delegates had not attended it.

Another opportunity came for Husák at the end of 1968 when Brezhnev decided that the time was ripe to settle accounts with Smrkovský, the old rebel who had been in trouble with Gottwald and Stalin and had spent many years in prison. He was perhaps the most radical leader of the reform movement. He was a Communist with a genuine working-class background. Under Dubček he had

become Chairman of the National Assembly and, what was even
more important, a member of the Praesidium of the Party. Now the
conservatives considered it imperative to deprive him of both
functions. This was particularly urgent because, on 1 January 1969,
when the new Federal Assembly was to be convened, he was likely
to be voted its Chairman. This was an awkward situation for the
Russians. Husák offered to find a plausible solution to the problem.
He argued that in the new federal structure it would not be politically expedient for the three highest offices of the state, that of the
President of the Republic, the Prime Minister and the Chairman of
the Federal Assembly all to be held by Czechs. He omitted to
mention the fact that the post of First Secretary of the Czechoslovak
Communist Party, which was more important than the three state
offices put together, was held by a Slovak – Alexander Dubček.
Husák insisted that the Chairman of the Federal Assembly should
be a Slovak. He declared that he had nothing against Smrkovský,
personally or politically. Meanwhile the trade union protest grew,
even threatening strike action if Smrkovský lost his posts in the
Assembly and in the Party.

In the end Smrkovský himself fell into the trap and accepted
Husák's argument. He made public statements to the effect that
he was sorry he had become the centre of a political crisis. He
almost begged to be allowed to step down to the less important job
of Chairman of one of the Houses of the Federal Assembly, the
Chamber of the People, and in this capacity to be Vice-Chairman
of the Assembly. On 1 January 1969 the Slovak Dr Peter Colotka
became Chairman of the Federal Assembly instead of Smrkovský. In
April 1969, at the time when Husák replaced Dubček, Smrkovský
was removed from the Party Praesidium and soon after that he lost
his membership of the Central Committee. He was expelled from
the Party during the purges early in 1970, by which time it was
considered completely irrelevant whether he was a Czech or a Slovak.
This had merely served as a convenient pretext for the gradual removal of a dangerous man.

Husák's behaviour in the Smrkovský affair did not impress most
Slovaks, though his views were intended to appeal to their
national sentiment. In the midst of the crisis which arose over
Smrkovský's future in politics, a conference of Slovak writers was
held in Bratislava in December 1968. The majority of the delegates
expressed views supporting Dubček's socialism, despite the efforts
of a few followers of Husák among the writers, such as Novomeský,
Válek, Mináč and Mihálik. The conference declared its firm support

for the post-January movement. The Slovak writers wanted to continue the drive for socialism with a human face in spite of the prolonged presence of the occupation forces. The conference resolution demanded that pressure be brought to bear on the leadership of the Slovak Communist Party, in other words on Husák, and requested the removal of all obstacles to the reform movement. The conference even approved of strikes and demonstrations with this aim. Some writers wanted their Union to become a second political centre for the Slovak intellectuals, which would concentrate and coordinate their efforts to achieve a better and more democratic cultural and national policy. There was a strong appeal that they should join forces with the Czech intellectuals and another speaker claimed that it would be much better for the new Writers' Union weekly if the members of the editorial board were not bound by Party discipline.[3]

Not until April 1970 did the Praesidium of the Slovak Writers' Union issue a statement condemning the December 1968 conference and denouncing the resolution and speeches. It repudiated in particular that passage in the resolution which referred to the Soviet Union as a prison of nations, and to politicians 'who no longer called a crime a crime'.[4] This was an allusion to Husák, who, unlike the Praesidium of the Party, which on 21 August had condemned the invasion as an act contrary 'to the fundamental principles of relations between socialist states' and 'a denial of fundamental norms of international law',[5] constantly referred to it in more euphemistic terms. Shortly after his election to the post of First Secretary of the Czechoslovak Communist Party in April he described the occupation of his country as an act of international solidarity. The Czech and Slovak people should be grateful to their socialist allies, especially to the Soviet Union, who came to save them from the horrors of counter-revolution.

[3] The new weekly was to replace *Kultúrny Život* which Husák banned in September 1968. It was supposed to appear on 1 January under the title *Literárny Život*. The first number came out a few weeks later but its publication was then stopped by the new Slovak Ministry of Culture, this being one of the first acts in the cultural sphere of the autonomous Slovak government established under the federal constitution. In Prague *Literární Listy* continued to be published until April 1969 when Husák's arrival there also brought about its demise.

[4] Passages from the resolution and references to individual speeches are quoted from *Nové Slovo* (weekly), Bratislava, 16 April 1970, which also published the statement of the new Praesidium of the Slovak Writers' Union denouncing the conference.

[5] Philip Windsor and Adam Roberts, *Czechoslovakia 1968*, Appendix V, pp. 174–5.

In the period when the press, although enjoying a certain degree of freedom, was silenced more in Slovakia than in the Czech lands, Slovak progressive articles were welcome in the Czech press. Thus the Praesidium of the Slovak Writers' Union, unable to publish its letter to Černík, who had become Prime Minister of the federal government on 1 January 1969, sent it to *Literární Listy* in Prague.[6] The Praesidium of the Slovak Writers' Union wrote that they

> had never permitted themselves any doubts. . .that the purpose of artistic creation was to fight for a humane form of socialism in Czechoslovakia, for the implementation of democratic laws and norms in our country on the basis of voluntary discipline and service to our nation. This, the fundamental ethical attitude of the Czech and Slovak nations, which came to fruition in January and in August of the tragically magnificent year 1968, will be deepened by our work together with our peoples and our governments. This attitude we shall never abandon.[7]

When the Czech student Jan Palach burned himself to death on 16 January 1969 he also kindled a flame in the consciences of the Czech and Slovak people and indeed the peoples of the whole world. The Slovaks cried out in anger and despair just as did their Czech brethren. The Bratislava daily *Práca* wrote:

> Those flames have reached out to us, they have burned us too and will continue to burn for a long time. It is not difficult to share the feelings and thoughts of that young man who committed such an awful and desperate action. Extreme solutions are sought and found only in extreme situations when the tortured soul sees no other way of saving itself.[8]

In the crisis that followed, the party leaders and Dubček himself made every effort to calm the disturbed emotions of the population. Husák tried to present the tragedy of Palach as a solely Czech affair, which did not concern the Slovaks. A group of prominent Slovak writers wrote to their Czech colleagues:

> We are writing to you, dear friends, at this hour, to demonstrate that we are. . .bound to you by more than ephemeral ties. We are united with you by destiny. . .We want you to know that no administrative measures such as those which have prevented us Slovak writers from publishing our own periodical, nor traditional barriers. . .can isolate us from you Czech

[6] *Literární Listy*, 16 January 1969.   [7] *Ibid*.
[8] *Práca*. Bratislava, 21 January 1969.

intellectuals who have refused to reconcile yourselves to limitations of the citizen's democratic rights, who have confronted the uninvited power, and those who have capitulated to it, with the unbreakable strength of spirit which derives from the greatness of culture, from national and revolutionary traditions...There is no need to preach to us constantly where our country lies on the map of the world. Who in this country is not aware that Czechoslovak sovereignty must take into account existing natural conditions, under which our nations have lived and will live for ages? Who does not know at the same time that in addition to those conditions there are limitations imposed on our nations against the will of every patriot? Only men who care merely for their own personal power...can agree with those limitations...In this sad situation it is necessary to reject Czech chauvinism and Slovak nationalism, because they isolate Slovak progressives from Czech progressives. All attempts to divide us by nationalist, social, religious or anti-semitic demagogy must be rejected. Whom could they serve? Only those who are willing to resign themselves to be the only proprietors of the country and of its history...This is not everything we want to tell you. We do not want to reiterate opinions which are well known; together with you we do not rely on providence, but on the independent and proud attitude of our nations, on our people's sense of liberty, truth and justice.[9]

In a postscript to this letter it is mentioned that it was written as a spontaneous response to doubts which had been expressed concerning the attitude of the Slovak public to the events following Palach's death. Because of limited time it was not possible to circulate the letter for signature by all Slovak writers. It could only be signed by those working in the Institute of Slovak Literature attached to the Slovak Academy of Sciences, and by those members of the Praesidium of the Slovak Writers' Union who were present at the time. The same issue of *Literární Listy* published a letter written by Slovak students, because, as its authors stated, it could not be published in any Slovak periodical. They wrote about Palach: 'His death is the responsibility of those who have brought our nation into a situation in which people are forced to take such desperate actions of resistance'.[10]

Another group of nineteen Slovak students went on hunger strike; they wrote: 'This act has marked an absolute frontier, an absolute

---

[9] *Literární Listy*, 30 January 1969.   [10] *Ibid.*

value in the face of which all reality crumbles – here, I stand, my whole personality, my hands, my lungs, my eyes, my burning body, I, a living man, I cry NO in the face of the inhuman reality which burns up the truth, and I cry that it is necessary to begin again from a human reality'.[11]

Professor Miroslav Kusý was dismissed from his post as head of the ideological department of the Party for expressing his democratic views in the Slovak mass media (amongst others, an interview in the trade union daily *Práca* on the dangers of Czechoslovakia once more becoming a police state, which was probably the immediate reason for his dismissal). In March 1969 he wrote in the Czech Party weekly, *Politika:*

> Federalization, in spite of all its advantages, contains within itself the danger that there will develop two different republics in Czechoslovakia – one more or less democratic and the other more or less totalitarian: that a policy of the tough hand will operate in the latter in the same way as before January 1968. Only it will no longer be the tough hand of Novotný[12]

Voices like these were more representative of the mood in Slovakia than any speeches made by Husák, or Bil'ak or, for that matter, any politician.

At the end of March 1969 a new crisis arose on the night when the Czechoslovak ice-hockey team won in a match against the Russians in the world ice-hockey championship in Stockholm. Disorders broke out during which the Prague office of the Soviet airline, Aeroflot, was set on fire. (This could have been caused either by an excess of enthusiasm, or by the action of agents provocateurs, or both.) These events provided the conservatives with a good excuse for launching an open attack on Dubček. They accused him of being unwilling or unable to suppress the 'right-wing counter-revolutionaries'. It looked as if Dubček's days were now really numbered.

On 11 April, at the centre of the political storm, Dr Husák spoke at a meeting in Nitra. Describing the Dubček era of 1968, he said:

> Our society was undermined and disintegrated. Various hostile and, let me say, anti-socialist, forces gained influence in our country, as we now see. The foundations of our society were shaken; political power in the hands of the working people was weakened. Anti-social and opportunist forces strove to crush and

[11] *Ibid.*
[12] Michael Hornsby, 'Warning of totalitarian Slovakia', *The Times*, 21 March 1969.

destroy the political power of the working people in this state, to undermine the leading role of the Party, the power of the state apparatus, to wreck the unity of the working people, to divide the working class and the peasantry so that their immense combined power, which is of such importance to our state, would be unabe to assert itself...We have no need of élites who despise the working man; what we need are millions of working people who really feel that they are the masters in this state, that they are free men, and we want them to know how to do away with disrupters.[13]

A few days later, at a meeting of the CPCz Central Committee on 17 April 1969, the former lawyer, Dr Gustav Husák, replaced the former worker, Alexander Dubček, as First Secretary of the Czechoslovak Communist Party. The worker Dubček had led the Slovaks and Czechs into a movement which was to make an end to, among other things, the old rhetoric about the power of the working class. The intellectual Husák reverted to a policy which preached antagonism to the élite, just as Novotný had done. The Dubček era was finally at an end.

[13] *Pravda* (daily), Bratislava, 12 April 1969.

24 EPILOGUE

Husák, who had suffered long years of imprisonment for his Slovak patriotic views, now volunteered to work for a power which still considers nationalism within its own boundaries as a political deviation and a criminal offence. Under the circumstances, what Husák was doing, whether willingly or under pressure from the Russians, was not just a personal tragedy. It was a strange instance of the irony of fate. Brezhnev displayed a crude sense of humour when in October 1969 he made Husák sign a common Czechoslovak–Soviet statement. This was after the first official Party and state visit in Moscow which was supposed to mark the final act of reconciliation. Both sides considered it to be 'their most important duty to strengthen Marxist–Leninist ideology, and to defend socialist democracy'. This aim seemed innocent enough in itself were it not for the ominous-sounding affirmation that 'this must be carried out in a bitter and continuous struggle against anti-socialist views and concepts within the communist movement', naming in the first place bourgeois nationalism, followed by right and left-wing opportunism and revisionism.[1]

Husák is too experienced in the matter of political deviations not to have appreciated the significance of this emuneration of anti-socialist views. He must have noticed the stress on bourgeois nationalism, the very deviation to which he had confessed in 1949. When soon afterwards he was imprisoned, he stubbornly refused to accept this self-criticism as a justification for the accusations of criminal activities, including spying for the imperialist West and conspiring with Tito against the Soviet Union – levelled against him.

After becoming First Secretary of the CPCz in 1969, Husák frequently promised that the Party would never revert to the practices of the Fifties. It would not stage show trials. Husák could afford to offer such assurances because in the Soviet Union itself, after the death of Stalin and the dramatic removal of Beria and his most prominent underlings in State Security, show trials had become a thing of the past. Khrushchev had introduced a new method of

[1] The passages from the Czechoslovak–Soviet statement are quoted from *Smena* (daily), Bratislava, 29 October 1969.

liquidating political opponents, possibly quicker than Stalin's but also more humane; by sending them to remote places in the diplomatic service (as he did with Molotov), or to insignificant posts in industry (as he did with Kaganovich and Malenkov). Brezhnev too, allowed Krushchev to retire with a certain amount of dignity. Husák was actually faithfully following the example of the Soviet Union in dealing with his political opponents. But his removal of his opponents has been more drastic than was expected even by the most pessimistic observers of the Czechoslovak political scene.[2]

First of all he dealt with the so-called 'right-wing opportunists'; Dubček fairly soon emerged as their leader. At first Dubček was accused merely of having been misled by worse anti-socialist elements like Kriegel, Šik, Smrkovský, Císař and other counter-revolutionaries who allegedly wanted to abolish socialism and restore capitalism in Czechoslovakia.

Fairly soon after Dubček's removal in April 1969 the remarkable feature of Czechoslovakia was the total elimination from positions of influence of all those who in 1968, and indeed until the change of leadership in April 1969, had expressed any kind of progressive views, including those who had been rather prominent in stressing the national aspect of developments in Slovakia. Once again they had been labelled as bourgeois nationalists. Almost all the members of the new Central Committee elected at the Fourteenth Extraordinary Congress of the Slovak Communist Party on 26 August 1968 were replaced by obscure men, or by notorious ones whose main principle was collaboration with the invaders. The most infamous was Viliam Šalgovič, the Czechoslovak Deputy Minister of the Interior, who during the invasion had been willing to work for the KGB, in whose ranks he had been a major. In May 1970 Šalgovič became Chairman of the Auditing and Control Commission of the Slovak Communist Party, a post which he had previously held under Novotný. Vasil Bil'ak, who had not been elected to the Slovak

---

[2] True to the more up-to-date Soviet methods of silencing dissidents, Husák staged, in 1971 and 1972, trials against well-known intellectual supporters of Dubček and sentenced them to long terms of imprisonment. Vehemently, but rather unconvincingly, he argued that they were being prosecuted not for their political attitudes in 1968 but for their more recent subversive activities against the Socialist state. According to *Rudé Právo* (1 August 1972) they had 'spread distrust among leading state representatives, disturbed political consolidation and relations with the Soviet Union, and maintained contact with hostile emigré circles abroad'. Such words sound ominous and suggest even worse things to come for those who decline to follow the Soviet line, and perhaps even for Dubček himself who so far refused to confess to any anti-Party or anti-Soviet activities in 1968 and after.

Central Committee in August 1968, soon became Husák's most faithful assistant in carrying out the harsh Soviet demands.

The former Commissioners of the Slovak National Council were probably well pleased that from 1 January 1969 they held the official title of Ministers of the Slovak Government. The Slovak new class found no shortage of opportunities to assert itself. More now than under Novotný they managed to attain positions in the much-coveted diplomatic service. Oddly enough among them were some of the prominent Slovaks of the reform movement whom Husák, at least in 1969 and 1970, had managed to send abroad as Czechoslovak representatives. It was a convenient way of depriving them of political influence at home. In March 1970 Dubček himself was made Ambassador in Ankara; within three months he had lost this post, his Party membership, and all his functions in the Federal Assembly and the Slovak National Council. All the other reformers suffered similar fates.

On the first anniversary of the Federation the Deputy Prime Minister of the federal government in Prague, Dr Karol Laco, a former Professor of Law at the Comenius University in Bratislava, who had drafted the constitutional law on the Federation, could not conceal the difficulties which had arisen in implementing it. He complained that national elements were over-emphasized. He asked that the federal, centralist, integrationist principle should now be given more prominence. In an interview with the Czech daily *Mladá Fronta* and the Slovak daily *Práca*[2] he was hardly able to hide his embarrassment when he had to explain that one year after its introduction the office of State Secretaries in the Federal Ministries was going to be abolished. It was one of the principal clauses of the constitutional law that a Slovak should be deputy in those federal ministries which were headed by Czechs and *vice versa*. The reason Dr Laco gave was far from convincing. He said that the Federal Boards, which co-ordinated Czech and Slovak national ministries, would now become full Federal Ministries. Instead of functioning in a collective manner as committees, as they did in 1969, the Federal Boards now became central administrative offices. Dr. Laco argued that it would be inopportune to introduce State Secretaries into these new Federal Ministries because there would be too many of them. Instead it was found necessary to abolish the offices of State Secretaries even in those Federal Ministries in which they already functioned. This sudden change was the decision of the Czechoslovak Party

[3] *Mladá Fronta*, 28 February 1970; *Práca*, 3 and 4 March 1970.

Praesidium headed now by Husák. The clauses in the constitution which had been so carefully thought out in order to guard against the possibility of the Slovaks being outvoted in the two Chambers of the Federal Assembly, seemed now to be of little consequence.

In contrast in June 1969 there was a welcome reorganization of the State administration, but this was not echoed in the Party structure. The regions were abolished.[3] (Slovakia had had three such regions: West Slovakia, Central Slovakia and East Slovakia.) The smaller administrative units, the districts, now came directly under the jurisdiction of the Czech and Slovak Ministries of the Interior, and ultimately under the Federal Ministry of the Interior. However, the Party regions, which correspond to the former state administrative regions, have so far remained intact. They were and are an important link in the so-called democratic-centralist structure of the Party: in other words they are instruments of the prevailing centralist element as against the democratic one. The Czechoslovak Communist Party was to remain modelled on the Soviet pattern. That was one of the main purposes of the invasion.

Dubček refused, and Husák eventually agreed, to hail the invasion as a fraternal act of international solidarity to preserve socialist achievements in the interest of world Communism. Dubček maintained throughout that the Czechoslovak Party was strong enough to deal with any threats to socialism, suggesting that no such danger really existed. That was why eventually he had to go, although in August 1968 Brezhnev hoped that he would recant, admit his errors and that by doing so he would discredit himself in the eyes of his people. Instead, it was Husák who duly discredited himself in the eyes not only of Czech reformers, but also of Slovak patriots.

Where there is no political freedom for individuals there can be no freedom for nations. With the Czechs and Slovaks, whom the Russians came to save from their illusions of freedom, whether individual or national, the situation once again came to resemble that in the Soviet Union. The granting of national freedom to the Slovaks was to have been an integral part of a social system, of a society which was striving to achieve more individual freedom. That was the main aim of the Czech and Slovak Communist reformers. In that sense their efforts were revolutionary. They were dangerous to the so-called socialist world, dominated by the Soviet Union. The ideas of the Czechoslovak spring might easily have spread throughout the world even though that was not the intention of their

[4] On 1 January 1970 the regional structure in the state administration has been reintroduced.

originators. The real counter-revolutionaries were those who killed the Czechoslovak dream which for a moment held out the hope of becoming, although bloodless, perhaps the most radical, revolution of our time.

BIBLIOGRAPHY

Barto, Jaroslav, *Riešenie vzťahu Čechov a Slovákov, 1944–1948* (Solution of Relations between the Czechs and Slovaks, 1944–1948), Bratislava, 1968.

Beer, František, and others, *Dejinná križovatka* (On the Crossroads of History), Bratislava, 1964.

Beneš, Dr Eduard, *Memoirs: From Munich to the New War and Victory* (translation from the Czech), London, 1953.

Bertleff, Erich, *Mit blosen Händen: Der einsame Kampf der Tschechen und Slovaken 1968*, Wien, 1968.

Blažek, Miroslav, *Hospodársko-geografický přehled Československa* (The Economic-Geographical Survey of Czechoslovakia), Prague, 1963.

Bokes, Frantisek, *Dokumenty k slovenskému národnemu hnutiu v rokoch 1848–1914* (Documents on the Slovak National Movement in the Years 1848–1914), Bratislava, 1965.

Bušek, Vratislav, and Spulbeer, Nicholas, *Czechoslovakia*, New York, 1957.

Carsten, F. L., *Revolution in Central Europe 1918–1919*, London, 1971.

Chapman, Colin, *August 21st. The Rape of Czechoslovakia with on the spot Reports from Prague by Murray Sayle*, London, 1968.

The Czechoslovak Crisis 1968 (Proceedings of a Conference held by the Institute for the Study of International Organisation, University of Sussex), London, 1969.

Daix, Pierre, *Journal de Prague, Décembre 1967–Septembre 1968*, Paris, 1968.

Dubček, Alexander, *Komunisti a národné dedičstvo: Vybrané prejavy k otázkam národnej histórie* (The Communists and the National Heritage: Selected Speeches on the Question of Slovak National History), Introduction by Ondrej Klokoč, Bratislava, 1968.

Dubček, Alexander, *Dubček's Blueprint for Freedom: His Original Documents Leading to the Invasion of Czechoslovakia*, Profile by Hugh Lunghi; commentary by Paul Ello, London, 1969.

Falt'an, Samo, Slovenská otázka v Československu (The Slovak Question in Czechoslovakia), Bratislava, 1968.

Faltus, Josef, and Prucha, Václav, Prehl'ad hospodárskeho vývoja na Slovensku v rokoch 1918–1945 (Survey of Economic Development of Slovakia in the Years 1918–1945), Bratislava, 1969.

Feiwel, George R., New Economic Patterns in Czechoslovakia: Impact of Growth, Planning and Market, New York, 1968.

Gadourek, Ivan, The Political Control of Czechoslovakia, London, 1950.

Garaudy, Roger, La liberté en sursis: Prague 1968 avec des textes d'Alexandre Dubček, Paris, 1968.

Golan, Galia, The Czechoslovak Reform Movement, Cambridge, 1971.

Golan, Galia, Reform Rule in Czechoslovakia, Cambridge, 1972.

Goldman, Josef, and Kouba, Karel, Economic Growth in Czechoslovakia, Prague, 1969.

Gosiorovsky, Miloš, Dejiny slovenského robotníckeho hnutia: 1848–1918 (History of the Slovak Working Class Movement: 1848–1918), Bratislava, 1956.

Haufter, Stanislas, Changes in the Geographical Distribution of the Population in Czechoslovakia, Prague, 1968.

Hitchcock, Edward B., Beneš: The Man and the Statesman, London, 1948.

Husák, Gustáv, Svedecto o Slovenskom národnom povstaní (Testimony on the Slovak National Uprising), 2nd ed., Bratislava, 1969.

Jarošová, V., and Jaroš, O., Slovenské robotnícto v boji o moc (The Slovak Workers in their Fight for Power), Bratislava, 1965.

Josten, Josef, Oh, My Country, London, 1949.

Kennan, George Frost, From Prague after Munich: Diplomatic Papers 1938–1940, Princeton, 1968.

Kirschbaum, Josef M., Slovakia: Nation at the Crossroads of Central Europe, New York, 1960.

Kočtúch, Hvezdoň, Economic and Social Development of Slovakia, Bratislava, 1968.

Korbel, Josef, The Communist Subversion in Czechoslovakia, Princeton, 1959.

Kováčik, Ján, and Válik, Bohuslav, Malý sprievodca Slovenskom (A Small Guide to Slovakia), Bratislava, 1965.

Křiženecká, Ružena, and Šel, Zdeněk (Compilers), Československo 1968: Přehled událostí (Czechoslovakia 1968: Survey of Events), Prague, 1969.

Kusin, Vladimír, V., *The Intellectual Origins of the Prague Spring*, Cambridge, 1971.

Laštovička, Bohuslav, *V Londýně za války; Zápas o novou ČSR, 1939–45 (In London during the War: The Battle for the New ČSR 1939–1945)*, Prague, 1961.

Lettrich, Jozef, *O Slovenskej národnej rade* (On the Slovak National Council), Bratislava, 1945.

Lettrich, Jozef, *History of Modern Slovakia*, New York, 1955.

Levine, Isaac Dar, *Intervention*, New York, 1969.

Liehm, Anton J., *Gespräch an der Moldau. Das Ringen um die Freiheit der Tschechen* (translated from the Czech), Wien, 1968.

Lipták, L'ubomír, *Slovensko v 20. storočí* (Slovakia in the 20th Century), Bratislava, 1968.

Littel, Robert (Editor), *The Czech Black Book* (Documents of the Institute of History of the Czechoslovak Academy of Sciences), London, 1969.

Löbl, Eugen, and Grünwald, Leopold, *Die Intellectuelle Revolution: Hintergrunde und Auswirkungen des Prager Frühlings*, Düsseldorf, 1969.

Löbl, Eugen, *Sentenced and Tried*, London, 1969.

London, Artur, *L'Aveu. Dans l'engrenage du procès de Prague*, Paris, 1969. (Also available in English.)

Ludwig, Emil, *Defender of Democracy: Masaryk Speaks* (translated from the German), London, 1936.

Mackenzie, Compton, *Dr Beneš*, London, 1946.

Masaryk, Jan, *Speaking to my Country*, Foreword by Rt. Hon. Anthony Eden, London, 1945.

Masaryk, Dr Thomas Garrique, *The Making of a State: Memoirs and Observations 1914–1918* (An English version arranged, prepared with an introduction by Henry Wickham Steed), London, 1934.

Mastný, Vojtěch, *The Czechs under Nazi Rule*, New York and London, 1971.

Mikuš, Joseph A., *La Slovaquie dans le drame de l'Europe (Histoire politique de 1918–1950)*, Paris, 1955.

Mňačko, Ladislav, *The Seventh Night* (translated from the Slovak), London, 1969.

Parrott, Sir Cecil, *Czechoslovakia: Its Heritage and its Future*, London, 1968.

Pelikán, Jiří (Editor and Introduction), *The Secret Vysočany Congress*, London, 1971.

Pomaizl, Karel, *Vznik ČSR* (The Creation of the ČSR), Prague, 1965.
Prečan, Vilém, *Slovenské národné povstanie. Dokumenty* (The (The Slovak National Uprising. Documents), Bratislava, 1965.
Pustejovsky, Otfrid, *In Prag kein Fenstersturz. Dogmatismus 1948–1962, Entdogmatisierung 1962–1967, Demokratisierung 1967–1968, Intervention 1968*, Munich, 1968.
Randle, Michael, and others, *Support Czechoslovakia*, London, 1968.
Reichcigl, Miloslav, Jr (Editor), *Czechoslovakia Past and Present*, 2 vols. The Hague, 1969.
Remington, Robin Alison (Editor), *Winter in Prague: Documents on Czechoslovak Communism in Crisis*, Cambridge, Mass., 1969.
Salamon, Michael, *Prague: La révolution étranglée*, Paris, 1968.
Schwartz, Harry, *Prague's 200 Days: The Struggle for Democracy in Czechoslovakia*, London, 1969.
Selucký, Radovan, *Ekonomické vyrovnání Slovenska s českými kraji* (The Economic Equalisation of Slovakia with the Czech Lands), Prague, 1960.
Selucký, Radovan, *Czechoslovakia: The Plan that Failed*, with an introduction by Kamil Winter, London, 1970.
Seton-Watson, George Hugh Nicholas, *The East European Revolution*, 2nd ed., London, 1956.
Seton-Watson, G. H. N., *Nationalism and Communism: Essays*, London, 1963.
Seton-Watson, Robert William, *Racial Problem in Hungary*, by Scotus Viator (pseud.), London, 1908.
Seton-Watson, R. W., *Slovakia Then and Now: A Political Survey*, London, 1931.
Seton-Watson, R. W., *A History of the Czechs and Slovaks*, London, 1943.
Shawcross, William, *Dubček*, London, 1970.
Šik, Ota, *Die tschechoslowakische Wirtschaft auf neuen Wegen*, Prague, 1966.
Slánská, Josefa, *Report on my Husband* (translated from the Czech), London, 1969.
Šlingová, Marian, *Truth will Prevail*, London, 1968.
Stránský, Jan, *East Wind over Prague*, New York, 1951.
Šujan, Juraj, *Mladý Štefánik a mladé Slovensko* (The Young Štefánik and Young Slovakia), Prague, 1932.
Swerling, Anthony. *The Rape of Czechoslovakia: Being Two Weeks of Cohabitation with her Allies, August–September 1968*, Cambridge, 1968.

Táborský, Edward, *Communism in Czechoslovakia: 1948–1960,* Princeton, 1961.

Tatu, Michel, *L'hérésie impossible: Chronicle du drame tchécoslovaque,* Paris, 1968.

Thomson, Harrison S., *Czechoslovakia in European History,* Princeton, 1953.

Tigrid, Pavel, *Le printemps de Prague,* Paris, 1968.

Weisskopf, Kurt, *The Agony of Czechoslovakia '38–'68,* London, 1968.

Windsor, Philip, and Roberts, Adam, *Czechoslovakia 1968. Reform, Repression and Resistance,* London, 1969.

Zeman, Zbyněk Anthony Bohuslav, *Prague Spring: A Report on Czechoslovakia,* Harmondsworth, 1969.

Zinner, Paul (Editor), *National Communism and Popular Revolt in Eastern Europe,* New York, 1956.

Zinner, Paul, *Communist Strategy and Tactics in Czechoslovakia,* London, 1963.

Frontiers of the Hapsburg Empire 1918

Kingdom of Hungary

Brünn is Present-day Brno
Pozsony is Bratislava
Kassa is Košice
Budweiss is České Budějovice

100 miles

Map 2   Czechoslovakia 1918–1938

Map 3   Czechoslovakia from Munich until March 1939

Areas occupied by Hunga

Areas occupied by Polan

Incorporated in the
German Reich

Protectorate of
Bohemia and Moravia
(under German occupati

The Slovak State
(Occupied by German
troops August 1944)

Map 4   Czechoslovakia during the Second World War

International fron
Czechoslovak reg
boundaries

Map 5   Czechoslovakia after 1945 (The regions as in 1965)

INDEX